Girls in Power

GIRLS IN POWER

Gender, Body, and

Menstruation in Adolescence

LAURA FINGERSON

STATE UNIVERSITY OF NEW YORK PRESS

Chapters 2, 5, and 6 contain revised sections of "Agency and the Body in Adolescent Menstrual Talk," *Childhood* 12 (2005): 91–110, reprinted with the permission of *Childhood* and Sage Publications.

Published by
STATE UNIVERSITY OF NEW YORK PRESS
ALBANY

© 2006 State University of New York

For information, address
State University of New York Press
194 Washington Avenue, Suite 305, Albany, NY 12210-2384

Production, Laurie Searl
Marketing, Anne M. Valentine

Library of Congress Cataloging-in-Publication Data

Fingerson, Laura, 1974–
    Girls in power : gender, body, and menstruation in adolescence / Laura Fingerson.
        p. cm.
    Includes bibliographical references and index.
    ISBN-13: 978-0-7914-6899-9
    ISBN-10: 0-7914-6899-2
    ISBN-13: 978-0-7914-6900-2 (pbk.)
    ISBN-10: 0-7914-6900-X (pbk.)
    1. Teenage girls—Psychology. 2. Menstruation—Social aspects. 3. Body, Human—Social aspects. 4. Sex role. I. Title.

HQ798.F56 2006
305.235'2—dc22
                                                                    2005037173

10   9   8   7   6   5   4   3   2   1

Contents

Acknowledgments

I had the impression when I began graduate school that research was an individual endeavor, particularly for graduate students whose primary objectives are to write "independent" and "original" research to earn their degrees. Luckily, my impression was false and I have never been truly alone in my research. During my time in graduate school and as a faculty member, I have managed to be involved in a community of collaboration and support that has been invaluable in not only my research but also my understandings of sociology and the wider world. This book has been significantly enhanced by conversations with and feedback from friends, colleagues, and advisors contributing their expertise and encouragement.

First and foremost, I thank my teen research participants and the directors of their community groups for allowing me to take a peek into their menstrual and body talk. Going into the project I knew the data would be interesting, but I had no idea how unbelievably fascinating and rich teen talk about menstruation and the body would be.

Second, I thank Paul Namaste Ruggerio who interviewed the male research participants. In preparing for this project, I quickly realized that the teenage boys would never open up to me as they would to a man. I cannot imagine a better interviewer for this project. I am deeply in debt to my transcriptionists: Kirsten Eamon, Emily Fairchild, Vanessa Hamilton, Tiffany Lynch, Julie Patterson, and Jill Stalowicz. The analyses would have taken much longer without the fabulous, accurate transcriptions of my data.

Vital funding to pay Paul and the transcriptionists came from: the Indiana University CONCEPT I program in medical sociology; the Indiana University Graduate Student Organization; the Kinsey Institute for Sex, Gender and Reproduction; and the Midwest Sociological Society.

Several people offered amazing insights and feedback on my data, analyses, and writing: Katy Hadley, Sandi Kawecka Nenga, Kris DeWelde, audience members at conference presentations I have given on this topic, Ellie

Miller, Stacey Oliker, Scott Long, Helen Gremillion, Jane McLeod, Brian Powell, and, most especially, Donna Eder. I have been lucky to receive support and encouragement in this from good friends Chad Menning, Lisa Kuriscak, and Jeni Loftus. Finally, I owe a deep gratitude to those in my personal life who have sustained and supported me throughout my academic endeavors: my parents and my husband, John.

ONE

Introduction

MENSTRUATION IS . . .

KASSIE (age 16): "Makes us stronger, in ways, I guess, like [we] deal with pain better than a lot of people, a lot of guys."

BRIAN (14): "When girls get really mean and they bleed everywhere."

JANE (14): "Something to make guys miserable . . . cause they have to put up with the whole PMS and all that."

ALLY (17): "It's messy, and it's gross, and I don't want to have to deal with it. . . . You have to deal with stupid boys and physics class and algebra 2 and I don't want more things to deal with."

From these quotes of mostly white, middle- and working-class teenagers today, we can see that the experience of menstruation, far from being private and secretive, is embedded in social relations. In this book, we will explore the social aspects of menstruation and the body and how adolescent girls today can use their bodies as sources of power in their social interactions with others.

I spent several hours a week volunteering at a local girls club in southern Indiana in the late-1990s. During this time, I was involved in a drug abuse prevention program for the teen girls in the club. One day, our topic of discussion was over-the-counter drugs and how they too can be abused. The girls said that, at school, kids take painkillers such as aspirin and ibuprofen even though the school nurse is supposed to administer all drugs. Students are not even allowed to have them in their bags or lockers. The girls understood the safety concerns behind this policy. However, during this discussion, Sierra, a tall, confident, 13-year-old working-class Black girl, talked openly about subverting school policy by getting some ibuprofen from a friend to soothe her

---

All respondent names used in this book are pseudonyms.

1

menstrual cramps. This in itself was not remarkable. What was unusual was how Sierra referred to her menstrual status. She clearly, loudly, and without hesitating a beat said, "When I became a woman" and continued clearly, loudly, and surely with the rest of her story. None of the other girls in the group seemed to notice or be surprised at either her "coming out" about her menstrual status or her choice of words. I, however, was floored. "What?" I thought, "Who in this day and age uses the phrase, 'when I became a woman' to refer to getting her first period?" Even more interesting, at age thirteen, Sierra was remarkably comfortable talking about her growing body and her period in front of the whole group of girls and adult women! Wasn't she embarrassed? Weren't the other girls embarrassed?

I immediately began describing this incident to my adult friends, who, like me, were in their late twenties and early thirties. They thought it was as unusual as I did. When we were in our teens, we were highly embarrassed by menstruation, sensitive about our bodies, and would never have discussed menstruation in such a public setting. Sierra brought menstruation easily and seamlessly into public social interaction and the other girls her age were not fazed. This comment indicated several things. Sierra is comfortable with menstruation. Sierra is comfortable with talking about her own menstruation in public. Because of this comfort, Sierra does not see menstruation as a negative thing to hide or as a source of powerlessness and shame. This is social power! Sierra does not submit to dominant cultural norms in the United States, which demand that menstruation be concealed from the public. She has a power over menstruation, her body, and the dominant menstrual discourse.

This led me to an intriguing set of questions about how girls can wield power in their social interactions with others. Are they using their female bodies as a source of pride, rather than shame? Are female bodies not seen as weaker or less powerful as they have been in the past? How do girls interpret and talk about menstruation? If menstruation is now out in the open, then it must enter into cross-gender interactions as well. How do boys interpret and talk about menstruation? Do girls talk about menstruation with boys?

In exploring the body and how teens feel about the body, many writers have examined girls' body images, weight concerns, sexuality, and self-esteem. What is missing are how girls might *use* their bodies in their social interactions, how the body might be a resource for power, and how boys might respond to this power. Studying adolescents' menstrual talk and experiences can shed light on these complex power issues. While menstruation may restrict girls' activities because it can be shameful, bewildering, and disempowering, girls might also use menstruation as a source of power.

Searches of academic research and popular literature turned up material on the cultural history of menstruation, girls' and women's individual attitudes towards menstruation, and a small alternative literature on celebrating menstruation, puberty, and womanhood.[1] Most of this research suggests that girls and women think that menstruation is gross, messy, shameful, and a negative and frustrating experience overall. Previous work has also demonstrated that boys have more power when it comes to body issues such as sexuality and appearance norms.

But menstruation is something that is unique to girls, something that boys do not have personal experience with. How does this special experience play out in cross-gender social interactions? When menstruation is out in the open, is it used as a source of power in social interactions? Are girls still teased about it or do girls turn the tables and tease boys about it?

As a sociologist trained in social psychology, I am interested in issues of social power, the body in interaction, language use, and adolescent peer culture. I conducted this study because I wanted to learn about how this aspect of the body, menstruation, is experienced socially in teens' everyday lives. As power is an underlying aspect of all social relationships, my research questions were fundamentally about power and how girls and boys can use their bodies and menstruation as sources of power in their social interactions.

SALIENT BODY EXPERIENCES

In Judy Blume's widely read book *Are You There God? It's Me, Margaret* (1970), one of 12-year-old Margaret's major complications in life is her much anticipated menstrual period. She quietly shares this eagerness with her friends, her mom, her grandma, and in her diary in the form of letters to God. When I talk about my research, invariably at least one adult listener will mention this book. Why has this book been a best seller since its 1970 publication?[2] Why do many of us think of it when we recall adolescence and puberty? Because menstruation is one of the most salient pubertal transitions in adolescence. Particularly in the 1970s and 1980s, at a time when menstruation was not discussed openly among adolescents, this book helped us understand what menstruation and puberty are all about.

In junior high and high school, and even in late elementary school, girls' bodies are transformed into women's bodies. For a brief time, menstruation is new and has a great impact on girls' lives. For a brief time, menstruation is salient. By adulthood, women's and men's management of menstruation has become routine. Thus, adults think that menstruation is not relevant to social life because it is not relevant to *adult* social life. However, in order to understand *adolescent* life, we must understand adolescent bodies, and menstruation is a salient experience to them. Adolescent bodies are changing and growing as they make the transition from pre to postpubertal forms. The body and the body's experiences shape human experience and human experience in turn shapes the body. Social researchers have a lot to learn about how our experiences of our bodies are transformed over the life course, especially in adolescence.

Interestingly, key to Margaret's journey through puberty is how and what she learns about menstruation from those peers and adults around her. Even as they are secretive about it, menstruation still enters into their social lives and thus, into their power relations. Today's teens, as I explore, have gone far beyond these tentative social steps.

Menstruation is often seen by dominant adult culture as an individual "woman's issue," not legitimate for sociological study or even appropriate for everyday conversation. Lots of research in girls' studies and women's studies has explored body image, self-esteem, eating disorders, appearance, exercise, and even issues of hair, body modification, and cosmetic surgery. But not menstruation. It is odd that such an integral and routine event in women's lives, which has significant implications for women's health and well-being over the life course, not to mention the salience it holds in adolescence, has generally been ignored in social research. Even though the general public tends to be uncomfortable with the topic of menstruation, researchers are trained to seek out and understand such public squeamishness; but researchers have not yet examined menstruation as relevant to social life or social science. Yet, *all* women, if they menstruate or not, manage menstruation in one form or another. Women who menstruate do so for approximately half of their lives. *All* men who have any interaction with women manage menstruation in one form or another.

Social researchers, including feminists, have a lot to gain from focusing on "essential" or "medicalized" properties of women's bodies. We are not talking heads, but we are all *embodied* actors, as the condition and form of our body affects our interactions. The body is a variable in social interaction. For example, having a cold can make us irritable and grumpy, being in shape can compel us to start up a neighborhood pickup basketball game, and having frozen toes at an outdoor football game can force us to retreat to a heated home before the game is over. Socially, we interact differently with elderly bodies or pregnant bodies or bodies belonging to those of a different race, ethnicity, dis/ability, or gender.

By learning about how adolescents experience their bodies and menstruation socially, we can learn about broader aspects of their everyday lives. We can learn about the shifting power in their gendered interactions, the resources from which girls and boys draw power, the ways in which they construct their social worlds, and the ways in which they define each other as gendered beings. Also, how do menstrual interpretations and menstrual talk affect other aspects of teens' lives, such as body politics, the gender order, and health? Rather than focusing only on the hygienic aspects of menstruation, we need to focus on the wide spectrum of experiences and interpretations of menstruation. Many of these connections have been suggested in various popular literatures[3] or suggested, but not empirically explored, in some social research work.[4] Using the example, or case study, of menstruation, this book is about the body and how the body enters the power relations of social life.

By exploring what goes on in teens' own peer groups and in teens' own thoughts through group and individual interviews, we can learn how teens see and experience the world. Menstruation is more relevant to teens' lives than even I thought initially. Through understanding their experiences with menstruation, we can learn about teens' peer interactions and power relations. We can learn what it means to be a girl or a boy at the beginning of the twenty-first century. We can learn how teens seek to assert control in their lives. We can understand how teens talk about the body. On a concrete level, this learning can help parents, community organizers, educators, and policy makers develop strategies to promote safer health and sexual practices, strategies that can take into account teens' own significant knowledge, experience, and agency. These strategies originate in teens' own language and their own culture. This book is based on the premise that academic research can and should be socially relevant and politically responsible.

To explore these questions, we have to ask the teens themselves. We have to learn what they are saying in their own words, with their own friends, and in their own social contexts. Instead of focusing on adult experiences or adult memories and reflections on menstruating in adolescence or at menarche, as much research has done, I will examine adolescents' current experiences.[5] Children, particularly girls, are an "outsider group" in our society, as they have substantially less power than adults do.[6] I follow the "new sociology of childhood," which seeks to uncover agency in children's lives and defines children as competent social actors. Children are not just adults-in-the-making, but have their own unique cultures. Childhood, including adolescence, is a permanent structural feature of society[7] that is intersected by adult-based institutions such as education, work, media, and family.[8] In recent years, childhood researchers have focused on children's own experiences rather than only on these larger institutions. In this research, I explore teens' collective, as well as individual, interpretations and discussions of menstruation. I explore how teens learn from each other in their peer groups.

What about boys' attitudes towards and experiences with menstruation? We know very little about how menstruation enters boys' lives beyond its relationship to sexuality.[9] In the interviews, I explore not only how the girls bring menstruation into their social lives, but also how the boys talk about menstruation. We will learn that, rather than being silent, these boys have a lot to say about menstruation and how it affects their relations and power interactions with girls.

As I explore teen menstrual talk, I follow the sociological approach of symbolic interactionism, which contends that people form their realities, beliefs, and interpretations through interaction with others.[10] Thus, an event itself cannot determine how people will understand the event. Instead, there are multiple potential meanings of that event and people assign significance to select meanings through social interaction and social experience. In short, in order to understand and interpret our world, we talk about it with others. Thus, through teens' social interaction and talk, they learn about, assign meaning to, and develop unique interpretations of menstruation and the body. In other words, our understanding of menstruation is socially constructed.

Following this thinking, William Corsaro (1997) developed the "interpretive reproduction" theoretical approach as a way to understand children's unique cultures. This theory was primarily developed as a response to socialization models (which concentrate on how children are socialized by adults, media, peers, and surroundings), which Corsaro sees as too individualistic and too focused on children as adults-to-be, rather than as an important focus of study in their own right. Central to Corsaro's theory is the importance of collective, collaborative, and communal activities in which children negotiate, create, and share cultures with each other and with adults. This theory is *interpretive* in that children actively interpret their worlds and adult information in creative and innovative ways. The theory is *reproductive* in that children are not viewed simply as the passive recipients of adult socialization and culture, but as actively producing and reproducing their own cultures through their negotiations with adults and with each other.

Fundamental to all social interaction is power. Power is both the ability to influence behavior and the capacity to use resources to achieve desired ends. For example, the teens use power to influence others' views, to control conversation, and to increase their social statuses. Teens use resources such as social status, their bodies, and their knowledge to achieve their interactional goals. I follow Michel Foucault's (1977) view of power as fluid in interaction, in contrast to the idea of one group or gender always having power and control over another. Power is indirect social control exercised over others in social interaction. Power is a process that people continually negotiate through relationships and language.[11] Power is a fundamental aspect of all social interaction and we can understand the processes and effects of power by studying social interaction.[12] Throughout the teens' narratives, we will see how girls and boys use menstruation and the body as power resources and how menstruation and the body affect girls' and boys' power negotiations.

In this book, I connect the related approaches of the sociology of childhood (childhood studies and the new developments in "girls' studies"), embodiment, and gender. While there is a large body of research that explores childhood in terms of gender, far less research has explored childhood and the body.[13] Children's bodies are constantly shifting and changing through growth and puberty. I strive to empirically and theoretically envision an embodied childhood as it is continually subject to power negotiations. Just as embodiment theorists argue that women and men are all embodied social actors, so too are children embodied social actors. In my research, I explore how important the body is in teens' experiences and social lives.

THE TEEN PARTICIPANTS

In this book, we will explore adolescent talk on menstruation and the body through an analysis of group and individual interviews with mostly white, high school age girls and boys living in southern and central Indiana. Although observational methods can access teens' "naturally occurring" talk, conducting an in-depth ethnography of adolescent everyday talk is not feasible given the relative sparseness of menstrual-related talk in everyday conversations that are readily witnessed by researchers. Published ethnographies note that menstruation issues come up in teens' talk; however, the occurrence of such talk, albeit important, is relatively infrequent.[14] Interview-based research can access issues that are highly salient to children and adolescents' lives, yet are not frequently talked about informally in settings accessible to researchers.[15]

Doing individual interviews allowed me to investigate each teen's own understanding of and experiences with menstruation. Following feminist research models, I was able to learn about their worlds listening to their own words and their own language.[16] It is vital to understand their individual histories in order to more effectively interpret the collective and collaborative discussions in which the adolescents engage with their peer groups.[17]

Group interviews grow directly out of peer culture where teens hang out and develop their views in collaboration with their friends. Many of the adolescent beliefs about life including the body and menstruation are culturally based and transmitted through social discourse. Adolescents learn and form opinions about the mechanics and experience of menstruation from each other through talk, storytelling, and jokes. In group talk, participants bring their own views, their own experiences, and their own understandings of the social phenomena under investigation to the interaction. In group interviews, teens build upon each other's talk and discuss a wider range of experiences and opinions than may develop in individual interviews. For example, one person tells a story that reminds another of a story and so on. As Mayall notes, participants can "follow on each other's leads, pick up points and confirm, comment or move on" (2000:123). Also, it is through talk that researchers can explore how power is displayed. Talk is a resource all people use for communicating power dynamics.

Importantly, the individual and group interviews were with both girls and boys. Teens live in a mixed-gender world and their bodies enter into their interactions with those of the other sex to a significant extent. In order to understand gender, we must include both girls and boys in our research. We cannot depend only on what girls say about boys; we have to ask boys themselves. In my interviews, for example, the girls made many claims about how boys respond when girls bring up menstruation. Although this is important in understanding the girls' own interpretations of the boys, the strength of interviewing boys is also that we can hear from the boys themselves how they respond. We can get both sides of the gender power plays.

I recruited the research participants from several ongoing teen groups in central and southern Indiana, including community groups, girls' clubs, boys' clubs, and teen councils. By drawing from existing groups, the teens in each group interview knew each other and had a shared history of experiences. Thus, the collective talk in the interviews was easier to generate and more "natural." We conducted the individual and group interviews with each group over one or two days. Sometimes these days were one or two weeks apart. The teens' opinions about menstruation (and most everything else) are constantly shifting, and these interviews reflect their feelings on those particular days of interviewing. We conducted the interviews in the first four months of the year 2000. The girls and boys completed both individual and group interviews. We first discussed how teens feel about their bodies, weight, strength, and athleticism. Then we explored how they feel about menstruation, what they know about menstruation, and their experiences with menstruation.

Twenty-six girls participated in this research in seven group interviews and twenty-three individual interviews. Eleven boys participated in two group interviews and eleven individual interviews. The size of the group interviews ranged from two to nine participants. The teens ranged from age 13 to 19. The teens were all in high school at the time of the interviews except two girls who had dropped out that year, their senior year. I wanted to focus on high school age adolescents because, while they have had experiences with menstruation, they are still learning how to deal with it in their daily lives. Menstruation is still somewhat new for them, but they are comfortable enough with it to discuss it. The different girls' groups were fairly homogenous by age and the boys' had a larger in-group variation. Even with the relatively wide age range (of 13 through 19), the older and younger research participants did not differ remarkably in their interpretations of menstruation and the body.

As the teens themselves acknowledge in the interviews, differences in interpretation would abound if we were to compare high school menstrual talk with that of middle school menstrual talk, when menarche[18] is so new and recent. Leslie, in her individual interview, said that her attitude about menstruation has definitely changed since she first started her period: "I'm more open about it, like, in there. Like, if I was in sixth grade and you would have come in [to her group] none of us would have said anything." The teens in our interviews, especially the girls, were amazingly forthcoming and comfortable with the talk about menstruation.

For example, at the end of the individual interviews, we interviewers would say that we were done with the questions and would ask the teens if they had any other comments about menstruation or anything else they wanted to say about it. Two of the girls in particular had a lot more to say about their own menstrual experiences. Sylvia took the opportunity to tell me how she experiences her own menstrual cycle. Jennifer ended up telling stories about when her period started, her nightmares about her periods, the experience of her period, her exercising, and even a story she read about an African girl getting her period. These added comments comprised over one-quarter of her entire individual interview. In one of the girls' group interviews, as well, the girls took the opportunity to talk about their own periods and their experiences after my questions were over. Overall, almost all of the girls were very forthcoming and comfortable talking about their menstrual experiences. Even the boys were generally very forthcoming, as I will show in this book. Although most had no questions or comments at the end of the interview, one group of boys launched into an extended sequence about why menstruants crave certain foods, like chocolate.

To compare, my friend's daughter, who just reached menarche at age ten, would not tell any of her close friends about it until she knew that they too had gotten their periods. She did not want to stand out or be different (although, someone has to be the first to admit menarche). As many women readers of this book will understand, this girl also spent a good deal of time checking her backside in the mirror to be sure the "giant" pad did not show through her pants. Another friend's daughter, who also got her period at age ten, was convinced her male classroom teacher knew she had gotten her first period because she needed to use the bathroom more often and she brought her purse. Every time she needed to use the restroom, she worried that her teacher would be looking at her knowingly. Once adolescents have reached high school, their interactions around menstruation have somewhat stabilized because menarche is in the past.

My sample is nonrandom and from a specific community in Indiana. All but three of the teens were white. One girl and one boy were biracial (white and Black) and one girl was a Korean immigrant. (Sierra, mentioned earlier, was not in my sample.) The girls' groups were exclusively either working or middle class and the boys' groups had some crossover, although most participants in each group were one socioeconomic class or the other. Appendix A provides a detailed list of the participants with their ages, grades, and social classes. The teens lived in homes representing a wide variety of family structures including two parent, single parent, biological parent, stepparent, and grandparent. The teens had brothers, sisters, step-siblings, and some were only children.

These teens come from a midwestern culture that other teens in the United States may not share. The way these teens speak of menstruation and their bodies might seem conservative or liberal to other teens. At the same time, from my experience I believe that these teens represent most teens from "middle America," a group from the "heartland," which plays a dominant role in U.S. identity and culture. Regardless, the goal of qualitative research such as this is not to generalize to the rest of the population, but rather to explore the theory, or explanations, of the data, and to think about how these explanations extend to other populations, other circumstances, and other contexts for social interaction. As such, the overall goal in this book is not to focus on these particular teens' experiences with menstruation, but rather on what these experiences can say about gender, power, and embodiment.

All interviews were audio-recorded, and during the group interviews I also ran a video recorder (to make transcription of the group interviews easier). I conducted all of the girls' individual and group interviews, and I hired a male research assistant, Paul Namaste Ruggerio, to conduct the boys' individual and group interviews. Paul's help was invaluable, as he was able to connect with the boys on the issues of body and menstruation in a way that I, as a female, never could. Other female researchers have interviewed both boys and girls on issues of the body, sexuality, and puberty, but I believe that the conversations the boys had with Paul were much more reflective of their "natural" talk than they would have been had I been the one conducting the interviews. (Appendix B provides more detail on the interview guides used). For more detail on methods of individual and group interviewing as used in this project, please see Fingerson (2005b).

THE INTERVIEWERS

In any social interaction, the participants involved negotiate and develop their interpretations of that interaction and respond accordingly. In interviews, the participants are not only the teen respondents, but also Paul and I, as we also contribute to creating the conversation.[19] It is thus important to examine our own roles in the research. First, interviewers, as with most researchers, have more power than the respondents because researchers control the conditions and topics of the interaction. They also control the interpretation and distribution of the research findings. Although group interviews help reduce power differences between adult researchers and child respondents because of the high child-adult ratio, the interviewer still has the power of an adult.[20] Second, the researcher's own preconceptions and prejudices can influence the interview. Thinking reflexively about this research, it is important to recognize that Paul's and my self-presentations and backgrounds influence the data.

I am a tall, white woman who at the time was 25 years old, average weight and not particularly athletic, although I lettered in varsity sports in high school and played intramural sports in graduate school. During the months of interviewing, I began a fitness program of healthy eating and exercise. This made me acutely aware of and sensitive to not only my own body, but also to the girls' bodies and their attitudes towards their bodies in our discussions of weight and athleticism. I was born to and raised by professional parents in the Minneapolis-St. Paul suburbs. My undergraduate degree in Sociology and Anthropology is from the University of Minnesota. I am straight, married, and my wedding rings were visible on my hands. The teen participants knew I was in graduate school in Sociology at Indiana University and that this project was for my Ph.D. dissertation. They knew that my hope was to turn the data collected into a book that they could some day read. I felt I connected well with the girls because I was able to relate to them on several levels, such as dating, relationships with friends, and dealing with parents, not just as a fellow menstruating woman who has issues with her body. My previous work as a girls' club volunteer and a summer camp counselor allowed me to easily enter into their way of talking.

At the time, Paul Namaste Ruggerio was a second year graduate student. I selected Paul as my research assistant because of his extensive experience with youth, his rapport with teens, his interest in education, and his enthusiasm for this particular project and life in general. He was also involved in research on women's experiences of infertility so I knew he was familiar with issues of the body. Paul is also very "cool" according to the teens that he regularly works with. He is young (age 31 at the time of the interviews), white, slightly balding, and has a Van Dyke (facial hair). He describes himself as heterosexual, of average male height, and has an athletic build with a bit extra around the middle. He is from the Boston area and participated in varsity sports in both high school and college. In addition, he is very comfortable with his body. Paul connected with the boys on many different levels, which significantly increased his rapport with them. For example, the boys would mention their hobbies or outside interests, such as the Boy Scouts, drama, fencing, and baseball, and Paul was able to share some of his own experiences in those areas.

ANALYSIS OF THE DATA

The interview data, both audio and video-recorded, were transcribed in full. Each utterance in the interviews was transcribed, including fillers such as "uh," "like," "you know," and "mm." Following DeVault (1999), it is important to include the "inelegant" features in these adolescents' talk rather than editing out seemingly extraneous words. Rather than being unnecessary, as some researchers have argued, these words highlight the structure and distinctiveness of adolescent talk about the body and menstruation. In addition, such fillers can indicate uncertainty and/or discomfort with a particular topic.

My thematic analysis followed a grounded theory approach using constant comparison. I read and reread the transcripts many times and marked passages that followed themes and patterns. These themes and patterns developed from the data themselves (such as the theme of agency) or they came from previous literature (such as the theme of negative attitudes towards menstruation). At each rereading, I would go back and find more examples of themes, shift some of the thematic categories, or rethink some themes entirely. It was a constant, and exciting, process of illumination and exploration.

Sociolinguistics is the study of language structure and use. Not only was I interested in what the teens were saying about menstruation, but also *how* they were saying it. In particular, sociolinguistics explores language within its social and cultural context and as it is embedded in larger discourse. It views language as a social resource and examines language in its larger social context. With my data, for example, in using sociolinguistic analyses I find that adolescents use language in their talk as a way of providing several types of feedback to their peers such as support, contradiction, and humor.

Sociolinguistics is also interested in how social-cultural competence and evaluative orientations are achieved through talk.[21] I examine how the teens collectively and collaboratively construct the body and menstruation through their talk and use this talk as resources of power. Through sociolinguistic analysis, we can explore what the adolescent talk represents, such as how it fits into gendered power relations, structures of resistance, and concepts of agency. By using sociolinguistic methods, we can understand the structure of the collaborative talk in the group interviews on a more general level beyond the specific issue of menstruation. Older children have been neglected in the study of sociolinguistics,[22] as the focus has traditionally been on infants and young children and their language acquisition and early use.[23] Sociolinguistic analyses of group talk are peppered throughout this book.

ORGANIZATION OF THIS BOOK

The central issues that came up again and again in the interviews were first, how teen girls and boys exert power in their social interactions, and second, how teens' social experiences are embodied. These two theoretical threads, gendered power and embodiment, weave throughout the interviews and analysis in this book.

In chapter 2, I start out with interview data on how the girls and boys show both negative and ambivalent interpretations and experiences of menstruation. Girls do a lot of management work to conceal and hide menstruation, are very concerned about leaking, worry about boys finding out about their periods, and are often uncomfortable with tampons. On the surface, girls and boys take certain aspects of larger cultural views on menstruation and integrate them into their own culture and their own social experiences. In chapter 3, I explore the cultural contexts in which teens learn about menstruation. I first look at historical advice books written for girls and their parents. These books encourage concealment, worries about hygiene, taboos, and a feeling of powerless due to their medicalization of the female body. Then, I explore the roles of schools, family, and media in influencing the teens' menstrual constructions. In chapter 4, I delve into issues of medicalization, gender politics, and the female body and how power is a component of gendered interaction on the body. Based on these dominant norms of menstruation, gender, and the female body, we would expect a reduction of power that girls experience in their interactions, as we will see in these first chapters.

However, as I explore in chapter 5, I find that at the same time, girls use menstruation as a source of power in their social interactions with each other and with boys and men. Menstruation can be a source of power because it is unique to girls and because, among today's teens, it has turned into a social event, rather than a secretive event. The girls are truly living in an embodied social world as they use their bodies as a tool in their social interactions. In chapter 6, I turn to how boys respond to this increased power. From dominant gender norms and their own past experiences, boys are used to having more power in social interactions with girls. When confronted with reduced power, because they do not personally experience menstruation, the boys develop and use several strategies to deal with this reduced power. In chapter 7, I conclude by discussing the common threads of gender, power, and embodiment that interweave the interviews, reflecting on the methods of inquiry I used and furthering our theoretical and analytical thinking on an embodied understanding of social life.

TWO

Negative and
Ambivalent Experiences

In their interviews, the girls and boys talked about and experienced menstruation in negative, ambivalent, and positive ways. To start, we will explore these negative and ambivalent experiences and attitudes. Often, girls want to conceal menstruation. They are afraid of leaking. Tampons can scare them. They do not like boys knowing that they are menstruating. At the same time, some girls do not think menstruation is that big of a deal and they do not stress about it.

CONCEALMENT AND SHAME

At the most basic level, the girls expressed feelings of both concealment and shame. Much of the work that girls perform to manage menstruation is done to hide evidence that they are menstruating from others. Girls put a great deal of effort into this, such as keeping pads and tampons in concealed places, wearing certain clothes so their pads do not show, changing their "protection" during regular class breaks so they do not have to ask the teacher for a pass, and changing their protection often to ensure that they do not leak through their clothing. In their private conversations with other girls, the girls are comfortable talking about their experiences menstruating. However, in public, many of the girls want to have the outward appearance that they are not menstruating and that their bodies are not doing anything "out of the ordinary." They want to maintain their private menstrual identity.

Concealing menstruation is a masculinist-based notion of the body because, for women, menstruating *is* ordinary. Women menstruate on average just under one week per month; thus, approximately one-quarter of all fertile women are menstruating at any given moment. Yet the dominant view of

15

what the body is and how it should act and look is that of the male body. Carol Tavris (1992) offers several examples of this myopic view on the body. Medical experiments are typically done on men as women's estrous cycle "disrupts" test results and increases variation. Imagine the dangerous side effects for women taking medications designed for the male body. The physiological changes of menstruation (and pregnancy and menopause) vary from one woman to the next and the hormone levels shift substantially during the cycle. Anatomy textbook illustrations typically show a male body, except when exploring the female reproductive system. Also, there is a huge pressure on girls and women to have low body fat although the female body is designed to have a much higher body fat percentage than the male body, including breasts and fat reserves in thighs, buttocks, and hips. Even the dangers of fat have been based on studies of men; excessive thinness for women can *increase* the risk of osteoporosis.

Cultural messages tell girls and women that menstruation should be hidden. Janice Delaney, Mary Jane Lupton, and Emily Toth (1988) find powerful messages in the twentieth century from health classes, product advertisements, and other media that tell mothers and girls to keep menarche and menstruation a secret while using the most deodorizing and sanitizing products. Not only is menstruation a secret, but it is a dirty, unsanitary secret. Compounding the problem, accurate information about external reproductive parts (such as the labia and clitoris) and internal parts (such as the hymen) were nearly impossible for the lay public to find until the first publication of *Our Bodies, Ourselves* in 1973.

Children, more so than adults, work particularly hard to fit in with others, as Allison James (2000) learns in her classroom ethnography. Children do not want to stand out as different from their peers. To do this, they must make their bodies appear a certain way:

> It is clear then that children's body work relies, therefore, upon two kinds of seeing: first, looking at the bodies of others and interpreting the information gained to judge the status of one's own body and, second, making one's own body look or seem '*as if*' it were another kind of body. Thus it is that in the classroom, children who wish to gain favor from their teachers straighten their backs, fold their arms, look straight ahead and sit still: they present their bodies for view '*as if*' they were the bodies of those who are orderly and well behaved. (p. 34)

In fact, children are not generally "orderly and well behaved," but children work to promote this view of themselves. This is similar to concealing menstruation. The girls are menstruating but they work to conceal this and act as if they are not since they do not want to be different from those around them. The high school-age girls wish to gain favor from the larger community, which includes boys and men.

In a sense, by hiding evidence of menstruation, such as keeping their menstrual products unseen and by not carrying purses to the bathroom, they present their bodies as if they were children's bodies, or ungendered bodies: bodies that are not fully sexual, or bodies not marred by blood and menstruation. The girls who conceal their periods are not outwardly acknowledging their womanhood or their maturing bodies. In her individual interview, Kassie said that when she first got her period, she thought, "Man, I'm a woman now." But then the cramps started and she wanted "to be normal again." For Kassie, being "normal again" was not menstruating but instead reverting to a child's premenstrual body. Also, girls present their bodies as if they are no different from boys' bodies. With no bodily difference, there is no place to base power difference. With no bodily difference, girls cannot be teased.

In line with the cultural emphasis on concealment, girls use various strategies to respond to their bodies' needs as they menstruate and prepare to menstruate. Shirley Prendergast (2000) writes about the work involved for a girl when she has her period:

> Most basically she must know in advance that her period is likely to start that day, and be prepared with appropriate supplies. She must learn how to keep these in a safe place so that they are both readily accessible but not likely to be found, deliberately or accidentally. After that she must judge the appropriate time to change in order that no accidents happen, timing this with lesson breaks, and finding a toilet [bathroom] that has the facilities that she needs. If a girl has any kind of negative effects from menstruation (which, as we have seen, they commonly do) she must assess how she is likely to feel and be appropriately prepared (for pain, for example) in order to stay alert and complete school tasks successfully. She must have considered the day's lessons, and brought a note if she wishes to be excused from any of them. (p. 117)

This exhaustive list, confirmed by the girls in our interviews, as we shall see, explains the complexities of managing menstruation during the school day for girls and highlights the fact that the menstrual experience is a constraining event. All of this work is done to keep menstruation concealed by maintaining its invisibility in public space. Other bodily functions must also be managed, such as defecation or farting, but they are not embedded in the tricky realms of gender and puberty as menstruation is. School, a central feature of children's lived experience, is a spatial context that is dedicated to the control and regulation of the children's bodies and minds.[1]

Girls do not want to call attention to themselves or their menstrual cycle. For some children, being invisible, unnoticed, and just a part of the group is a daily interactional goal. One effective punishment for kids who misbehave in school is to physically segregate and mark them. For example, in one research study, a child who was talking while the students were lining up for lunch was punished by being told to stand in the main passage with his back to the rest of the school. He was put on display bodily.[2]

As Shirley Prendergast learned in her research, schools in particular fail to provide conditions for girls where menstruation can be managed adequately, much less positively. Imagine the frustration and anxiety for Kasey, one of the girls in my interviews, when she got her first period (menarche is a very unpredictable event) in "the first week of seventh grade, the first week in a new school, first week with a new schedule, first week with forty-five minute class periods, and with only four minute passing periods"! There is a large amount of management work in handling menstruation that girls must learn and negotiate. At the same time, the girls rise to the challenge of this responsibility, exert power over their bodies and their social situations, and use both individual and collective strategies for managing menstruation. This management also highlights how menstruation is a personal bodily event that girls experience within their social contexts and interactions.

THE HORRORS OF LEAKING

Several girls discussed their concerns about leaking through their clothes. Leaking not only gives evidence of the "secret," but also makes a mess that is difficult to clean up at school where girls do not have access to bathing facilities or a clean change of clothes. In one group interview, Leslie's first reaction when I brought up menstruation was a concern and reflection on "accidents" that she and her friends have had. Leslie delved into an extended narrative as she described how she leaked during her period at school in seventh grade. She was crying in the classroom, she was so embarrassed and frustrated. She leaked on her jeans and had to call her mom to bring her fresh clothes. This story elicited a great deal of sympathy from the other girls, as leaking is the thing they are probably most afraid of.

Ally said, "I've heard people talking about girls that have, like, bled through their pants or something. And I've always been terrified of doing that, because they're like, making fun of her." Although Ally does not specify their gender, "people" can be either boys or girls. Ally keeps a sweatshirt in her locker to wear around her waist just in case she does leak through. On a collective level, Marcia described how she will help a menstruating friend. Marcia told us in her group interview that, "I had a friend in middle school; she kept making me check her butt to make sure she wasn't leaking through." Girls band together to help their friends.

Leaking is gross and messy. But, leaking is a major concern for girls because they are not exactly sure when their periods are going to come. Teenagers' cycles have typically not stabilized yet (women beyond puberty tend to have regular cycles while teenagers often fluctuate between shorter and longer cycles). How can you be prepared when you do not know when it will come? By bleeding on an often unpredictable schedule, the body is an actor in girls' lives. The body acts without a girl's consent and regardless of a girl's wishes. Being aware of their bodies and being prepared for their periods is an important first step in managing menstruation. As the girls in one group interview said, it is important to try to keep track of when it is coming:[3]

LAURA: *What would make it easier to be a girl menstruating?*

. . .

LACEY (16): If you knew, like, to the second, when, without having to take birth control [pills], like in two hours, I'm going to get my period, you know. You could prepare yourself, you could—

KASSIE (16): It's like a war, you don't quite know when they're going to attack.

LACEY: That's a good—

LESLIE (16): Not if they're attacking early or late, or—

LINDA (16): Yeah.

GRETA (15): If we're not having it at all.

KORRINE (15): Mine likes to play hide and seek, I don't know how else to describe it. You always think, like, when you end, and then it like surprises you, you're like, 'Okay, next time, okay this is when I stopped, I'm going to keep track until next time so I'll know.' And then you're like— you just forget.

LESLIE: See, my mom and I are on the same cycle now, so she's, like, 'Leslie, we're getting close to our period.' I'm like, 'Thanks mom.' She, like, circles it on the calendar.

Using sentence completions and agreements, the girls form a supportive mode of talk where they sympathize with each other and talk about the unpredictability of menstruation. Interestingly, they use war metaphors for menstruation, talking about sudden, early, and late "attacks" of their periods on their unsuspecting selves.[4] It is frustrating for the girls that the timing of menstruation is so out of their control. The "hide and seek" metaphor brings a children's game into the discussion, which could indicate a connection to childhood that these girls still feel. This talk highlights how the body acts on its own while the girls have no control over what the body does and when it chooses to act. The girls show how distanced they can feel from their bodies because of menstruation. At the end of the transcript, Leslie talked about a solution she has found to this problem. Although frustrating, the unpredictable bleeding has given Leslie the opportunity to learn how to plan ahead and work with others. This also shows how comfortable Leslie is talking about her period with her mom, something I would never have been able to do when I was her age, a mere 15 years ago.

These girls also work to prevent leaking in response to gendered social norms to keep menstruation hidden. Leaking prominently announces menstruation. In addition to maintaining cleanliness, girls want to manage menstruation to conform to dominant U.S. cultural norms of keeping menstruation concealed, especially from boys. Most girls do not want to call attention to themselves and their menstrual cycle and prefer to hide their bodies and slip to the bathroom unnoticed. As I will discuss in more detail later, in mixed-gender settings such as schools, girls are subject to teasing and embarrassment because of their periods. For example, Jennifer talked about how boys tell "gross" and "nasty" jokes about menstruation. Several girls described how boys will rifle through their backpacks and tease girls about the menstrual products they find.

"WHY I NEVER CARRY A PURSE"

Of course, the boys and other girls know that girls menstruate. In their menstrual management, girls must deal with this collective knowledge and awareness of menstruation. In her group interview, Jennifer said that simply leaving the classroom during class can be cause for notice and speculation:

> JENNIFER (14): Sometimes you'll hear like a girl leave the room and you'll hear a whisper around the room like, 'it's a girl thing and it got out of control' and everyone will be like, 'oh, her period started and she wasn't ready.' Heh heh.

Since most adolescents do not want to stand out in the first place, being noticed for menstruation can be doubly frustrating. In response, girls conceal their supplies to prevent others from knowing what is happening, as described by Kasey and Jane in a group interview:

> KASEY (13): Everybody can tell when a girl is on her period, because most of them, they won't carry a purse, and then they'll carry a purse that week.
>
> JANE (14): Yeah.
>
> LAURA: *Oh really?*
>
> KASEY: And it's like totally obvious. That's why I never carry a purse.

By using purses to carry their supplies, the girls are planning for and managing menstruation in what should be a concealed way. But even then, they can be teased. The girls are embarrassed that others know what their bodies are doing and how their bodies are acting. The girls must not only manage their own bodies but must also attempt to manage the social situations in which their bodies, unintentionally, become actors.

Schools are a place where many stories about menstruation, particularly embarrassing stories, are circulated. As a social institution, schools intersect with teens' peer cultures and influence their interpretations of and management of menstruation. During school hours, girls must manage their menstrual products, and many girls told narratives about handling this responsibility. In one group interview, the girls collaboratively shared embarrassing stories about unsuccessfully concealing their menstrual products:

GRETA (15): Wasn't like Sue Heinz or Allison or somebody that was in eighth grade algebra, and—

LESLIE (16): That would be me.

LACEY (16): And, in her folder—

LESLIE: Tell it.

LACEY: I almost forgot about that.

GRETA: Who was I talking to—

LACEY: I don't know, but it was—

GRETA: Sue was, like, 'Can I have the English notes?' or something. I was like, 'Sure.' So, I rip out my folder, and my pad had somehow, it was just loose in the bag, it had gotten stuck in the folder. So, I was li—I think there was somebody between me and Sue. I think it was a guy, too, and I was like, 'Can you pass this to Sue?' And it, like, falls out. It hit her in the head, too, it, like, it just flew to her forehead.

LACEY: I was looking ( ). And I was like, 'Well, here it is,' pull out my pad, and it flies across, 'That's mine.' I had to, like, go over, like, pick it up. It was so embarrassing.

KASSIE (16): You know what they did to ( ) freshman year. She was sending one to me, so I was like, 'That's it.' So, I reached in my bag, and it was in Mr. Berry's room. And, like, someone, I don't know, we were sitting there doing class work or something, and I pulled it out, and I threw a pad across the room, and it landed on her desk. She was like [ ], but, like, no one else around her noticed. And, then, remember that when I pulled that pad out, and I was just like, 'Pa-ching.'

LESLIE: You got me.

KASSIE: Oh, did it hit you?

LESLIE: No, it hit my desk or—and I was like, 'Here.'

KASSIE: Yeah, and then everyone was like, 'What the—?' It was funny.

This sequence is a storytelling session where one story builds upon another, all in the mode of supportive talk. First, Greta brings up a story that Leslie and Lacey immediately recognize. Greta and Lacey collaboratively tell the story and share their experiences with this embarrassing moment. This story reminds Kassie of a similar story that she shares. The first story is particularly embarrassing. Pads or tampons end up where they are not supposed to be: in public space. However, in the second story Kassie challenges this nonpublic nature of menstrual products as she explains how she was sick of trying to conceal it, so she openly tossed a pad to a friend during class. She laughs at the incident precisely because she broke the norms of handling menstrual products. By having and displaying a pad, Kassie identifies herself publicly as a menstruant. "Third wave" feminists (a current generation of young feminists) argue that by claiming their own identities and claiming and using terms such as "sexy" and "cunt," they prevent others from having the power to label them.[5] By claiming this identity, Kassie prevents others, particularly boys, from turning the menstrual identity into something embarrassing. She defines the situation as "not a big deal." As we will see later in this book, there are many examples throughout the girls' stories where the girls actively take on the identity as menstruant in order to gain some sort of power advantage.

In both of these stories, the girls collectively decide if pads in public spaces are embarrassing (as Lacey evaluates the first story) or funny (as Kassie evaluates the second story) or both. In contrast to Lacey's feelings, Kassie thinks that having pads out in public should not be embarrassing and actively resists this embarrassment. Also, in each of the stories, it is the determination of the incident as embarrassing or funny that marks the end of one story and signals that another line of talk may begin.

In their interviews, some of the boys recognize the responsibility and work involved in menstruation. Even though many girls are embarrassed by the boys' knowledge of their cycles and actively work to prevent the boys from knowing when they are menstruating, some of the boys are sympathetic with the girls' situation. Larry thinks that, as a boy, not menstruating is "one less thing to worry about." He hears the complaints from girls about the work and frustrations involved and is glad he does not have to deal with it. He said it would be good if girls did not menstruate because "it would save them some hassle." Martin also thinks that if girls did not have to menstruate, "then they really don't have to worry about buying products, or uh, just worrying about when it happens." He talked later about girls having to worry if "any of the fluid leaks or anything like that." Although many girls are concerned with what the boys think, some of the boys are quite understanding. However, these boys do not discuss their own roles in embarrassing girls. They stick to sympathizing about the bodily experience and management of menstruation.

THE BODY AS ACTOR

Menstruation is a constant reminder that the girls are embodied beings, as the girls must respond to their bodies' actions. In these examples, the girls show that, in response to their bodies' needs, their desire for cleanliness, the school structure's limits on bathroom breaks, and teasing by boys, girls use both collective and individual strategies to manage the work of menstruation. These girls develop subcultures of management strategies in response to the deprivations imposed by the dominant structure (in this case, the limits the school places on bathroom breaks).[6]

These examples show a complex relationship between agency and cultural norms. The girls continue to follow their culture's prescription of keeping menstruation concealed, as the "standard" body is a male body. This body can release a multitude of bodily substances such as through sweating, blowing one's nose, and using the bathroom. But menstruation is something that must be hidden and kept secret in public. Yet, at the same time, the body is an active agent in these girls' lives and the girls must respond to the body's needs. This agency is both resistant to social structure and reproductive of social inequality.[7]

The body's unpredictable actions demonstrate what I call "agency *of* the body," where the body itself is an actor as it actively bleeds (Fingerson 2005a). The body is the active subject and the girl is the object that is acted upon. Menstruation is a constant reminder that girls are embodied social beings and that the body is an independent actor in their lives and not always within girls' control. Girls' bodies directly affect girls' social interactions. In response to the bleeding, which is both messy and constrained by cultural expectations of concealment, the girls must actively manage their bodies. This is what I call "agency *over* the body." Here, the action is inverted from agency *of* the body, as the girl is the active subject and the body is being acted upon (Fingerson 2005a). Although they do not dismantle the norms of cleanliness and concealment by freely bleeding all over their classroom chairs (such as in Ani DiFranco's [1993] third wave song, "Blood in the Boardroom"), these girls work within the system and exert power over their bodies by managing menstruation.

These ideas enhance and extend R. W. Connell's (1995) notion of "body-reflexive practices," where bodies are both objects of practice and agents of practice (such as in sexual encounters). Bodies have a materiality and are embedded in history and in social processes. It is through social interaction, for example, that bodily difference between the genders becomes social reality. Bodies are not merely natural, but are actively involved in social interactions, as they can shape the course of people's behaviors. As Connell (1995) and Prout (2000) point out, thinking about the body as agentic has not been theorized enough, and scholars need to think about the agency of bodies, not just discourse and behaviors, in social processes. I help extend sociological understandings of how bodies are agentic in social processes by showing how girls experience agency of the body and agency over the body in dealing with menstruation. Later, I will discuss how girls use their bodies, gendered through menstruation, as sources of power in gendered interactions.

WHAT IF IT GETS STUCK?

Nothing about menstruation makes adolescent girls more nervous than tampons. In Judy Blume's (1970) bestselling book *Are You There God? It's Me, Margaret*, Margaret and her sixth-grade classmates watch the "period movie" at a special girls-only gathering in the school auditorium. After the film, sponsored and shown by a sanitary napkin company, "the lady in the gray suit asked if there were any questions" (p. 97). Margaret's friend asks about Tampax, which the film did not mention. "Gray Suit coughed into her hanky and said, 'We don't advise *internal protection* until you are considerably older'" (italics original). That was the only (non)information Margaret, her friend, and the rest of the girls in the auditorium received. The girls in my interviews, thirty years after this book was published, experienced a similar dearth, although not as extreme, of information on tampons and a reluctance to try or depend on them.

Girls lack knowledge and language about their own internal reproductive anatomy and they show discomfort with their genitalia. Many girls I interviewed, both older and younger, are unfamiliar with their bodies and not comfortable dealing with or touching "down there." Karin Martin (1996) finds that girls in the United States are denied knowledge about their bodies and, in particular, their genitals, from early childhood through puberty. Parents, for example, give boys names for their genitalia such as "wee-wee," but are much less likely to offer specific names for girls' genitalia. Girls are taught to refer to "down there" or "private parts" rather than being offered a language to describe the various parts of their genitals such as vagina, clitoris, or labia. Without language, there cannot be comfort or full understanding. How can we fully experience something if we do not have the language to describe it?

According to the theory of linguistic relativity, language profoundly shapes our perceptions and experiences of our worlds.[8] Through language, we formulate the cultural categories by which we define and interpret our experiences. The language and words that we have predispose us to seeing the world in a particular way. For example, "sanitary napkin" makes us think about sanitation, keeping clean, and the dirtiness of blood. Talking about "down there" does not name the vagina, clitoris, or vulva, and in fact, suppresses the individual importance and distinctiveness of each.

Further placing the girls at risk, Karin Martin argues that because of the lack of both cognitive and subjective knowledge about their bodies, girls may feel that they have little control over their bodies. For example, Deborah Tolman (2002) argues that adolescent girls are limited by their language in expressing sexual desire. They are not given language or space to express sexual pleasure or to positively explore their sexuality. This lack of sexual subjectivity limits girls' sexual agency, which makes girls susceptible to sexual and domestic abuse and unfulfilling sexual relationships throughout the life course. In sexual relationships, girls often have less power precisely because they are often unfamiliar and uncomfortable with their own genitalia, and they do not have access to comfortable language to express either discomfort or pleasure. Girls are thus more vulnerable in sexual situations and when being pressured to do things they do not want to do. Boys, on the other hand, are culturally supported in their sexual explorations and sexual knowledge. They use their knowledge and language in sexual interactions with girls to gain and hold the upper hand.

None of the mostly white girls I interviewed used "vagina," "clitoris," or other specific terms for their genitalia when talking about menstruation and the body. Rather, some said "down there" and the rest avoided the reference completely. Unlike boys who can refer to their genitalia in pop culture-accepted everyday language such as "dick" or "balls," girls do not have an equivalent colloquial language for their genitalia. For example, "cunt" is certainly colloquial, but it is considered vulgar and offensive (although some third wave feminist writers such as Muscio [1998] are reclaiming the term). This discomfort with their bodies is particularly evident during their discussions of tampon use. To use tampons, girls must touch their genitalia and be intimately familiar with their own vaginal anatomy. It requires girls to touch and manipulate "down there," which is something the girls were neither taught nor encouraged to do. Many of the girls expressed discomfort with tampon use, and thus they rely on pads. The girls' lack of cognitive and subjective knowledge about their bodies not only affects their sexual power and safety, but has direct and often painful and frustrating effects on their management of menstruation.

Katie, one of the youngest girls at age 14, uses pads exclusively, saying that "tampons are scary—we don't use tampons." Interestingly, she removes her own self in this discussion by referring to herself in the plural. Her mother and her sister both use tampons, so she is not using "we" to refer to her family. Later, Katie talked about how she really dislikes going to the gynecologist. "The whole idea of putting anything 'up there' is like really scary." Katie does not say "vagina," rather, she uses the vague and nondescriptive term "up there." Briana, age 16, also shows her discomfort with "up there." When I asked her if she used pads or tampons, she said, "Just pads, I mean, I don't like the idea of tampons." I asked her why and she responded with, "I don't know, I just, I don't like the idea of how you wear one."

Some of the more experienced girls talked about their first times using tampons and how they were confused and often used them incorrectly. Trying to get a tampon in position is often the first experience girls have in handling their vaginas and labias. Leslie does not swim and avoids wearing tighter shorts during her period because she "can't wear tampons." She said that she tried a couple of times to wear tampons, but she "was like hhheeee [screech] and I freaked out, like, right before I got it [in]." Interestingly, Leslie said that she *can't* wear tampons rather than that she *doesn't* wear tampons. In her group interview, the other girls talked about their problems wearing tampons:

> LACEY (16): Oh my gosh, I got a tampon when I went to the movies one time.
>
> KASSIE (16): Oh, wow.
>
> LACEY: It was my first time ever wearing one.
>
> KORRINE (15): Sucks.
>
> LACEY: It got stuck, and I had to call my mom.
>
> KASSIE: Stuck in?
>
> LACEY: Yeah, it was in all the way.
>
> LESLIE (16): Do you guys all, like, wear them?
>
> ERICA (15): No.
>
> KASSIE: Yeah, I do, I wear them. I don't slee—
>
> REBECCA (15): Over spring break was my first time with them.
>
> LACEY: And so, I had to call my mom to the movie theater in [the next town]. 'Cause there were people around me, she said, 'What?' I was like, 'Stuck.' And she was like, 'Oh. Oh, all right.'

During this conversation, Leslie is curious about her friends' experiences and asks if all the other girls wear tampons or not. She wonders if she is the only one who does not wear them. The girls in this group talk about the problems with tampons and how, initially, they were unsure of how to use them. As Lacey said in the transcript, she does not like tampons because "my first time I got it stuck." She described her situation later in the discussion; "I put it in wrong, first of all. There's like two cardboard pieces and the tampon inside one of the cardboard pieces. I put it in there with it, 'cause I didn't know. And I found that uncomfortable." Lacey did not know how to insert a tampon properly and that the cardboard applicator is used only to insert the tampon, then it is pulled out and thrown away. If she were more comfortable with her vagina and its anatomy and how a tampon works, she may not have had these troubles. The girls are particularly interested and engaged during this quick-paced conversation. Lacey starts out with her story, but the other girls are so eager to share their own experiences that they interrupt her. Lacey is finally able to finish her story at the end of the sequence. Notice at the end of the story, Lacey conceals her menstrual status from the "people" around her and uses a code word, "stuck," with what was, I am sure, a meaningful glance to her mother. Her mother immediately knew what had happened. Leaking and getting a tampon stuck are probably among any girl's or woman's greatest fears.

Erica's mom uses tampons so Erica "always knew, like, what tampons were." When she started her period, her mom gave her tampons and told her how to use them. But Erica did not like them and uses pads instead: "They made me feel uncomfortable, like I can't, like, not think about the fact that, like, something's inside of me that shouldn't be there. And I don't like it at all. And I'm always afraid it's going to get stuck or something bad is going to happen so, heh, I just don't like them." She adds a nervous giggle, "heh," to the end of her story.

The "something bad" Erica mentions could be a fear of getting the tampon stuck inside, but Toxic Shock Syndrome (TSS) is often brought up by the girls when talking about tampon use. TSS, discovered in 1979,[9] is a rare but serious disease that can cause death. Medical researchers believe it is caused by the combination of tampon use and the presence of a bacterium (staphylococcus aureaus), which is found in the vaginas of some women. To reduce the risk of TSS, women are advised by tampon manufacturers to use tampons with the lowest absorbency that meets their flow needs, to wear the tampon for no longer than six hours, and to alternate tampon use with pad use. The girls' fears are warranted according to the TSS information inserts placed in every box of tampons, but I find the girls are much more concerned and vocal about their fears of the disease than adult women are in their everyday talk. Most likely, adult women who use tampons are not only significantly more experienced with handling their vaginas, but they also have more rational (i.e., minimal) concerns about contracting TSS and are used to managing their tampon use accordingly.

Briana is afraid of TSS because she "heard early on from my sister that like, you, if you don't, like you have to change it like every couple of hours and if you don't, you get like really sick." Briana does not use the term TSS or give any name for the disease, but she is clearly frightened to use tampons and concerned about contracting TSS. Ally knows the name "Toxic Shock Syndrome," but admitted that she does not really know what it is: "I know it's not like a big thing, I don't even understand what it is, I just know it sounds bad and I don't want to get it." The terms "toxic" and "shock" are indeed not very benign. As in the linguistic relativity theory, our language affects our interpretations, particularly in this case. Ally said she does not "really like using tampons" because of this fear. These girls' semiawareness and concern about contracting TSS reflects confusion about tampons, how they work, and for how long you can leave a tampon in. These girls feel they have little control over their susceptibility to TSS. They might also be using TSS as one more reason, a medical, official-sounding reason, not to use tampons, something they are uncomfortable with anyway.

Kassie, on the other hand, shows a more complete understanding of TSS, although she does not remember the name. She said that she wears tampons every day but that she sleeps in pads. She said, "I just don't want to get that, you know, thing. What's that disease called?" I responded with "Toxic Shock Syndrome." She said yes, and then continues to describe how "I'm always paranoid about that, if I leave it in for more than eight hours, I'm like, 'Oh no!' I'm just, like, freaking out." Kassie understands that TSS can only be contracted by wearing a tampon for an extended amount of time. Ellen also shows a more complete understanding of TSS. She said, "I kind of worry about TSS" because "it's really unlikely, but if you wear it too long, and I worry about forgetting or something." She is careful to not wear a tampon "more than four or five hours." Not only do girls have to manage carrying protection and not leaking, but tampon users also have to keep track of how long a tampon has been in.

Overall, tampons were an important feature of the girls' menstrual discussions, no matter if the girl was a younger or older teenager. Some older girls, like Nancy and Kassie, use tampons regularly with no problems. Nancy even remarked, "the bigger the better" because of her heavy flow. However, most of the discussions about tampons reflect girls' unease with and lack of understanding about their own bodies and gynecologic anatomy. They are afraid of getting tampons stuck, using tampons improperly, manually handling their vaginas, and TSS. This lack of knowledge can be detrimental to their comfort with their own bodies, which can affect girls' sense of bodily control and confidence in their sexual relationships. If girls are afraid to use tampons because of unfamiliarity with their vaginas, how will they react to pressure from boys to have sex? How will they be able to assert sexual agency, particularly when boys act more confident in their sexual knowledge?

Tampon use is a highly salient issue for many adolescent girls, as it deals with the insides of their bodies and their vaginas, areas they are uncomfortable with and know very little about. At the same time, talking about menstruation and tampons can be one of the few spaces where women, particularly adolescent girls who are not sexually experienced yet, feel free to talk about their reproductive anatomy in very intimate ways. The girls talk about tampon use with each other, albeit in single-gender groups, and this can foster a discussion about body and sexuality that might not occur otherwise. If girls can talk more openly about tampon use with each other, perhaps this can extend to further discussions of genitalia and sexuality. This could lead to more knowledge and comfort with sexuality, which might bring a more equal balance to sexual relationships with boys than currently exists.

TAMPAX ADS IN A ROOM FULL OF BOYS

Even though we will explore instances of mentstrual discussion between girls and boys, some girls want to keep all discussions of menstruation, not just tampon use, in women-only spaces. For example, the mass media, a powerful social institution intersecting teens' lives, is pervasive and enters into our lives in all moments, when we are in all different types of social situations.[10] For some girls, mass media can be intrusive because it brings up menstruation at seemingly inappropriate times, such as in cross-gender situations. These girls do not think that menstruation should enter their interactions with boys, possibly because they are afraid of being teased or because they are embarrassed. They want to retain their private menstrual identity. This adds a further layer of complexity to girls' attitudes towards menstruation. Even if a girl thinks that menstruation is not a big deal, she still might be embarrassed about it and not want it talked about in front of boys. Wearing a bra, for example, is not a big deal to many girls, but they still might not want to talk about bra sizes with boys.

Krissy, in her individual interview, told a story about her male cousin and how he was confused about the menstrual products he saw on television. She did not want to explain the products to him, preferring that another male handle it:

KRISSY (16): Heh heh. When my—ok, it's really funny because when my cou—when I was—my cousin was like 11. I was 12, I think. We were having this conversation I was staying the night at his house about—

LAURA: —He's a boy

KRISSY: He's a boy. About commercials and he goes, he goes so what are these commercials I keep seeing with these chicks on them and they're talking about something that has wings and I just—I just like didn't know what to say I was like, ok, because I knew that his mother like intentionally did not put him in sex education, like—

LAURA: —Really

KRISSY: They intentionally didn't like sign something or didn't sign something so he wouldn't go into it or something like that which I really thought was stupid 'cause we had to explain everything to him. But, so, what I did actually I think was I had another guy explain it to him.

Krissy thinks that these topics are better shared in single-gender interaction rather than in mixed groups. She equates a discussion of menstruation with sexual education (which she believes is important to learn in school) and may be too embarrassed to discuss these topics with her cousin.

Ally is quite a talker both in her interviews and in my conversations with her before and after the interviews. She is a senior and already has a scholarship from a nearby college. When I asked at the end of her individ-ual interview if she had any other comments about menstruation, Ally shared that she does not like the Tampax commercials that are aired on tele-vision. This is particularly salient to her since she offered it without me ask-ing a question about it.

> ALLY (17): I don't see what the big deal is, everyone's all like, everyone's so uptight about it, except for the Tampax commercials. They're so dumb. And I don't see what the big deal whenever a woman's all, like, uptight, and not wanting to talk about it. But, I don't see why people have to, like, throw it in our face when we're on the couch, trying to watch TV. So, like, you go to your boyfriend's, and it's you and your boyfriend and his brothers and his mom, and then Tampax comes on, heh heh.

Later, she adds, "that's just how I look at it. It's not a big deal, don't make it a big deal." Ally has mixed feelings. She first said that menstruation is not a big deal, yet then says that women should be able to talk about it and not be uptight with the topic. She then added that Tampax commercials bug her because they talk about it during her leisure television viewing time. I believe that Ally's irritation is because the media mention menstruation during her time in mixed company with her boyfriend and his family. During her individ-ual and group interviews with girls only, Ally was very forthcoming and talka-tive about menstrual topics. She may believe that menstruation should remain in the women's realm, rather than being broadcast on television where it enters a mixed-gender world. With boys, there is the potential for embarrassment and shame about menstruation, a topic that is for her, supposed to remain private and shared among women only. Additionally, boys see menstruation as a sex-ual topic, as we will explore later, so these advertisements bring sex into a set-ting where Ally is with her boyfriend, his brothers, and his mother.

THE CHECKOUT BOY

Kasey and Jane said in their group interview that one of the difficult things about menstruation is buying menstrual products from male store clerks and keeping them organized and concealed from boys at school. Keeping men-struation and menstrual products in the realm of women only is important. Kasey and Jane suggested ways of making this easier for girls:

> KASEY (13): Like, having to go to the store and buy your own pads and having to go through the line with like male cashiers.

> JANE (14): Yeah. That is, like, totally embarrassing. I think we should just create a women's store. Women can go there and have, like, and have, like, like we'd help the guys that had no clue that were coming in there.

KASEY: Or during each time during school, and then you have to, like, write a pass out of class, and go through all this junk in the bathroom, and those really thick things that they have in the bathroom. It's just annoying.

JANE: I think we should have a place in the lockers, like, where you can, like, have a little compartment.

KASEY: I do, now.

JANE: But there is like nothing ( ).

KASEY: I keep them in my backpack, like in the bottom, and my locker.

Kasey and Jane discuss some of the biggest difficulties in managing menstruation in public: male cashiers, asking for a pass during class, keeping menstrual products hidden, and the bulky pads that are sold for a dime in public restrooms. (Even with today's space-age technology of thin pads, those sold in restrooms are notoriously large and thick, which makes them both uncomfortable and certain to show through pants.)

Similarly, returning to Judy Blume's (1970:135–37) classic book, Margaret and her friend, Janie, experience the embarrassment of purchasing pads from a male clerk. The girls, in anticipation of their first period, "inspect the sanitary napkin display" at the drugstore. Margaret suggests that they buy a box, "just in case." She thinks to herself, "It was something I'd thought about for a while, but wasn't ever brave enough to do. Today I was feeling brave." Margaret takes a box off the shelf. She also grabs "a purple pocket comb to make it look like we were really shopping." The girls walk over to the checkout counter and "walked away just as fast when we saw that there was a boy behind the cash register." Janie gets scared, almost starts to cry, and says she cannot go through with it. Margaret, still feeling very brave, approaches the register and pays for "the box" and comb while avoiding any eye contact with the clerk. After she gets her change, which she does not take the extra time to count, she and her friend leave in triumph. Margaret thinks to herself, "That was all there was to it! You'd think he sold that kind of stuff every day of the week."

"SURFIN' THE CRIMSON WAVE"

The language that the high school-age girls and boys use to describe menstruation reveals their negative and ambivalent feelings about menstruation and shows how some girls are more positive and direct about menstruation. Although the teens are forthright in their peer discussions, they still do not use "adult" terms like "menstruation" or "menstrual cycle" in their conversations. The teens assign meaning to and interpret their worlds through their language and terminology. Terminology today has changed since even the 1940s, when women did not use the term "menstruation," but instead preferred and used terms such as "the curse," "I'm sick," and "being unwell."[11] Using such terms expresses the attitude that menstruation is an illness and not something talked about in public conversation.

Most of the girls and boys in our interviews did not refer to menstruation as "menstruation" because they see the term as formal, medical, and used by adults, not a term that is part of their own adolescent language and discourse. (I asked in the pilot groups if Paul and I, as the adult interviewers, should use the term "menstruation" or another term such as "period." The teens said since we were adults, using "menstruation" would be best.) The girls in one group interview said that they use the term "menstruation" only in health class. Although teens medicalize menstruation to a certain extent by, for example, comparing it to a chronic illness, in their own peer interactions they reject the explicitly medical term. Some researchers believe that using code words indicates that girls lack a standard language to express themselves and are thus alienated from their bodies.[12] For example, girls have little language with which to express their sexual desire, because the dominant culture defines girlhood and femininity as not sexually assertive. Other research finds that girls use code words and other linguistic strategies to maintain the concealment of menstruation from outsiders while still being able to talk about and share information about menstruation with friends.[13]

However, the girls in our interviews were relatively comfortable with menstrual talk and they discussed menstruation, their experiences, and their bodies. The "code words" the girls use do not serve to keep menstruation a secret from others who might overhear. It is clear to all teens what "getting it" means and why girls have to run to the bathroom with their purses in the middle of class. I believe that by using alternate, but not secretive, terminology, the girls claim menstruation as their own, make up their own terms for it, and reject the formal medical terms they hear nurses and teachers using. They may find that the available terms, such as "menstruation," do not adequately express their own feelings and experiences. For example, "vagina" is a formal, adult term, used in health class and by doctors, that does not hold intimate significance for girls' own subjective experiences.

The teens used a variety of different names for menstruation, both in everyday conversation and in humorous storytelling. During the interviews, both group and individual, both girls and boys primarily referred to menstruation as "period." However, occasionally other terms arose in the discussion such as "drop an egg," "ragging," and "that time of the month." When Paul, the male interviewer, and I asked specifically about the different terms teens use when talking about menstruation, a variety of other terms were offered by both the boys and the girls. The table below lists the terms the girls said they use and boys said they use.

The terms in this list reflect the whole range of negative, neutral, and positive feelings about menstruation. The boys' list is quite short compared to the girls' list, suggesting that boys do not talk about menstruation in as much detail as do girls. The girls' list is more extensive because girls experience menstruation on a regular basis, and it enters their talk as part of a more thorough and elaborate discourse than it enters boys' talk. Janice Delaney, Mary Jane Lupton, and Emily Toth (1988) contend that the more openly menstruation is accepted in a social group, the more words there are to describe it. The list includes most of those from the boys' list, but the girls add more terms and versions of the terms. Interestingly, "she just dropped an egg" is not on the girls' list, possibly because, for girls, the experience of menstruation is with blood, not a microscopic egg.

MENSTRUAL TERMINOLOGY

TERMS GIRLS SAID THEY USE:

bleeding
I'm bleeding again
period
I'm on my period
the monthly thing
time of the month
it's that time of the month again
ragging
the rag
I'm on the rag
monthly visitor
Aunt Flo
Aunt Flo is visiting

Aunt Flo has come for an unannounced visit
my little friend's in town
surfing the crimson wave
crimson tide
riding the crimson tide
floods
I'm flooded
mens
PMS
Bloody Mary
it's the white flag with the red spots
flag day (referring to Japanese flag)

TERMS BOYS SAID THEY USE:

period
having her period
on the rag
ragging

riding the crimson wave
she just dropped an egg
Aunt Flo is visiting
that time of the month

Most of the terms are self-explanatory and are used by adults and teens, such as versions of "period," "that time of the month," or "ragging." However, "Aunt Flo" (referring to the "flow" of a menstrual period) is more unique to girls' culture. I had never heard the flag metaphors before these interviews and I had to ask what the Japanese flag had to do with menstruation (it is a red sphere, or spot, on a white background, which can look like blood on underwear or a pad, the teens explained to me).

The different words used for menstruation can indicate the type of feelings the speaker has towards menstruation. In her individual interview, Anne said that she hears boys refer to girls' periods as "when the red river's up" and "take the dirt road." Both refer to sexual relations with girls, offering added evidence that the boys Anne interacts with define menstruation in sexual terms and in terms of how menstruation affects their interactions with girls. "When the red river's up," boys cannot cross the river or, in other words, engage in sexual intercourse. "Taking the dirt road" is the alternative path of anal intercourse, which boys might take instead of vaginal intercourse when their female partner is menstruating. For the boys, "riding the crimson wave" can also be a sexual reference to when a male "rides" a female in sex. Yet the girls offered their own versions of the crimson wave, possibly referring to sitting on a red wave of blood.

In the girls' list, some of the terms are passive and others are active. "Bleeding" and "I'm bleeding again" are straightforward ways to talk about menstruation where the girl is doing the acting. In contrast, "Aunt Flo is visiting" or "my little friend's in town" are passive, more coded terms where menstruation is happening "to" the girls. "I'm flooded" is an even stronger and more overwhelming term than "bleeding." Other terms use clever metaphors, such as "flag day" or "monthly visitor." These terms mask the real process, unlike the term "bleeding." Terms such as "flag day" also indicate creative ways of describing menstruation. For the girls, it can be cool to find new and different ways to refer to menstruation.

None of the teens used the term "sanitary napkins" or "sanitary products" when referring to pads and tampons. Although the teens' use of "pad" and "tampon" is not a code, their overt rejection of the "sanitary" terms indicates a mode of language with which they are uncomfortable. In her group interview, Lacey told a story about asking the school nurse for a "pad" and the nurse responded with, "You mean a sanitary napkin?" The group collectively laughed at the use of the term "sanitary napkin," recognizing it as a term that is not a part of their own cultural language patterns, but belongs to nurses, doctors, and health class.

Both girls and boys engaged in the use of alternate terms; however, they may do so for different reasons. For boys, the use of code names for menstruation might add to the mystery of menstruation since they do not know very much about the process or the experience of menstruation. Using code names might also imply that the boys know more than they actually do. In our interviews, the boys were not only less sure about the process of menstruation, but were sometimes embarrassed and uncomfortable discussing menstruation in a way the girls were not. I asked the girls what terms boys use when they talk about menstruation. In one of the group interviews, the girls recognized that boys use different words because they are embarrassed:

LAURA: *Do guys talk about it differently than girls do? Like, do guys use different words than girls do?*

Kasey (13): Yeah, 'cause they can't say the words that we say, because they're embarrassed about them.

LAURA: *So, what do they say?*

Kasey: Uh—They go, 'Uh, that thing that they go through, uh, you know.'

Jane (14): 'That monthly thing.'

Kasey: And it's funny, in our health classes, they way all the guys fidget in their seats whenever we're talking about it. It is so funny.

The root of the boys' embarrassment, I believe, is their lack of knowledge about menstruation and how girls manage their periods. The girls have more power in these interactions because they have the experience and knowledge. Kasey enjoys laughing at the fidgety boys. The boys also talk less about menstruation so it makes sense that they do not have or use as many alternative terms. As Larry noted in his group interview, "I just say period. But, it's not something we talk about too much, so we don't need too many words."

Kathleen O'Grady and Paula Wansbrough (1997) claim that, for girls, using code names adds to the mystery for younger girls not familiar with menstruation yet and affirms the place of menstruating girls in the larger community of women because they share a special language. As we will see later, some girls do see menstruation as an entrée into an exclusive and special club of older women. A small number of the girls in my interviews preferred secret code words because they want to conceal their menstrual status from the public, but share it with selected, in-the-know friends. Andrea shared in her group interview that her friend "always" says "I have a math test" when she is on her period. Andrea admitted that it was confusing, since she never knew if her friend indeed had a math test or not!

Dave said in his individual interview that he had asked a girl friend "if she had a secret system" for referring to menstruation. He said, "She said they [she and her friends] had like entire systems of codes worked out so guys have no idea what they are talking about." Dave's friend continued to explain to him, "They'll sit there and be like 'yep, my red lipstick arrived in the mail.' And so, other girls will know that they're on their period and we'll be like, 'Okay, you got lipstick, whoopdeedoo!'" In his group interview, Jim said that girls have alternate terms for menstruation. He said, "I've heard girls—they'll name it so that way they don't have to be like 'I'm on my menstruation cycle.' They'll name it like a goofy name or something between their friends." In these cases, the boys are aware of these "secret" codes used by the girls. However, the codes still function to create an in-group among the girls. They create a way of sharing their experiences in a private way that most boys, or other girls, do not readily understand.

Not all girls like to use code names. Interestingly, in the same group interview where the girls said they do not like the term "menstruation," Korrine admitted that she says, "I'm on my menstruation cycle," but immediately afterwards apologized to the group saying, "sorry guys." She apologized for her use of the term "menstruation," as if she was abandoning her peers and aligning with a different group of people who use a different language. Later, during the discussion of different terms, she defended herself again and said, "I don't use any little names." By referring to the codes as "little names," she belittles the other girls' code words and positions herself as more adult and mature.

"IT'S NOT A BIG DEAL"

Like Korrine, some girls find that menstruation is not a big deal. Rather than seeing it as a negative experience that they feel they must conceal, these girls prefer to just deal with it and move on. Not all teens feel that menstruation should be defined as a shameful embarrassing event. Those that see menstruation as not a big deal show how they do not let menstruation or menstrual-related comments define their experiences. As we have seen, many teens resist the medical term "menstruation" in favor of lay language such as "period" or "ragging." At menarche, there is much anxiety and ambivalence about puberty and menstruation, but, as the girls age, they get used to menstruation and see it as a part of their normal everyday lives. Katie's comments directly reflect this when she would tell a young girl that menstruation "is kind of scary the first time it happens, but you get used to it after a while." Many girls agreed with Katie's sentiments and would tell a young girl that although it is important, menstruation is "not a big deal" and is "perfectly normal." As Rebecca said, "it's nothing to be alarmed about."

Although Ally was fairly negative about menstruation during her interviews, she still sees it as not a big deal in her life: "Yeah, like breathing. You know, it's like second nature. 'Oh look,' blood, pad, done." Later she added that, "I don't see what the big deal is, everyone's all like, everyone's so uptight about it." In one of the group interviews, the girls expressed similar sentiments:

LESLIE (16): I think it's just weird, because people are like, 'It's disease.'

LACEY (16): Yeah.

KASSIE (16): And, you know, really, I don't know, girls that are all like, they don't, like, want to talk about it, it's, like, some big secret or something. It's just like, it's just your freaking period. I mean, it is a big deal, but at the same time, you shouldn't be like- [interrupted]

Kassie displays the tension between seeing menstruation as not a big deal, but at the same time recognizing that "it *is* a big deal." Later in this same group interview, the girls talked about how they wish society was not so "hush-hush" and "dirty" about menstruation.

Some boys also talked about menstruation in this way. Don said that he is surprised that menstruation is "really kept under wraps and on the down low" because he does not see menstruation as that problematic. Jim asserted that he is comfortable with menstruation and talking about menstrual products, but recognizes that many of his guy friends are not. He reported that even the sight of a tampon wrapper "grosses 'em out or something, I don't know why, but it does." Walter would tell a young girl who knew nothing about menstruation that it is "a natural thing, that there's nothing to worry about." He does not see menstruation as deviant or medicalized; rather, it is a normal occurrence. Similarly, Larry would tell a young girl that menstruation is not "weird or bad or anything, it's not something to be ashamed of, it's just something you've got to deal with."

These teens resist the power that menstruation holds over their lives. It is not a major issue to tease about, be embarrassed or secretive about, or show superior knowledge about. Thus, by defining menstruation as "not a big deal," at the same time knowing that menstruation in fact is important, these teens do not engage as overtly in the power plays surrounding menstruation between girls and boys in cross-gender interactions that we will see later (although this is not so easily cut and dried). Menstruation simply does not hold as much sway in their lives. Rather, they see menstruation as normal and not something with which to be concerned. Although this does not directly empower girls, it does show how power is negotiated in interactions and is not absolute. Menstruation provides opportunities for girls to interpret their bodies in an agentic way. Girls can draw on their bodies as a power resource in their social interactions.

This attitude, particularly among the girls, could be partially due to their age. The girls have already gone through puberty, they are experienced with menstruation and their adult bodies, and they are more confident around boys. It would be interesting to compare these teens' opinions with interviews from younger girls at or near menarche because they may be much more sensitive and susceptible to boys' teasing and want to conceal menstruation to a much greater extent.

As we have seen in this chapter, girls and boys have both negative and ambivalent experiences with and views about menstruation and girls' bodies. Where do these views come from? What cultural norms are their experiences based in? In the next chapter, I explore what our dominant western cultural history tells us about girls' bodies and menstruation and how this can affect teens' experiences of menstruation, social interaction, and power.

THREE

Cultural Contexts

The cultural context in which we all live affects our attitudes and behaviors. In order to understand and contextualize adolescent social power relations and how adolescents use their bodies as sources of power, we must take into account the larger cultural context in which adolescents live. Adolescents learn their attitudes about the body from a variety of sources including family members, teachers in schools, health textbooks, works of fiction, and the media. Adolescents' own cultural contexts and understandings are embedded in each of these sources or social institutions.

As Alan Prout and Allison James (1997) and many other contemporary sociology of childhood theorists[1] contend, childhood is a social institution, a permanent structural form in society. Children are active agents in determining their own lives and in influencing those around them. Childhood is a social construction and our understanding of childhood is dependent upon the context in which children live. At the same time, as children grow from infancy through adulthood, their lives are continually intersected by the other social institutions of larger society, such as schools, family, economy, media, peers, and government. They are also embedded in the ways that age, gender, class, race, and ethnicity structure their lives. Children do not live entirely in their own cultures in a vacuum, but they participate in and are constrained by larger society.

William Corsaro's (1997) "Orb Web Model," based in his theory of interpretive reproduction, conceptualizes these intersections. Interpretive reproduction highlights how children participate in their own unique cultures by appropriating information from the adult world, being constrained by larger society, and at the same time actively contributing to cultural production. As they age, individuals move along a spiraling path that starts at its center with birth in their family of origin and spirals out through their peer cultures of preschool, preadolescence, adolescence, and adulthood. Intersecting this large spiral are several radii, or spokes, which each represent the various social institutions in an individual's life. Thus, it is within these institutions that "children will weave their webs" of their lives and peer cultures (p. 24).

The teens' talk about menstruation illustrates these intersections of other social institutions in their lives. The girls and boys are active agents negotiating and interpreting their own definitions and understandings of menstruation. At the same time, they live in a world constrained by not only their peers and peer cultures, but also by the family, media, school, and the health and medical industry. The teens' social interactions surrounding menstruation are not determined by them alone, but are also affected by these institutions and the numerous actors within these institutions. Girls must request bathroom passes from their teachers, boys and girls learn about menstruation from health class and media advertisements, girls are embarrassed when tampon commercials come on during a date, girls complain that school nurses do not stock Midol, and boys and girls engage in the medicalization of menstruation. In thinking about childhood as a social institution, we can envision this tension in how childhood is intersected by these other institutions even as children retain a measure of control in their own lives.

CULTURAL HISTORY OF MENSTRUATION

One intersecting spoke shaping current views of menstruation in the United States among adolescents (and adults) is the cultural history of menstruation in western thought and practice. Based on previous literature that has explored girls' bodies, sexuality, appearance norms, and menstruation, we would expect the negative and ambivalent attitudes girls and boys show towards menstruation, as we saw in the last chapter. We would expect that girls have reduced power in their gendered interactions when it comes to body issues.

Throughout the existing work on menstruation are descriptions of children's and adults' negative attitudes toward menarche and menstruation.[2] Many people see menstruation as dirty, "gross," messy, and basically an overall nuisance. For example, several studies find that women remembering menarche said their first menstruation made them feel dirty, unclean, ashamed, and even fearful.[3] In some religions such as Judaism, there are ritual purifications for women to complete after menstruation. A majority of girls report that menarche had a negative impact on their lives and almost half of menstruating girls have a negative view of menstruation.[4] Also, women perceive themselves as stigmatized by males when they are menstruating compared to when they are not menstruating.[5] Interestingly, girls who receive more information about menstruation from male sources are more likely to view menstruation as more negative and debilitating than girls who learn less from males are.[6] Younger girls in particular are more susceptible to negative attitudes and superstitions about menstruation because they have more limited experiences with menstruation than older women have.[7] Researchers attribute these negative attitudes to lack of information[8] or the cultural stereotypes and beliefs about menstruation.[9]

CONCEALMENT AND HYGIENE

Dominant cultural norms that are steeped in U.S. history are generally negative and encourage girls to be embarrassed about menstruation. Girls, compared to older women, are particularly susceptible to taboos and such negative norms because they dare not question them and have little experience of their own with which to counter such claims. To explore this history, I conducted analyses of a sample of advice books written for mothers and girls about puberty and menstruation during the early- and mid-twentieth century. Two principal themes emerged in these books: concealment and hygiene.

Concealment is a top priority. Many girls and women are concerned about odors. There are constant admonishments in the historical advice literature about the odor of menstruation and tips on how to contain this undesirable smell. Valeria Parker (1940) cautions her readers to thoroughly clean their vulvas several times a day so "that no odors from menstrual blood will offend others" (p. 67). Karl Karnacky (1943), writing around the same time, directly addresses a solution to the "smell" problem by suggesting that girls use tampons since he believes that they "overcome the problem of menstrual odor" (p. 152). The primary concern in many books is with other people and what they might smell, know, and think about the menstruating girl.

In 1975, Ellen Voelckers advised her young readers to be very cautious about menstrual odor and to change their "sanitary" pads often to avoid this problem. She argues that other people notice this foul odor and it is of utmost importance to conceal it, partially through using scented pads or talcum powder. Voelckers constantly reminds her readers to remain clean and fresh during menstruation. Identifying the socially created shame involved, Lenore Williams (1983) contends that "the idea that menstrual blood is a bad odor is evidence of a sociocultural norm that is perpetuated by the feminine-products companies and the reinforced perceived social need to hide any natural body odor" (p. 146). In fact, menstrual blood often only smells when it comes into contact with menstrual products. Rarely can it be smelled by others, even after such contact.

Today, western culture conveys images of disgust for menstrual blood, such as seen in everyday advertisements for "feminine hygiene" products to clean, deodorize, and conceal menstruation.[10] Menstruation is seen as a hygienic crisis for girls and, conveniently, this crisis sells a lot of single-use sanitary napkins and tampons.

In the historical advice literature I examined, there has been a constant concern with hygiene during menstruation, possibly dating back to the public health concerns of the late-1880s through the 1920s in response to the new germ theory, which posited that illness was passed by germs in unhygienic conditions, rather than by humors or vapors.[11] Menstrual blood, which had certainly been taboo prior to this time, was now considered even worse, a potential contaminant. In the 1940s, several advice books discussed hygiene including Valeria Parker's (1940) warning to keep the vaginal area regularly clean and Marion Faegre's (1943) suggestion to "keep fresh and clean by bathing frequently" (p. 29). In 1948, Lester Kirkendall wrote that cleanliness is particularly important during the menstrual flow and that girls should bathe at least once per day. Not surprisingly, Tampax reports from 1945 advise use of tampons to increase cleanliness and hygiene, and even discuss the pre-WWI era when "the life of the menstruating woman was a miserable one" because disposable pads and tampons had not been invented yet. Disposable pads, called "sanitary" napkins, and tampons are frequently associated with cleanliness as well as frequent bathing.

This discussion continues in the 1970s with Hilary Maddux (1975), who focuses on the logistics of menstruation, including cleanliness, "sanitary" napkins, and tampons. Ellen Voelckers (1975) tells girls that, just prior to menstruation, they "may feel the desire to be really clean, like cleaning your bathroom or bedroom" (p. 78). She argues that "during menstruation, cleanliness matters" and recommends that her readers shower more often and to "be as sanitary as possible" (p. 79). Voelekers also refers to menstrual pads as "sanitary protection," reinforcing the idea of hygiene and sanitation during menstruation. In their research article, Loudell Snow and Shirley Johnson (1978) find that this strong emphasis on hygiene and cleanliness has been detrimental to women's physical and emotional health and has even been manifested in "an overdependence on douching," which can actually damage a woman's body (p. 66). This cultural history of hygiene and cleanliness underscores contemporary girls' feelings of bodily embarrassment and shame surrounding menstruation.

These negative attitudes in western culture can be traced back to Greek and Roman antiquity in the writings of Aristotle and Pythagoras. These men believed menstrual blood was an excess of unwanted materials that is dirty and toxic.[12] In Eugene Mozes's (1955) list of menstrual taboos, he describes one ancient culture where women who were menstruating had to "cry out in warning *Mi Kay! Mi Kay!*—'I am unclean! I am unclean!'" In the Bible, Leviticus 15:19 tells believers that women are impure during their menstrual periods and anyone who touches them is rendered unclean. Among some orthodox Jews, menstrual impurity taboos (*niddah*) and postmenstruation purification rituals (*miqveh*) are in current practice, although some writers argue that the *miqveh* is solely spiritual and has nothing to do with physical cleanliness or negative images of menstruation.[13]

TABOOS

For many women in older generations, menstrual taboos were central to their experiences of menarche and menstruation. Taboos through the 1900s included restrictions on swimming, physical exertion, sexual intercourse, and even restrictions from certain high-pressure jobs because of fears of how women's hormonal cycles would interfere with their ability to concentrate. Prior to the twentieth century, menstrual taboos were even more restrictive and supernatural.

Menstrual taboos are based in gender politics and have a rich and long history in western culture. "Taboos" are restrictive laws that use exacting imperatives ("yes," "no," "you must," or "you must not") that exist to protect people from perceived danger.[14] Menstrual taboos thus help people to avoid the menstruant's "dangerous power" and help the menstruant get through her period without succumbing to her own "dangerous power."[15] For example, B. G. Jefferis and J. L. Nichols wrote in 1894 that, during menstruation, women have an enhanced psychic influence over themselves and their surroundings. Most of these superstitions and taboos developed because of the perceived power women and their menstrual blood had during menstruation. Taboos were a way of isolating that power from the men of the community. Many societies imposed restrictions on menstruating women, denying them privileges normally granted. Menstrual blood was feared as it was believed to be contaminating, yet magical at the same time.[16]

Eugene Mozes (1955) provides a list of "ancient" taboos that includes such things as:

- "if a menstruating women came close to a warrior, his sword would be dulled"
- being near menstruating women would cause men to become impotent
- women who fail to warn their husbands when they are menstruating can be put to death
- if a menstruating woman enters a sugar refinery, the sugar would blacken
- menstruating women walking among crops can destroy them

Oddly, Mozes adds that menstrual blood can be used as a love potion. Writing in 1955, Mozes also lists some "contemporary beliefs":

- if a menstruating woman does canning, the food will spoil
- a permanent wave for the hair will not take if the client is menstruating
- if a menstruating woman holds a flower, it will wilt

In extreme superstitions, menstruation is seen to cause women to be violent. In 1970, David Reuben, a medical doctor writing an advice book about "everything you wanted to know about sex but were afraid to ask," reported that when women commit violent crimes, it is most often during their menstrual periods. This type of writing makes menstruating women sound not only emotionally out of control, but physically quite dangerous. When girls and boys hear this, it is bound to have a negative impact on their overall views of menstruation and the "power" of girls' bodies.

Interestingly, there is no evidence of *who* started the taboos: women or men.[17] There are very different implications depending on if women are restraining themselves, giving themselves some time off to rest their bodies, to talk, and to share experiences with other women, or if men restrict women because men want to protect themselves from this unknown power and are afraid of women's bodies given this inexplicable loss of blood. Generally, when people bleed, it is because of injury or illness. Most likely, given women's lower social standing throughout most of western history, men developed and perpetuated the negative beliefs and taboos as a further method of social control of women.

CONTEMPORARY VIEWS AND ADVICE

In the last 15 years, a more positive and open discussion about menstruation has emerged in the advice books. The focus is not on concealment, hygiene, or taboos, as it once was. I also explored contemporary advice publications for girls and their parents such as Karen Gravelle and Jennifer Gravelle's (1996) *The Period Book*, Kathleen O'Grady and Paula Wansbrough's (1997) *Sweet Secrets*, and an article for parents in *New Moon Network* by Bridget Grosser (1998). These publications discuss a wider variety of experiences and beliefs than the historical ones I examined. For example, they do not write for mother-daughter pairs alone, but also include other adult-girl relationships, such as those with fathers. They also include a recognition of other cultures, such as in *The Period Book* where the authors state that in the United States, people are more concerned about body odor than in other countries (this might explain the earlier mention of obsession with menstrual odor). In these publications, menstrual taboos are not provided. Instead, they include explanations of the biological processes along with the experiences of and the social and cultural meanings of menstruation. They also highlight ways of celebrating menarche and menstruation, along with explanations of how girls can learn about themselves, their health, and their bodies through an understanding of menstruation. Similar to the girls' stories and narratives in our interviews, these contemporary publications emphasize the practicalities of managing menstruation, the pride that comes with knowing how to handle menstruation, and the social connections and bonding that girls can engage in because of their shared experiences.

Other researchers find evidence of menstrual taboos in contemporary U.S. society, where menstruating girls and women are prohibited from certain activities or contact with certain things.[18] Interestingly, in our interviews among mostly white, working- and middle-class teens in Indiana, I found no evidence of such menstrual taboos. There are examples of attitudes and practices that are unique to interacting with menstruants, such as when boys are afraid of making eye contact with menstruants as if they could catch it, as Kassie says. But such avoidances are not taboos. In the individual interviews, I asked directly if the girls do anything different while they are menstruating. Several mentioned not swimming or participating in other sports, but the girls attributed this to their fear of tampon use and clumsiness of pads, not to any sort of "taboo" or people telling them what they can or cannot do during menstruation. This contrasts with previous research, which finds that contemporary teenage girls think menstruation is a time of debilitation and restriction.[19] Our girls are certainly aware of their menstrual cycle, but they do not frame it in terms of limitations and taboos.

This recent change in views may reflect our increased physiological understanding of menstruation, ovulation, and the role of hormones in girls' and women's bodies. We now know where the blood comes from and its role in reproduction. Medical science also shows that hormones and chemicals in the human body affect our behaviors in multiple ways, such as clinical depression or feelings of euphoria, and that these are tied to females and males. Many of the girls in our interviews felt that menstruation did not restrict or debilitate them to any significant degree. Taboos are also more rampant when there is little public discourse or openness about a topic. Today's teens live in a media saturated, AIDS-epidemic, post-Clinton-Lewinsky, third-wave-feminist world where women win the soccer world cup, and menstruation, body, and sex are frequently talked about in the media, their families, and their peer groups. Even so, it is important to note that other subcultures in the United States and elsewhere may still circulate such taboos.

HISTORICAL CONTEXT OF HEALTH AND MEDICINE

The health and medical industry is a powerful social institution that intersects the lives of all people (particularly those with chronic illness or the elderly), including adolescents. Medical science has increased our knowledge of menstruation. At the same time, medicine's increased presence in our lives can have negative effects. Medical science and how we learn about menstruation affects teens' interpretations and experiences of menstruation. If menstruation and menstrual experiences are "medicalized," that means that, rather than girls and women having power to define their own bodies, the medical realm defines their bodies for them. Also, girls are seen as subject to the physicality of their bodies. Generally, when menstruation is medicalized, it is defined as an illness with physical and psychological symptoms. I will discuss medicalization in further detail in the next chapter, but here I offer a discussion of the teens' shared western cultural history of the pain and illness.

In my analysis of early- and mid-twentieth-century advice literature, girls were frequently warned about feeling ill and the pain that would come with menstruation. This stems from the late-nineteenth through early-twentieth century medical "fact" that women's normal state was to be sick because the female functions, including menstruation, are inherently pathological (luckily for continued U.S. gross domestic output and the survival of most U.S. families, this frailty did not extend to working-class women or Blacks).[20] Since antiquity, menstruation not only defined womanhood, but also signified women's inferiority (see Delaney, Lupton, and Toth [1988] for more detail). According to Aristotle, women's role in reproduction was passive (the soul of a baby comes from the male, only the physical part comes from the female) and thus menstruation, a part of the female reproductive system, was another indication that women were inferior.

In one extreme case, A. J. Ingersoll, a medical doctor writing in 1899 (republished 1974), argued that the pain of menstruation comes directly from anger. In one woman's case, he writes that her pain and spasmodic attacks were "caused by her anger with God for creating her a woman, and thereby subjecting her to menstruation; that her anger must cease, for she was beyond relief until she became reconciled to this function" (pp. 47–48). However, by 1900, most physical education teachers in the high schools, an important source of information on menstruation for adolescents, believed that menstruation was a natural, not a pathological process, although moderate variations were common.[21]

More characteristically of this time, B. G. Jefferis and J. L. Nichols, also writing at the turn of the century in 1894, argued that "most girls and women feel badly during the periods and absolute rest is necessary during the first two days" (p. 70). They believed that any trouble with menstruation stemmed from overexertion during a previous cycle. Girl Scout manuals from the 1920s instruct girls to tell their scout leaders when they were menstruating so they can be assigned reduced activities because of their more delicate condition.[22] Verbrugge (2000) reports that the mechanical models of menstruation available to the lay public between 1900 and 1940 claimed that poor posture, restrictive clothing, and too little or inappropriate exercise would weaken the uterus's structural integrity and cause it to be displaced or collapse entirely. The goal was to reduce mechanical strain on the uterus. Thus, physical education teachers did not want their girls engaging in competitive sports and other activities that had risks of falling or collisions, particularly before and during the menstrual flow.

Throughout the 1930s, people believed menstruating women should restrict their activities to save their energy for the process of menstruation.[23] The body, it was said, can never do two things well at the same time. In particular, girls who are menstruating for the first few times must be confined, as their bodies are especially sensitive and the processes are new. This confinement included not only restrictions on physical activity, but also on things such as education and reading. This type of belief dealt a serious blow to girls at a time when women were becoming more actively involved in the public sphere as a result of the recently successful suffrage movement. In fact, these restrictions may have been a backlash against this increased feminist activity, a strategy by those in power to relegate women back to the home.

In the 1940s, these attitudes about sickness and pain continued. In Valeria Parker's 1940 handbook, she writes that "Most girls feel better during menstrual periods, however, if they avoid violent exercise, such as basketball, tennis, horseback riding, jumping, and long walks" (p. 66). Similar to B. G. Jefferis and J. L. Nichols's warning at the turn of the century, Parker warned that not paying heed to these instructions could cause future menstrual periods to be painful. In Marion Faegre's (1943) advice pamphlet for young boys and girls, she wrote that reduced activity is not necessary for girls during menstruation but still warned girls against getting fatigued or chilled. She also advocated an extra amount of rest during the first day of the period should the girl feel the need for it. In 1948, Lester Kirkendall also warned against fatigue and overwork: the menstruant "should guard against overwork, nervous tension, too much exertion, and especially against chills and extreme changes in temperature" (p. 12).

New attitudes began to emerge in Shailer Lawton and Jules Archer's 1951 advice book. They told girls not to follow "old wives' tales" by restricting themselves to their beds or withdrawing from normal activities. However, following the pattern of earlier writers, they warned against pool swimming. In a rather optimistic advice book for mothers and daughters written in 1955, Abraham Beacher asserted that "each period should be painless and should cause no discomfort" (p. 698). He does not mention menstrual cramps or backaches as a part of most women's menstrual experience. As most women experience such pain, Beacher's attitude would make them feel that something is medically wrong with them.

Helen Southard (1967) continued along the path set by her 1940s predecessors by writing that menstruants might not want to engage in "strenuous physical activity or being outdoors for a long time in extremely cold weather" (p. 24). In their research among low-income and poorly educated women in Michigan, Loudell Snow and Shirley Johnson (1978) learned that many still believed that during menstruation, girls and women should avoid the cold and avoid strenuous exercise or household tasks. All of these restrictions underscore the understanding of menstruation as an illness and warn girls about potential trauma during menstruation. "Culturally induced" beliefs of pain and illness during menstruation and the stereotypes about menstruation in general can lead girls to actually feel more pain and emotional trauma. In a sense, it can become a self-fulfilling prophecy.[24] Also, these limits on activities assume a middle-class audience where girls and women can afford to take extra "leisure" time to rest during their periods. These restrictions give primacy to a docile femininity, one where girls and women are not bold, sporty, or engaged in any strenuous activities.

Most of the advice literature I examined focused on the medical model of menstruation, inundating the reader with facts and medical terminology. For example, Hilary Maddux, writing in 1975, argued that "Any discussion of menstruation should begin with a description of the female reproductive system and the various functions of its parts" (p. 35). David Reuben, in 1970, used the medical explanation to advise his young readers about menstruation. In terms of complexity and timing, he states that "controlling the menstrual cycle is roughly equivalent to launching a space vehicle" (p. 30). This metaphor even further distances and alienates the girl from an event happening within her own body, especially given that science and technology are traditionally (and certainly in 1970) the realm of men. Space travel, in the 1970s, was the most technologically advanced process known. Instead of first discussing maturity or sexuality, the books start by medicalizing the process, which places distance between the girl's feelings and this "medical process" that is occurring inside her body. Instead of happening *within* their own bodies, girls often feel like menstruation happens *to* them. This is a method of social control of girls and women by "experts."

In sum, our cultural history medicalizes menstruation and can render girls powerless over their bodies. How can a girl feel that she has power over her own body and her own bodily experiences if menstruation is compared to the launch of a space vehicle? How can she see her body as a source of power in her interactions if she is alienated and judged by her body?

SCHOOLS

Education is another social institution which intersects teens' lives and, as such, affects their social interactions and power relations. In schools, where they spend an enormous amount of time, teens interact with teachers, staff, other teens, textbooks, classrooms, and the temporal and physical structures of the school. Teens learn a significant amount about menstruation within the cultural context of schools, and school experiences are brought up frequently in their individual and group interviews.

Male teachers are often embarrassed about menstrual issues, but some female teachers are forthright about menstruation in their classrooms. Dave said that he can tell when one of his teachers is menstruating because "she gets so damn bitchy. It's not even funny. Like, she has like, actually thrown stuff at us before. She gets pissed off!" Dave said that his teacher tells her students that her moods are attributable to her menstrual cycle. Another teacher of his is also forthcoming to her students about her cycle saying, as Dave reported, "I just dropped an egg."

Several girls said the structure of the school day makes managing menstruation more difficult. Bathroom breaks are difficult because time between classes is so short. They plan to go before school, during lunch break, and after school. They hope that is all they will need. They have to negotiate their time, their menstrual supplies, and the adult world telling them when they may go to the bathroom. Greta said that "you really have to plan ahead for it" and that having "more time in school to be able to go to the bathroom" would make things much easier. Andrea said that during her period, she wants to "stay close to a bathroom . . . 'cause, just in case there's an accident." Similarly, in explaining menstruation to a young girl who knew nothing about it, Leslie would say that menstruation is "something that happens like once a month that requires a lot of like responsibility, 'cause it does like, even like today like now I still forget to bring pads to school or something like that." Although adult women also worry about having supplies, most have the freedom to go back home, go out and purchase supplies, or have the confidence to ask a friend or co-worker.

Alyssa described the difficulties and frustrations of managing bathroom breaks, saying that in "high school, you have like hour classes and you have, like five minutes of passing period, and you can't even go to the bathroom and change it, and it's like, really hard." Katie said in her individual interview that when she menstruates, she alters her schedule:

KATIE (14): I change my schedule a little bit because like, you have to change pads and stuff so then that changes, like what—like, when you do things like. And then, like, depending on—like I usually change them at lunch but depending on when lunch is sometimes you have to change it before and then you have to like—like know when you're going to the bathroom so you have time to get to class on time and stuff.

In some classes, Jennifer said, the teachers will not let the students leave the room to go to the bathroom. Not allowing students in the halls during class is "a school policy because someone could be carrying a gun in the hallways and if you're out there. It's one of those little paranoia stupid rules." Because of this post-Columbine rule (the Littleton, Colorado shootings of twelve students and one teacher by two fellow male students at Columbine High School occurred in April 1999), girls who have their periods at this school have even larger hurdles in managing their bleeding. A few of the girls directly referenced Columbine when talking about restrictions in school hallways.

Not only does the school setting influence girls' and boys' interactions about menstruation, other settings also make it difficult to manage menstruation. In one group interview, the girls spoke about camping and how they think it is gross to carry out their own trash when they have their periods.

Klara said that she was so glad she got her period before the group went on their last camping trip because "I was all worried. I was like, for once in my life, I actually want to start my period, please, and it happened, and I was like, 'Yes!'" Nancy expanded on the discussion of difficult times to get your period. She said, "And see, the times you don't want your period, like whenever you know that you're going to be somewhere where changing is not going to be as easy, or if it's like prom or something where you have enough to worry about, let alone bleeding, or spots. That's what I hate, is when, like, you go right through all your protection and it gets on your clothes. I hate that." These girls feel out of control when it comes to the timing and management of menstruation.

The physical settings of teens' lives do not always allow for comfort, privacy, and ease of managing menstruation. Children and adolescents have very little freedom over their time and movements during school and other adult-run activities. Children are told where to sit, when to get up, and when to go to the bathroom. Structured settings such as school and camping can frustrate girls and foster more negative attitudes towards menstruation. Additionally, teachers who are comfortable or uncomfortable with their own menstruation or teen girls asking them for permission to go to the bathroom can influence girls' and boys' feelings about menstruation. These attitudes and restrictions can influence the amount of power girls feel over their own bodies (very little if there are no bathroom breaks) and how they feel about their bodies compared to boys' bodies.

THE FAMILY

Many of the teens talked about interactions with their families, another key social institution in teens' cultural contexts, in their individual and group interviews. These interactions tend to deal with menstruation in a different way than peer interactions, yet the family still influences the language, attitudes, and power resources teens bring to their peer interactions. Girls, in particular, and boys learn about menstruation in their families, talk to their mothers about menarche, menstrual symptoms, problems they experience with their periods, and menstrual products. Much of the interaction in the family deals with learning about menstruation and experiences with early menstruation.

Just as girls enjoy sharing in peer talk about menstruation, one of the girls said that she looked forward to menarche so that she could share in the menstrual talk of her older sisters. "I was 12," Cindy said, "and I was excited at first, heh heh, 'cause both my older sisters had already started their periods and they were always, like, talking about it. And I was like, well, we can't wait 'til I'm big enough to have my period, and you know. And then I started it and I was like really excited."

Many of the girls learned about menstrual products in their families. Several share bathrooms with their mothers or older sisters and saw menstrual products under the sink or in the cupboard. Lacey does not remember learning about menstrual products specifically; rather, she says there was always a supply of pads in the bathroom she shares with her two older sisters and her mom. Briana also learned about menstrual products from the bathroom she shares with her mom as she "saw pads and tampons everywhere."

Many girls' mothers or older sisters taught them how to use menstrual products when they reached menarche. Katie uses the pads her mom buys, but her sister taught her how to put them on. Erin and Rebecca each learned how to use tampons and pads from their mothers. Cindy said that "mostly my mom told me and taught me about—about them," but she also learned about products from television advertisements and browsing through store shelves. Kassie's mom showed her how to use pads, but her aunt also gave her Instead™ "things," which are cups inserted into the vagina to collect the blood. Kassie said neither she nor her aunt were sure what Insteads were, but Kassie thought you could only use them if you have had a baby (which is inaccurate). She even offered to bring them for me to have since she said she was never going to use them.

Boys also learned about products from their families, although to a much more limited and vague extent. Dave sees tampon wrappers in the bathroom trash but does not ask his sister or his mom about it. He is uncomfortable either asking or admitting that he does not know what they are for. Don, one of the boys, related a story during his individual interview about when he found his sister's pads in the bathroom before he knew what menstruation was. In his narrative, he is confused about what the purpose of the menstrual products are and even in this description, he confuses pads and tampons (he is talking about pads, which have adhesive on the back to stick to a menstruant's underwear, rather than tampons, which have strings to grasp when the tampon is soaked and ready to be pulled out and replaced).

> DON (18): I remember one time, actually I was just thinking about this, heh heh, this was before I knew what menstruation was or anything, and I don't know, the little—I don't know how they were like, applied or anything, but the little pink things, you know, and you push 'em up and then there's like, the little pad and then it exp—I remember it was little pad and I remember I was like, 'okay, what is this for?' I thought I was like some makeup application thing and it was in my sister's bathroom. I know it had a little sticky tab at the end and then a long string and this little pad that kinda had an hour glass shape to it. And I don't know why I did it, but I like, lined the whole toilet, this was when I was like, I don't know, second grade, I like, lined the whole toilet with these little pads, and they were like, up under the sides, and I just thought it was funny,

and so, they were in my sister's bathroom, and so when you flushed the toilet, they would all like, rush into the center but they were attached at the little sticky end, and then they'd just expand in the center of the toilet. Heh heh. I remember, I thought I was the funniest thing. So I did this and then my sister came in, first of all, all her tampons were like missing, then she flushed her toilet. And I remember getting all that and my mom being like 'Donny, your sister needs those, da da da.' I didn't really know what they were for or anything, and that was my first experience with menstrual products.

Through experimenting, Don learned how much menstrual products really can soak up. From the narrative, it sounds like Don was dealing with pads, not tampons, since tampons do not have adhesive tape. Don learns about menstrual products in a very vague sense, but since he was not a girl, he did not ask about the products and neither his sister nor his mother explained the products further. One source of girls' power over boys is the boys' lack of knowledge about menstruation, as we will explore later in this book. Interestingly, Don had been thinking about this experience not long before the interview, which shows the salience of this moment in his own life, unprompted by interviewer questions.

One important role of the family in shaping girls' experiences of menstruation is when girls go through menarche. Most of the girls told their mothers when they got their first periods. Some would first tell friends, others would first tell their mothers, but overall, most of the girls at some point said that they shared their menarche with their mothers.

Katie, like many of the girls, found blood in her underwear when she went to the bathroom and so she went right away to tell her mother. Her mother gave her a pad and showed her how to put it on. Many of the girls, like Katie, recalled that their mothers were very matter-of-fact and simply got their daughters a pad upon hearing the news. Nancy and her mother had already bought tampons for Nancy in anticipation of Nancy's menarche so Nancy was prepared and ready. Nancy said, "I had my stash and everything and just had to get it [her period]." Menarche was not a big deal for her or her mother. In addition to giving her pads, Greta's mother also told her where the Advil was, but, as Greta said, her mom "didn't make a big deal about it." This is similar to the attitude that many of the girls have—that menstruation is not that big of a deal.[25]

How a girl reacts to her first period can significantly affect how she feels about her body and femininity for years to come. In addition to the "not a big deal" attitude, some of the girls had positive reactions to their menarche. Kasey, for example, said that when she first got her period she told her mom that "I feel kind of proud." Her mom then asked what Kasey meant, and Kasey shared that "I started my period."

Other girls had mothers who responded positively to their daughters' menarche. When Andrea got her period, she told her mom, a nurse, and her mom "got me a present, actually, and I thought that was a little weird, but heh heh." Andrea is not sure how she feels about her mom's positive reaction, but is pleased with the necklace her mom gave her. When Kassie got her first period during a sleepover with a friend, her mother called her own friends to tell them of Kassie's new status. For Kassie's mom, attaining menarche was a positive event and the good news should be shared with other women. Rebecca's mom also celebrated Rebecca's menarche. Her mom "made up a song" for her with words "like, 'she's a woman now.'" When Rebecca's dad came home from work, her mom started singing the song again and Rebecca recalled that it was "so embarrassing." Rebecca was embarrassed about the attention and unsure about menarche, but her mother saw it as something to celebrate and tell others about.

Some of the girls also talked about how they share menstrual symptoms with their mothers or other female family members. Kasey and her mother both crave chocolate during their periods. She said "it's this mother-daughter thing" and that "we always have chocolate in our house for at least two weeks a month." It is clear that she and her mother are telling each other about their cravings and finding a common bond. Klara knows that during her sister's menstrual period, she experiences mood changes. Anne knows that her mom and her aunts never have cramps. Anne hears her friends talking about cramps and does not experience them herself, so she talked with family members to see what their experiences were. This interaction can reassure Anne that her experiences are not unusual, in spite of her friends' experiences. This sharing of menstrual symptoms is similar to interactions girls have with peers, the purpose of which is to reassure girls that their experiences are normal and that others share their cramping, cravings, and frustrations. This leads to a shared bond with other women about something that boys and men cannot fully understand or experience.

MEDIA, ADVERTISING, AND MERCHANDISING

Teens' lives are also intersected by the larger cultural context of the media and advertising industries. Many teens learn about menstrual products from media long before they learn more general information about menstruation. Disposable pads were developed at the end of World War I, but it took until the 1930s for Kotex to convince women's magazines to run their ads.[26] Prior to then, such products were deemed too private for mass media. Most ads for pads, tampons, and deodorizers used euphemistic terms (such as "those difficult days" or "feeling fresh") until fairly recently. Now we see graphics and absorbency ratings (albeit with blue fluid rather than red, like blood) and ads offer detailed information on the products and how they work. I have to admit that as a child, when I watched television advertisements in the mid-1980s for the douche Massengill, which depicted a mother and daughter talking quietly in a kitchen filled with soft light, I was convinced that Massengill was a dishwasher detergent. I asked my mom why we used Cascade and not Massengill.

Many girls and boys said that they learned about menstruation and menstrual products from advertisements they see on television or in magazines. Brian said that from advertisements, he knows that there are different kinds of pads and tampons and that some women take pills for menstruation. Dave learned about "reusable tampons" being sold for the concern over Y2K from reading *Time Magazine*. (Y2K refers to the worldwide concern over failures of computerized systems, including basic services such as water and electricity, during the turnover from Dec. 31, 1999 to Jan. 1, 2000. Older computer systems stored only the last two digits of the year, never anticipating that the systems would still be in use in the year 2000. The fear was that any calculations involving dates after Dec. 31, 1999 would return errors, and that these errors would lead to a massive failure cascade that would shut down all these systems on New Years Day, 2000. "Y2K" means "Year 2000.") In describing menstrual products, Don referred to specific television advertisements. In one, a pad "has the wings that flap with the blue background so it looks like it's flying." These flying pads have been a popular ad since the late-1980s. He described another with a "little glass tube and you turn it upside down" on the pad to show its absorbency. He said, "it's just funny how they depict it in commercials."

Girls also learn about menstrual products from media and advertisements. Sandra, Klara, and Anne each said in their individual interviews that they learned about products from television commercials. Jane said that advertisements for products are "everywhere" on television and in magazines. Kasey said that she learned about menstrual products not only from media, but also from product placement in stores. She said that there is "that whole big aisle in the store that has this product and this product and this product, all listed in a row, and it's like they're all right there." Like Margaret in Judy Blume's book, it is hard to pretend you are shopping for something else when there is nothing else in the aisle. In this last phrase, Kasey expressed slight distress that all the products are shelved in such an obvious fashion. Cindy learned about products from television but also from stores: "you know you go to the store and check it out and stuff like that."

Krissy referred to another source of direct merchandising in her learning about menstrual products: "those vending machines that they have in ladies—women's restrooms." In the women's restroom on my floor on campus (shared with Sociology and Women's Studies), there is a sanitary bag dispenser by the sinks. It is painted metal with the words: "Sanibag. For Sanitary Napkin Disposal. For Personal Hygiene and Cleanliness. Preferred by

Discreet Women Everywhere." Such dispensers can be found in public women's restrooms everywhere. Today, most of these dispensers are empty, although their prevalence indicates that, at one time, they were filled and women (discreet women, of course) were expected to use them, instead of wrapping toilet paper or the product wrapper around a used pad or tampon, as women do today.

Girls also report learning about menstruation in general, not just about menstrual products, from the media. In one of the girls' groups, they reported learning about menstruation from commercials. Others talked about learning from teen magazines they read. Leslie said that before her mother told her about menstruation, she had "already started to get, like, the teen magazine and there were a couple things in there" about menstruation. Rebecca said that in learning about menstruation, "I guess I probably saw like commercials like on TV, you know . . . Always, and all this kind of stuff." Linda also referred to magazines as an important source of information:

> LINDA (16): It was in like third grade . . . me and one of my friends, she was actually my neighbor, we were looking through one of the magazines like, *Seventeen* or something like that just cause we were curious and we were reading about this we were like 'oh my god, what's going on?' you know. We're reading about all this stuff we're like 'oh, I don't want that to happen to me.' Heh heh. But that's when I first heard about it, but when I actually learned about it . . . was in school . . . we had it in like fifth grade.

Later, Linda said that when they read about menstruation in the magazine, "we were scared." Linda shared the magazine and her fears about menstruation and what it was all about with her friend.

The way that products are presented in stores and in the media can greatly influence how teens view and understand menstruation. Using blue dye rather than red dye to show the absorbency of a pad in a commercial can sanitize the pad for the viewer, as well as confuse those who are not familiar with the experience of menstruation. Shelving pads in drugstores can either contribute to girls' feelings of discomfort that the pads are so obvious or can contribute to a girls' comfort that menstruation is not something of which to be ashamed. The advertising strategies for menstrual products separate the product from the actual physical experience of menstruation. Menstruation is a disease, a dirty thing that must be sanitized, freshened, and hidden.

Additionally, the teens did not mention television programs or movies as places they learned about advertisements. Unlike 30 years ago, when the television menstrual taboo was first broken by the program *All in the Family* (in "The Battle of the Month," first aired in 1973) and when Stephen King's bloody short story *Carrie* was released on film (1976),[27] today, menstruation, sex, orgasms, and any other physical function are frequently heard not just on cable or in R-rated films, but also on network television and in music videos.

In sum, the cultural contexts of teens' lives, which they bring to their peer interactions, are rich with meaning and messages about menstruation and girls' bodies. Throughout this book, the quotes from teens show how the social institutions of history, schools, family, and media have influenced teens' attitudes and social interactions with their peers. These, in turn, influence the gendered power relations among girls and boys.

FOUR

Medicalization and
Gender Politics of the Body

Girls' power over their own bodies is reduced by the imbalanced gender power structure of our society. Put simply, boys' bodies are powerful, and girls' bodies are not. One source of this reduced power starts with the medicalization of the female body, which begins with menarche.

MEDICALIZATION OF MENSTRUATION

As briefly described earlier, the female body and reproductive functions are "medicalized" in our culture to varying degrees, which means they are defined as medical issues, medical problems, or requiring of medical intervention. Medicalization places women's bodies in the hands of "expert" doctors, usually male, rather than valuing women's own knowledge and care of their bodies. This takes power away from women. The medical community, including individual practitioners and large organizations, generates and perpetuates medicalization. Yet, girls and women also participate and support medicalization. For example, women in the United States welcomed medical intervention into childbirth in the early 1900s, as births were attended by male doctors instead of women midwives. Midwives were highly experienced, but did not have institutionally backed medical degrees. Not only can women now choose various methods of pain relief, but rates of infant and maternal mortality have plummeted over the last century.

The medicalization of menstruation generally means that menstruation is defined as an illness with physical and psychological symptoms. This medicalization in part stems from our cultural history, as discussed in the previous chapter, because menstruation was understood as an illness and as a deviation from a "normal" bodily state. As we saw, most of the advice literature from the last century defined menstruation in terms of pain and illness, restricted menstruant's physical activities, and focused their descriptions of menstruation on the medical model while inundating the reader with facts and medical terminology. This definition of menstruation as an illness may also be because menstruation is one part of the reproductive cycle, and for many women throughout time, childbirth often meant death. Girls' and women's bodies were socially controlled by the medical "experts."

As the social institutions of health and medicine intersect teens' lives through outlets such as the media and health classes in schools, the teens we interviewed engage in the medicalization of menstruation in their own peer cultures. First, menstruation is presented to teens in a medicalized context, from parents and in health class, which results in an initial definition of menstruation as a medical issue. Second, in their descriptions of what menstruation is, the teens focus on menstruation's role in reproduction, rather than on the experiential aspects of menstruation that pervade the rest of their interviews. Third, the teens' descriptions of the process of menstruation, although quite medical, rarely include blood. Last, menstruation is often referred to as a chronic condition defined by symptoms that require treatment.

FIFTH-GRADE HEALTH CLASS

In the early twentieth century, most girls learned about menstruation from their mothers and other older women. The Girl Scouts of America was one of the first groups to teach girls about menstruation in a systematic fashion. Among the tasks to earn the "Health Winner Badge," a girl scout had to learn about the physiology of menstruation and privately talk with her troop leader about it.[1] By 1940, menstrual education was firmly established in the schools and often provided by the physical education teacher.[2] Reproductive health, of which healthy menstruation was a large component, was seen as vital for middle-class women in particular, given early-twentieth-century concerns over recent immigrants' birth rates outpacing those of U.S. citizens. The teachers, along with many white middle-class professionals and reformers, equated reproductive health with overall physical health and encouraged exercise and sports that would protect a woman's reproductive system (although many of the recommendations were based on faulty information, such as the worries over uterine collapse from competitive sports). It was this connection of hygiene, physical activity, and menstruation that compelled PE teachers at this time to take on responsibility for menstrual education.[3]

The influence of gym teachers, who often double as health class teachers, continues today. Throughout their interviews, many teens explained menstruation using the medical terminology and language they learned in health class. When we asked the teens how they would "explain menstruation to a young girl or boy who knew nothing about it" and what the "point of menstruation" is, most teens did *not* include a discussion of menstrual blood or menstrual products that referred to the actual experience of menstruation for girls, which they focused on in the rest of the interviews. Rather, they discussed menstruation in terms of the ovaries, fallopian tubes, uterus, and, most often, the egg and failed reproduction. These are issues that girls do not "feel" during their periods, but are organs and processes that happen inside the girls unseen.

In their talk, the teens do not connect the medical terms and information they learn in health class and the girls' everyday experiences of menstruation. The teens distinguish between the process of menstruation (medical) and the experience of menstruation (e.g., managing the blood). The physiological events they describe do not illuminate or inform the girls' actual experiences of menstruation.[4] This medical approach could be an artifact of the way we asked the question ("How would you explain menstruation to a young girl who knew nothing about it? To a boy?"), but the question does not ask for the process of menstruation, merely how the teen might explain what menstruation is.

One of girls' and boys' earliest and primary exposures to menstrual knowledge comes from health class where the focus of the course is on medicine, biology, and physiology. Most of the teens in our interviews talked about fifth grade health as one of their primary sources of information about menstruation. For example, as discussed earlier, some of the boys couched their descriptions of menstruation in terms of sex and reproduction as it is presented in health class. At the first mention of menstruation in one of the boys' groups, one boy said, "I can remember health." He instantly connected the topic of menstruation to the medical issues learned in health. Many of the boys and girls had heard about menstruation earlier than fifth grade and had developed a "half-knowing" about menstruation, but almost all discussed health class as an important source of early information.

For example, in response to my question, "why do girls menstruate?," Klara mimicked her fifth-grade health teacher and provided a medicalized explanation. She started her narrative with, "Well, when I was in fifth grade, 'my teacher taught me' [sarcastic tone] heh heh." She continues her narrative, presenting information on fallopian tubes, the uterus, and the egg. Linda described menstruation in very uncertain terms, using medical terminology such as "releasing the tissue" and "eggs" but she did not quite understand it or remember how it all fits together. She said that menstruation is, "releasing of like the tissue and stuff, right, and like the eggs like, you know. I don't know how to say it. Like getting rid of the eggs or whatever. Like, you know what I mean." She learned about menstruation in health class and attempts to use this medical terminology, rather than her own teen culture's language of "bleeding" and menstrual symptoms, in her description. She is unable to recount it fully or with comprehension.

When I asked where she learned about menstruation, Briana responded that it was "probably" from her sister because "she was in college to be a nurse, so she naturally was the one that taught me." Even though Briana does not remember how exactly she learned about menstruation, she defined menstruation as a medical issue that her sister, who is in a medical profession, would have "naturally" explained to her.

The adult group leader described Ellen as a very quiet girl and she was impressed at how much Ellen opened up in her group and individual interviews. (This was a rare case where the group leader was in the room during the individual interviews. I found no inhibition on the part of the girls when a group leader was present, testifying to the comfort these girls feel with their adult leaders and the comfort they felt talking about these issues.) Ellen is at the top of her class and throughout her interview, her language and words reflected her academic prowess. In her explanation of menstruation in her individual interview, she recognizes the tension between medical "scientific" and lay "how to deal with it" descriptions.

ELLEN (17): I could go for the really scientific thing, or I could just say what you have to do to deal with it, um, I guess I'd say, 'Once a month, um, you will ovulate, which means you will release an egg, and your uterine lining would build up in preparation for your having a baby, and you probably won't have to deal with that, heh heh, hopefully, for several years down the road. But, um, you're going to have the cycle going anyway, and, um, you're going to need pads to catch the bleeding. I guess, um, uh, it'll last about five days or so, more or less, and it can be a pain, but it's just a part of life,' and I don't know, that's about it.

Sylvia and Andrea, long-time friends, would each describe menstruation in terms of medical terminology and body parts. When responding to the question, "why do girls menstruate?," Sylvia said in her individual interview:

SYLVIA (18): Well, I guess it's so that, I mean, whenever the ovum comes down and it—Like you know, it needs the insulation or whatever and then, whenever the egg doesn't become fertilized the body sheds the protective layer. Whatever.

It is clear that Sylvia is unsure of her explanation, yet she persists in using medical terminology that she is unfamiliar with, most likely heard in health class. She does not describe menstruation in terms of the experience of menstruation. By saying "whatever," she indicates that this medical process does not affect her or is not important to her own experience. Her friend, Andrea, would describe menstruation to a young girl by drawing a diagram:

ANDREA (17): I'd probably like draw her a picture of like, uterus, and like, you know, like fallopian tubes and like explain the whole thing, and then like, I don't know, be like, this is all inside of you and every woman and so eventually you're gonna have to deal with this, like, and this is— I'll be like, this is why it happens, like, how you make babies or whatever, you know?

Andrea's mother is a nurse and her stepfather is an obstetrician/gynecologist, so such medical terminology may be familiar from her home environment.

Her younger sister, Katie (also interviewed but in a different group), recalled in her individual interview that she, her sister, and mother had a conversation about menstruation where her mother drew the uterus, ovaries, and blood to explain menstruation. Andrea did not mention this incident, but it may explain why her description is couched in medical terminology with an accompanying diagram. Katie, in her individual interview, also said she would explain menstruation to a young girl in medical terms:

KATIE (14): I would say, um, depending on how much she knew about sex in general. I would probably like start with like talking about, just like, how, like, like their body parts and like the uterus and how you have ovaries and all that stuff like that. And how like every month, you have like a million thousand eggs in your ovaries. And then every month one comes down and it's waiting to be fertilized because that's the whole point, to have children. So it's waiting to be fertilized and when it isn't fertilized, it, ah, the body has to get rid of it so that you can have a new egg come down and wait to be fertilized. Because they only last so long, they're like chicken eggs, they get bad after a while. So, it has to go away, and you've been like—building up, your body is pre-preparing to have a child so it's got all these nutrients and like, like I was saying. ( ) lining in your uterus. And it has to get rid of all that so the new egg can come down and prepare itself again. So then it all—then it um, your body just gets rid of that by flushing it out. It just goes away.

LAURA: Okay. So you'd explain it to her and then your very—exactly step by step what's going on with your body

KATIE: Yeah, then I'd be like, it's kind of scary the first time it happens but you get used to it after a while. And if you have cramps take ibuprofen, heh heh.

Interestingly, Katie not only uses medical terminology in her explanation, but includes, at the end, the practical side of dealing with cramps. However, Katie also does not mention "blood." Rather, she talks about the "lining in your uterus" and the eggs that "get bad after a while," neither of which would explain to a young girl why women bleed during menstruation.

The medicalized discussions of menstruation are an unanticipated (and possibly unintended) consequence of fifth-grade health class. It is arguably a good thing that national guidelines require sex education in the schools and that students are learning about their bodies in a safe and informative way. Yet, what this means practically is that the fifth-grade health teachers, who are generally the regular PE teachers, now control the definitions of the body and health. The teens gave Paul and I the "right" answers, learned from school, as to what menstruation is. These definitions stem from dominant U.S. cultural stories of women's bodies and gender politics (as we will discuss further below). The way that teachers present the material, from our interviews with teens, has clear, lasting effects on students and their own understandings of the body and health. Additionally, how health teachers, gym teachers, and other teachers respond to menstruation (such as excusing a girl from gym class) affects students' understandings of the body and health. The definitions the teachers present of menstruation directly affect the teens' social constructions of women's bodies and femininity. Eggs that are not fertilized are bad eggs that must be flushed away. Women's bodies are made for reproduction and the whole point of the ovulation cycle is to create babies. This proscribes morality for the students, telling them that women are supposed to have children and that sexual behavior is supposed to be heterosexual. These images are very powerful for students in fifth grade because many girls have not started their periods yet and so do not have personal experience with the subject matter. The boys, as well, are learning much of this for the first time and will never have personal experience with menstruation.

Interestingly, these medicalized constructions from fifth-grade health class do not match up with the teens' actual experiences as seen in the rest of their interviews. There is a distinct separation between the cultural story of process and reproduction and the teens' own experiences of menstruation and their social interactions about menstruation. Their experiences are completely separated from the "right answer" given in health class. This may be relatively harmless on the surface, but it can lead to discomfort with menstruation, which can directly affect girls' comfort with their own bodies and their sexuality. Similarly, do teens understand sex in a clinical way from health class? Is this clinical understanding removed from their own experiences? This can tie directly into our adult discomfort with adolescent sexuality, which we pass on to our teens. This can result in a whole host of negative consequences for teen sexual health.

MENSTRUATION AS A REPRODUCTIVE ISSUE

When we asked the teens to describe what menstruation is, the teens focused on menstruation's role in reproduction. Again, this is in contrast to the rest of the individual and group interviews, where the teens focused on the experiential aspects of menstruation, such as managing the bleeding and menstrual products.

In the examples in the last section, the girls referred to menstruation as the body's passive response to failed reproduction. The lining prepares for a fertilized egg and when that does not happen, menstruation occurs. In Don's individual interview he also referred to menstruation, not only in medical terminology, but in terms of failed reproduction when he answered the question, "what is the point of menstruation?":

> DON (18): The point of menstruation. Okay, well. A—a woman, she ah, it's part of the monthly cycle it happens around every month, you know. A woman ovulates, the egg goes down the fallopian tubes and so it's— that's when a woman is supposed to be impregnated, fertilization is supposed to occur. And that's when the lining of the uterus forms. Um, you know, so that the egg can join. And if it's fertilized. And then, a baby forms. If that doesn't happen, though, the lining breaks down and s— bloody, and then it like comes out every nine months. I don't necessarily know how it happens, like—I guess you like, it like bleeds. And that's what the tampons are for and whatnot.

Don added later, "I guess the reason they menstruate is because a boy hasn't had sex with them."

Our cultural history, discussed above, continues to influence our current medical understandings of menstruation. Emily Martin (1991) describes the "scientific fairy tale" used by medical texts that refers to the female cycle as a productive enterprise, the sole purpose of which is to produce a baby. Given this definition, menstruation denotes a failure. Conception did not occur and there is no baby; thus, women menstruate. Martin finds that this medical and scientific discourse has created the view of menstruation as failed production, with menstrual blood defined as waste and scrap.

Many of the teens in our interviews discussed menstruation in terms of failed production, possibly because they are exposed to the details of menstruation in the medicalized context of health class and sex education. In Katie's narrative, above, menstruation is the result of a failure; the egg sat around, waited, and nothing happened so it "goes bad" and must be "flushed out." Many other girls and boys also talked about menstruation in terms of reproduction, saying that the point of menstruation is, as Jennifer said, "to have kids" and "to reproduce." Erica went further and said that, "to have kids" is "what the female body is made for." Claiming menstruation in terms of reproduction alone relegates women and their bodies to the role of child bearer. This limits girls' views of their bodies; rather than thinking about their bodies as, for example, martial arts experts or cross-country runners.

Some girls think they do not want to have children, so they are frustrated that they must endure menstruation. For Erica, menstruation is "awful and pointless" unless you have children. Krissy said that the point of menstruation is so "you can get pregnant, but I think we kinda got screwed in that deal because I don't want to have kids anyway, but I still have to go through this." Menstruation is happening to these girls for a reason they understand, but of which they are not convinced. For them, menstruation currently has no use and just happens to them once a month. Although these girls are correct biologically in that menstruation indeed results from a lack of conception, menstruation is also shown to be a cleansing process that cleans the uterus and vagina of foreign and potentially dangerous pathogens.[5] Additionally, for these girls, menstruation could be seen as the *desired* outcome of the ovulatory cycle because they most likely do not want to get pregnant at this time in their lives.

These statements also reflect the tension between essentialism and embodiment, which I will discuss more fully later in this chapter. Essentialist arguments posit that the physical body determines gender difference and gendered experience. Embodiment, however, recognizes that we live our lives and experience our social worlds through our bodies. Using embodiment theory, for these girls it is not menstruation as an essential phenomenon that defines them as girls, but rather how they experience menstruation and the lived body that are important to them as girls.

WHAT ABOUT THE BLOOD?

The menstrual cycle is in fact the "ovulatory cycle," but we refer to it in terms of menstruation in our lay language because it is the blood, not the egg, that we can see and interact with in everyday life.[6] The importance of the cycle for reproduction is ovulation and the ovary's release of the egg, not the shedding of the endometrium. However, for girls and women, the blood is absolutely central to the experience of menstruation. Blood is visible. Blood must be managed. Thus, I would expect that the menstrual explanations given by the teens would include descriptions and explanations of the blood. However, when we asked the teens to describe menstruation, although their descriptions were quite medical, most of the girls and boys interviewed did not mention blood. The teens often referred to pads and tampons and how they have to manage menstruation (without saying "what" it is they are managing), but most did not discuss the actual blood that exits the body.

A few teens, such as Ellen and Don above, *did* refer to blood in their descriptions, yet the source of this blood is unclear. For example, Ellen said that girls need "pads to catch the bleeding." Even so, Ellen still does not explain that the uterine lining is the source of the blood. Klara also talked about "extra tissue" that is in the uterus, but does not explain that the tissue she describes is the same as the blood that is expelled during menstruation. She explained menstruation as "the blood builds up in the uterus to support the fetus for in cas—when the egg gets, um, fertilized in the fallopian tube I think. And then it travels down and then, if it's not fertilized the uterus notices that and so it sloughs off the extra tissue and starts building it up again."

Most boys also do not explain where the blood comes from. Jim said that girls menstruate "for reproduction . . . the egg passes down through the fallopian tubes and through the uterus and then it connects to the, uh, uterus wall, I believe, and then that's there for fertilization and if it doesn't stay there, then it just passes through." This is a fairly accurate explanation, but it makes it sound like menstruation is only the expelling of the unfertilized egg, rather than including the blood and tissue from the uterine lining. This also does not describe the everyday experience of menstruation, which centers on the management of blood.

Briana is one of the few girls who talked about where the blood that "leave[s] the body" comes from. In her description of menstruation, she said: "Well, like technically it's like, all the blood vessels, 'cause your body gets ready for a baby, and like all those little blood vessels get ready and when you don't have the baby, they have to leave the body somehow." Ally also connected blood to the uterine lining and provided the most accurate descriptions. She said, "the egg has to be fertilized by a certain time, and if it's not, then it's like, dead and it has to go away." She continued, "the blood's just, like, the lining, that way if the egg was fertilized—I sound like a TV special, heh heh. If the egg was fertilized, then it would have the nourishment layer, and then, when that doesn't happen, the nourishment layer goes away." Not only does she joke about the formality of her language, but she correctly identifies menstrual blood as being from the "lining," the "nourishment layer." Interestingly, she later credits a television program she saw rather than fifth-grade health for her knowledge. Briana, who is 16, probably saw this program much more recently than fifth grade and after her own menarche, so the information would be retained much better.

Why do most teens not discuss the blood when explaining the menstrual cycle? First, blood in everyday experience signifies injury, not health, for most adults and children.[7] When we bleed, it is because we are injured. When we bleed, we require medical attention. Marcia said in her group interview that her "little brother's theory on life" is that "he doesn't trust anything that bleeds for seven days and doesn't die." Second, blood and injury signal a passive role for children when they must then find an adult and be taken care of.[8] When menarche occurs, it is a confusing event because now, blood is good. Bleeding, for the first time, occurs when there is no injury and the blood is normal and healthy. It is a *lack* of menstruation (amenorrhea) that is now unhealthy. This requires a significant alteration of

children's and adolescents' thinking about girls' bodies. The shift in thinking from blood loss as an indicator of illness to blood shedding as a healthy
process may help explain the lack of references to blood.

Third, blood is gross for most teens. They may want to sanitize their
descriptions of menstruation by concentrating on the unseen "clean" items
such as ovaries and fallopian tubes. Finally, many teens might honestly have
no idea where the blood comes from. They may have heard it in fifth-grade
health, but at the time (often premenarcheal), it was not salient to their
everyday lives, so they quickly forgot.

EVERY SINGLE MONTH FOREVER AND EVER

At the same time as the teens do not describe the blood, the teens still often
describe menstruation in terms of chronic illness. This shows the complexity
in teens' understandings of menstruation—both as healthy, because in this
case blood does not signify injury, yet as a chronic illness. This occurred
throughout their interviews.

Menstruation is often talked about by the teens in our interviews as a
"condition" defined by "symptoms" that require "treatment." This definition
is based in the medicalization of menstruation and models of chronic illness.
Dave thinks that it would be good if girls never menstruated again because
then "guys wouldn't have to deal with them" and also "toxins didn't build up
in them." Earlier in his interview, he referred to menstruation as something
that serves to "cleanse the body" and "get rid of the poisons." Dave defined
menstruation as a toxic, poisonous buildup of bad blood, an unhealthy condition, which is released (and thereby cured) through the monthly menstrual flow.

In Jim's individual interview, he described how he would explain menstruation to a girl or boy who knew nothing about it. As shown below, he
defines menstruation in medical terms:

PAUL: *How would you explain menstruation to a young girl who knew nothing about it?*

. . .

JIM (18): I don't know, I wouldn't break out like the health book, or an
encyclopedia and I'd just, you know, cartoonerize it and show 'em, well
this comes from the ov—like the ovaries and little, you have two of
them you know. And then, the egg come, you have—they have a limited supply of eggs. And something, if I remember something rubs on
the ovary and then, it—it cuts it open or something like that I believe.
And then the egg is released through the fallopian tube. And then I'd
show 'em like, if there's a picture I'd able to just like show 'em where it

was and then where it travels through and then where it connects. And then, if it doesn't get fertilized through that period of time, then it passes through.

PAUL: *Ok. How would you explain menstruation to a young boy who knew nothing about it?*

JIM: Probably the same way. I mean, yeah, pretty much the same way. I mean, I wouldn't, wouldn't really go into detail with him, I mean, unless it's, unless he's gonna grow up to be a doctor I mean, I could show him a little bit more from what I know on a book or something. But, I mean, there's real—no real use for him to know about it, just to know exactly what they go through, pretty much just to show 'em what happens and what they go through, symptoms, ah, wha—

PAUL: *What kind of symptoms?*

JIM: Uh, just their, the cramping, uh, breast enlarged, like, the hurt, the tenderness of the breast, that's it. Uh, lets see, if they get, you know, get headaches or anything like, that. The only thing I know is just the tenderness of the breast and cramping in the—the abdomen.

This follows the pattern discussed earlier—that many boys understand menstruation in terms of girls' symptoms, which boys experience through social interaction either directly, such as girls' mood swings, or from listening to girls talk. Jim describes menstruation medically, yet says that boys do not need to know this level of detail. Interestingly, Jim says that unless a boy is going to be a doctor, he would not need to know any detail about menstruation. Jim's own knowledge is pretty sparse and this may be his reasoning for why he himself does not know the details.

Some of the teens talk about menstruation as a disease that is ongoing and continues until menopause when it is finally "cured." Don talked about menstruation as a chronic illness in his individual interview. He said, "I see [menstruation] as something that women deal with, you know. I can kind of parallel it with my diabetes. It's just something that's kind of a pain at first, but you just deal with it and move on." He frequently referred to menstruation as a "woman's issue" during his interview and said that menstruation "identifies women from men." He discussed his diabetes at length in his individual interview and used chronic illness to frame his understanding and interpretation of menstruation. He said menstruation, like diabetes, is a nuisance and a pain to deal with, but then you "move on" with your life. Don explains menstruation as an embodied experience, but with essentialist overtones since it is a "woman's issue."

The onset of menarche and the monthly experience of menstruation can be compared to the experience of chronic illness. Those with chronic illness

live in a particularly embodied world. Kathy Charmaz (1991) finds that being
diagnosed with a chronic illness involves a redefinition of the self. The
chronically ill must deal with altered bodies that are turned into medical phenomena, calling for a reorganization and management of their usual activities. Their embodied experiences are significantly altered. They must accommodate new physical and mental limitations and attempt to preserve the self
during a time when they must redefine themselves in terms of their illness.

Following Charmaz's terminology, menstruation can be seen as experienced by girls as: an alteration of their girlhood bodies into womanhood bodies at menarche, the medicalization of their bodies, a chronic intrusion into
their lives that demands attention and accommodation (e.g. carrying tampons, planning bathroom breaks), and as a time when they must preserve their
sense of themselves while being redefined as sexual and feminine beings. Of
course, the girls and boys do not see menstruants as "patients" or requiring of
a doctor's care. Yet, even in "common" chronic illnesses such as diabetes, the
sufferers generally do not think of themselves as "patients" (Zola 1991).

According to Charmaz, people with chronic illnesses are very private
about their illness, treatment, and condition with the public, but are freer
giving information to their close friends and families. The privacy surrounding menarche and menstruation is similar in that the girls I interviewed relate
their experiences to their friends and mothers but not to the larger "public"
world. Many are embarrassed when, for example, boys know about their periods from finding pads and tampons in their bags or when they must get up in
the middle of class to use the bathroom. These are violations of their privacy.

Finally, Charmaz says that there are certain identifying moments in the
experiences of those with chronic illnesses, through which they realize that
they are ill and that this is a part of their self-identity.[9] A parallel is that of
menarche, staining, or cramps, which can be identifying moments in a girl's
life where she is compelled to acknowledge menstruation and what it means
to her identity and sense of self. The girls can and do compare their bodies
before and after menarche, before they suffered the "chronic illness." They
talk about how their lives have changed and how they learned to manage and
be responsible for menstruation and its symptoms.

Premenstrual syndrome (PMS), billed as a "chronic" medical condition,
is heavily publicized, legitimized, and pervasive in our culture. Our culture
constructs it as a negative condition that women suffer once a month when
they are under the control of their hormones and therefore have emotional
and physical upsets. This image of PMS has allowed women and others
around women (such as husbands, children, doctors, co-workers, and even
lawyers and juries) to use it as a legitimate physiological excuse for their
behavior prior to and during menstruation. Although some women reject
using PMS as an "excuse," many women contribute to this use and medical
culture has accepted PMS as a type of chronic illness.[10] The images of PMS

and menstrual symptoms are often used by boys in their understandings of menstruation and by some girls, as we will see later, to manipulate social situations to their advantage, such as getting out of gym class. Positive images of PMS are rare. Janice Delaney, Mary Jane Lupton, and Emily Toth (1988) argue that there are positive effects of PMS and menstruation, yet our negative cultural construction of PMS inhibits such views. For example, rather than a "Menstrual Distress Questionnaire" (devised in 1969 and still in circulation), why not have a "Menstrual Joy Questionnaire," which asks questions about happiness, increased creativity, or self-confidence?

To sum, the teens medicalized menstruation to a large extent in their individual and group interviews. However, this medicalization is not all-encompassing nor is it necessarily an entirely negative trend. Women and girls who embrace the medicalized constructions of menstruation are not necessarily devoid of agency and autonomy, as can happen when medicalization occurs. The teens actively participate in the medicalization of menstruation and develop their own peer-based interpretations. Medicalization is also not necessarily limiting for girls, as I will show in later chapters. Girls demonstrate agency and power in their interactions with others about menstruation.

MENSTRUAL SUPPRESSION?

Recently, there have been debates in the popular and medical literature about the use of the contraceptive pill to suppress menstruation.[11] Women taking Seasonale, currently the only FDA-approved "extended cycle" oral contraceptive, menstruate only four times per year. Seasonale was approved in September of 2003 and has generated a large amount of media attention from both critics and supporters. The contraceptive pill ("the Pill") suppresses ovulation and menstruation when it is taken. Why should women have to menstruate once a month when they could take the Pill every day and stop taking it to menstruate only once every four months, or every six months, or not stop taking it at all? This line of recent thought has used the medicalization of menstruation found in the dominant culture to support the extreme position of using medical technology to "cure" the body of menstruation.

Menstruation is often seen as a "condition," a "chronic illness" defined by "symptoms" that require "treatment." There is a loss of control over the body, issues of cleanliness and hygiene to deal with, and often pain and cramping. Menstrual symptoms can make some women feel victimized and powerless and they feel they need pharmaceutical drugs to resolve these symptoms. In the dominant model of health, where the body is unchanging and stable, menstruation is a deviation and a problem. This definition provides a contradiction in thinking because we know menstruation is normal and healthy, yet it is often accompanied by symptoms of "sickness" like pain, cramps, bloating, and mood changes.

Elsimar Coutinho, a medical physician, is the author of a controversial book titled *Is Menstruation Obsolete?* (1999). He claims that menstruation is a disorder that brings only disease, discomfort, and disruption for women. Coutinho goes back through history when women menstruated much less frequently due to later menarche, more pregnancies, and longer periods of lactation. For example, in one tribe in Mali, the women menstruate on average about 100 times in their lives and live into their seventies and eighties. In contrast, contemporary western women menstruate about 350 to 400 times. Supporting Coutinho's theses, Malcolm Gladwell (2000), in a *New Yorker* article, explained how the inventors of the contraceptive pill chose the 28-day cycle. Having three weeks "on" and one week "off" for women to menstruate was a decision not based on medical science; rather, the inventors thought that women would be reassured by the continuation of their monthly bleeding and thus accept the pill as a "natural" method of contraception. They wanted to make money on their invention.

Menstruating this frequently, Coutinho believes, places women at risk for many physiological conditions, some of which are quite severe. Coutinho provides a long list of potential conditions related to or aggravated by menstruation (in addition to a "needless" loss of blood) such as: premenstrual syndrome, endometriosis, anemia, dysmenorrhea, ovarian and uterine cancer, asthma, menstrual thrombocytopenia, porphyria, arthritis, epilepsy, insomnia and hypersomnia, myomas, and menstrually-related pneumothorax. What a frightening-sounding list! Coutinho claims that the regular monthly menstruation that today's women experience is not the "natural" state. This trend has occurred only recently with the demographic transition from high to low fertility (pregnant and most breastfeeding women do not menstruate).

Menstruation can and should be "treated" with medical advances in hormone and contraceptive medication, Coutinho argues. Following traditional western notions of science and biomedicine,[12] Coutinho believes that women can overcome nature through medical technology. His orientation towards menstruation is that of "risk," which legitimates medicalization and physician control and intervention. Using hormone therapy to prevent or reduce the frequency of menstruation, he says, will make women's lives easier and women will be healthier.

Coutinho also argues that menstruation can also be suppressed through not only hormonal methods, but also through rigorous physical exercise. However, this type of amenorrhea found in ballet dancers and long distance runners, for example, is an indicator of dangerously low body fat, where the body does not have the energy it needs to menstruate. This condition is also found among underfed and starving women.[13]

I believe these positions are extreme and that they violate the biological structure of reproduction and the healthiness of menstruation as argued by most medical and social researchers. Susan Rako, M.D. (2003), for example, finds that there are physiological hazards of menstrual suppression such as increased risks of osteoporosis, heart attacks, strokes, cancer, reduced sexual interest and pleasure, and depression. She recognizes that these risks have not been proven, but that the risks of suppressing menstruation have also not been medically proven. Coutinho focuses on the negative aspects of menstruation, forgetting the positive and productive health benefits. For example, according to Natalie Angier's (1999) search of the research literature, women are not necessarily less competent and ill around their period. Instead, the premenstrual phase is often accompanied by "heightened activity, intellectual clarity, feelings of well-being, happiness, and sexual desire" (p. 107). Emily Martin (1992) finds that many women report being more creative, more understanding, and more emotionally aware during their periods.

I believe views such as Coutinho's also negate and devalue the enriching social experience that menstruation can be for women. If women do not have periods, they lose this potential for social interaction, community building, and power, as I find among the teens interviewed for this book. Of course, not having the mess, the worry, or the responsibility of monthly menstruation certainly sounds appealing. But, when I asked the girls in the individual interviews if they would choose not to menstruate again but could still have children, four of the twenty-three girls said either "no" or provided conflicted responses. These four want to menstruate. They like the power and connection menstruation brings to their lives.

For example, Kassie would miss having funny stories to tell and having an excuse to be grouchy. As I discuss later in this book, she feels it is an important rite of passage into womanhood. Nancy also sees menstruation as something that is "part of me" and "who I am." Yet, she is conflicted because she "hates" menstruation, but still considers it "part of me" and "who I am." She said, "It's just always there. Kinda like one of those old friends that you don't really like anymore, but you just can't get rid of."

Greta and Lacey both say they would miss the power that menstruation provides. Greta said that without menstruation, she would not have something to complain about. Complaining to others is a source of interactional power. For example, the girls engage in one-upmanship where they complain about having the worst symptoms. This provides a glimpse into the interactional power that Greta has, potentially in both single- and mixed-gender groups, because she menstruates. Lacey agreed and said that without menstruation, she would lose a power over boys since "it's just like so funny to you know tease them about that." She also, along with Kassie, would miss the "funny stories that come out of it [menstruation]."

These four girls answered "no" directly in response to my question. However, throughout this book we see additional evidence, although the girls and boys may not realize it directly, that menstruation brings much more to girls' and women's lives than just the ability to have children and the hassle of dealing with it. The interactional power that girls (and boys) can attain because of menstruation is something that Coutinho and other menstrual suppression supporters do not take into account.

Through menstruation the girls learn about their bodies and reproduction; they learn to manage their bodies; they learn about larger power relations in society; they learn how they can use menstruation as a power source in their interactions with boys; and they learn that menstruation connects them to other girls and women. Although not discussed in my interviews, menstruation is also reassuring evidence of nonpregnancy for those girls who are sexually active and do not want to bear children.

It is important not to silence girls' and boys' talk about menstruation and the body. It is important that we give girls and boys space to speak about their own experiences and to learn from each other's experiences. Through this type of consciousness-raising, girls and boys learn about what they have in common, how larger society and its social structure works in their lives, and how they in turn can influence society. For example, through sharing their experiences, the girls in my interviews learned that the school nurse does not stock Midol. They explored the reasons for this and recognized the gendered structure of our society. They can then resist this by either carrying their own Midol (against school rules) or by complaining to the nurse.

It is through talking with one another that we gain knowledge. It is through knowledge that the processes of empowerment and social change begin. How we understand our worlds depends on our access to the range of ideas and experiences that exist and are possible. By not talking with one another about menstruation, the body, sexuality, or any other issue teens are interested in, a source for empowerment is lost. By talking with their friends about menarche, for example, girls can learn that some families celebrate menarche with a party and cake. Girls can learn that not everyone responds negatively with shame and secrecy. They then have the power to rethink and redefine their own views on menstruation and the body.

We must support teens in their quest for knowledge and understanding, particularly in issues relating to the body. As adults, we must answer their questions honestly and provide safe spaces for them to explore their own interpretations of their worlds. This gives teens the power to enact social change in their worlds.

THE VALUE OF FEMALE BODIES

Gender is a powerful social institution that intersects teens' everyday experiences and peer cultures. In her classic essay, Gloria Steinem (1978:110) asks what "If Men Could Menstruate"? "The answer is clear," she writes, "Menstruation would become an enviable, boast-worthy, masculine event." Steinem continues: "men would brag about how long and how much," "sanitary supplies would be federally funded and free," "men would convince women that intercourse was more pleasurable at 'that time of the month,'" and, one of my personal favorites:

> Military men, right-wing politicians, and religious fundamentalists would cite menstruation ("men-struation") as proof that only men could serve in the Army ("you have to give blood to take blood"), occupy political office ("can women be aggressive without that steadfast cycle governed by the planet Mars?"), be priests and ministers ("how could a woman give her blood for our sins?") or rabbis ("without the monthly loss of impurities, women remain unclean").

Steinem's commentary highlights the role of menstruation in our culture as a site of gendered power interactions. Menstruation is not an event confined to the physical body, but one that has social and political implications. Teens interpret and talk about menstruation in gendered ways in their everyday social interactions, but some teens are also cognizant of the larger gender structure and recognize the body as a site of this social order.

In western culture (and in many other cultures), the female body is devalued compared to the male body. This devaluation is passed from adult culture to children's and adolescents' interpretations of their own and their peers' bodies.[14] In the search to understand the well-established drop in self-esteem as girls reach adolescence,[15] some researchers blame the negative cultural discourses about women's bodies and female sexuality.[16] Puberty magnifies the differences between girls' and boys' bodies. Menstruation in particular is one concrete point at which girls' experiences are distinguished from boys' experiences. As one of the girls interviewed, Sandra, said, menstruation is when girls "are becoming a woman and they are capable of having children," unlike boys. Menstruation can be frustrating because girls are excited about menarche and impending womanhood, yet many who are new to menstruation feel that they must conceal and hide the evidence of menstruation from the public world.

Girls learn as they pass through puberty that the "normal" female body is derogated and not as important or valuable as the male body. They thus often develop feelings of shame about their bodies that are tied to feminine cultural concerns of weight, attractiveness, and cleanliness. Gloria Steinem (1978) contends that because it is women who menstruate, anything menstrual-related is of less value because it is a characteristic of the powerless. In contrast, boys, although at first uncertain of their bodies' changes, learn through cultural discourse and early sexual experiences that their increasingly masculine bodies are sources of power, pride, and self-worth.[17]

Girls' and women's bodies are also less understood physiologically. Western medicine has been slow to explore and understand the ovulatory cycle. For example, not until the beginning of the twentieth century did doctors learn why menstruation occurs or that it relates to ovulation.[18] The ovum was not "discovered" by western medicine until 1827.[19] In the seventeenth century, western doctors believed in the economy of blood within the body. Thus, they thought, by menstruating, women were disposing excess and potentially toxic blood. Otherwise, why would the blood be expelled? As we saw, this view was mentioned by some of the teens in our interviews. These doctors believed too little or too much menstrual flow was a cause of many diseases affecting women. The lack of understanding by medical science and "experts" about menstruation made it ripe for misunderstandings, taboos, and negative beliefs. We fear what we do not understand.

Even today, there are competing medical explanations of menstruation's role in the ovulatory cycle. The dominant view is that menstruation is a passive activity. The uterine lining builds up and awaits a fertilized egg. When this does not occur, the lining disintegrates and falls away "like so much mildewed wallpaper" or "ruddy bathwater," as Natalie Angier (1999:109) describes. Angier explores alternate explanations where menstruation has a more active role in the female cycle. Some medical research has shown that menstruation is a defense mechanism that rids the uterus of potentially dangerous pathogens that enter the female body with sperm, a foreign substance. The endometrial lining is shed during menstruation to cleanse women's bodies of these pathogens. Additionally, women sometimes bleed at ovulation and conception, and all women bleed during and after birth. Blood carries the body's immune cells that can find and rout out the pathogens. Angier admits that there are many critics of this new research; however, this debate highlights the lack of scientific knowledge and agreement about menstruation.

In public discourse, menstruation is not a valued subject of discussion. The girls in the following group interview saw this dismissal of menstruation as a lack of sympathy about the symptoms of menstruation. Most interestingly, they recognized that it is based in gender politics:

LAURA: *Is there anything that you guys would change about our attitudes as far as menstruation? Like, is there anything, any changes that would make it easier to be a girl menstruating?*

ALLY (17): No cramps.

ELLEN (17): Yeah, that would be nice.

LAURA: *No cramps.*

ALLY: They have a cure for impotence, but they don't have a cure for cramps. That's about the dumbest thing I've ever heard of.

ELLEN: The only thing they do is they have Midol, which is supposed to take care of cramps.

ALLY: But they don't have that at the school. They're not allowed to give us anything but Tylenol.

LAURA: *Why not?*

ALLY: Because our school's run by a bunch of guys—no, I'm serious. They say that we don't have the money to stock our medicine cabinet with something like that, because it's not extremely important.

LAURA: *Really?*

ALLY: Well, like half the school needs that stuff, you know.

These teenage girls recognize that medical research and funding prioritize the physiological problems of males, such as impotence and the newly (at the time) FDA-approved and heavily marketed Viagra pill, over female issues such as menstrual cramps. Ellen and Ally see these same gender politics working in their high school.

WHAT IF MEN COULD MENSTRUATE?

The girls discussed the gender politics of menstruation when I asked what might be different if men menstruated. Erica showed in her group interview who she feels has the power in society: "If guys could get pregnant, there wouldn't be anything, like, about abortion. Like no one would protest or anything, because they'd wa—they would, like, understand why you should be able to have that choice, you know." Erica feels that the reason abortion is so contentious is because it is a woman's issue and the men are the ones in power. The girls continued this line of talk in their group discussion:

LAURA: *Do you think there would be any differences, if guys could menstruate and women couldn't?*

LESLIE (16): Yeah

KASSIE (16): Yeah.

LACEY (16): It wouldn't be as—

KORRINE (15): Like, there'd be a lot more male products.

KASSIE: What?

KRISSY (16): I think you'd get days off work for menstruating?

LESLIE: Yeah.

KASSIE: Yeah.

ERICA (15): Me, too, yeah, definitely.

LINDA (16): It'd be national take-a-day-off for your period law.

These girls recognize the gendered power structure in our society and that it affects their lives on a daily level: in dealing with menstruation. Because men generally have the power, there is a lack of institutional understanding and support for menstruation. This also reflects the salience of menstruation at this point in girls' lives. Women who are older and see menstruation as not a big deal might not need or want a day off from work.

It is not just girls who recognize gender politics based on gender inequality. Some of the boys do as well. Larry is a tall, attractive athlete who had many thoughtful things to say both in the individual and group interviews. The girls in his community group predicted that Larry would have a lot to say—apparently, he has somewhat of a reputation for being mature, considerate, and attentive. This particular community group's mission is to teach teens about the medical field, so these teens were already interested in and familiar with the body and physiological information. In his group interview, Larry referred to gender inequality as a reason for the lack of attention paid to menstruation in research and development funds.

> PAUL: *What if men could menstruate and women couldn't, what differences might there be?*
>
> LARRY (18): I figure they'd probably have a lot better products, 'cause it seems like men kind of dominate the market, you know. At least that's what my mom, she always says. She's like, talking about, you know, how all the products for women are designed by men, and so she doesn't think they're good or whatever. And I always, whenever I'm with girls, and we dress in like—it's a dressy occasion, and they wear dress shoes, I've never heard a girl say that their dress shoes were comfortable. They're always, like, complaining about how uncomfortable they are. And I'm like, 'Well why don't you just wear a pair of comfortable shoes?' And they're like, 'Because, men design the shoes and men don't design the shoes to, like, be comfortable.' And I was like, 'Okay.' So, obviously, I think, if men had, like, need for the product, then I think they would make it.

Larry is astutely aware of who holds the power in our society and has learned about these politics from his mother and female friends. Walter, also in this group and also 18 years old, offered his own response to the aforementioned question: "It would probably be talked about more, you know, females and males would talk about it more." In saying this, Walter recognizes that menstruation is not talked about and valued as a conversation topic in our culture because it is a "woman's issue." However, if men menstruated, then *both* men and women would be interested in talking about it, rather than just the women.

Male teachers do not want to discuss or deal with menstruation, some girls said. They attempt to silence menstrual discourse and not let it enter their classrooms. This may be due to teacher discomfort or to the threat of parental lawsuits or discipline from the school district if such issues are discussed outside of health class. Regardless, by not allowing menstrual discussions or talk about girls' needs, the teachers devalue girls' bodily experiences. Although the teachers may simply be uncomfortable with the topic, by silencing it they indicate that it is not a valued experience or one they want to understand.

UNDERSTANDING GENDER

To frame the discussion of how girls and boys talk about menstruation in their social interactions, it is helpful to understand the two interrelated concepts of gender and the body. In this book, I follow the complementary approaches of gender as process and gender as a social institution, and I use the embodiment approach to understanding the body. There are many different approaches to gender and the body that each rely on different assumptions. The approaches that I describe here fit best with what the girls and boys themselves said in their interviews.

The girls' and boys' talk about menstruation in their cross-gender interactions shows how they experience gender in their everyday lives. Their talk shows how girls and boys understand gender and how gender affects their everyday social interactions. In order to understand the complexities of boys' and girls' talk, we need to think about how gender is constructed. What does gender mean? What does it mean to be labeled a "girl" or a "boy"? There are two complementary conceptualizations of gender: gender as a process and gender as a status. Each is based in feminist theory, which takes both gender and power into account in understanding people's everyday lives.

First, following Candace West and Don Zimmerman's (1987) "doing gender" approach, gender is a situational accomplishment that we are constantly "doing" in our interactions. Gender, rather than being a property of individuals, is produced and reproduced in everyday social interaction. We show our gender by the way we talk, the way we dress, and the way we present ourselves to the world. For example, when a girl wears barrettes in her hair, lip-gloss, and a midriff shirt, she is performing, or "doing," her gender. Others react to her based on this performance. Following symbolic interactionism, gender is socially constructed. This means that we interpret others' actions based on their gender and what we feel are appropriate gender behaviors. All interactions are based on symbols, such as language or dress, and we learn how to interpret those symbols of gender from others. Together, we create definitions of what it means to be a girl or a boy. These definitions are fluid and are continually being created and recreated in social interaction.

At the same time, following Judith Lorber (1994), gender is a social institution. Not only is gender a process that is emergent in social interaction, but gender is an existing social structure that is developed by human culture, not merely by biology. As a social institution, gender orders social life, establishes gender roles, and is a component of other social organizations of society, such as school, work, and the family. The gender social structure can also be thought of as our society's belief systems about gender and the status of men and women in various situations.

It is within the institution of gender that individuals interact and "do" gender. The processes of gender work within this larger social structure. It is dominant society that deems it appropriate, for example, for girls and not boys to wear barrettes and lip-gloss. Importantly, these belief systems structure girls' and boys' (and women's and men's) expectations in interaction. Gendered individuals are constrained by this gender order. The two socially recognized genders, or gender roles, are defined by expectations for their behaviors, gestures, language, emotions, and physical appearance.

So, not only do girls and boys create and sustain gender in their micro interactions, but they also expect each other to behave in certain ways based on their roles as "girls" and "boys." Similarly, social interaction produces gender inequality as differences between "girls" and "boys" are marked, interpreted, and acted upon in everyday life; and, at the same time, social structure produces and sustains gender inequality through our role expectations and gender stratification system. For example, the boys and girls use different language to talk about menstruation on a micro level. However, this language is embedded in the larger gender structure that places a higher value on boys' bodies and boys' experiences than on girls' bodies and girls' experiences. Anywhere there is difference among people, there are power plays. Difference is a base from which some people gain power and others lose power. In cases of high school sports, for example, male basketball stars are more powerful, as they have higher paid coaches, a cheerleading squad, and more fan attendance at their games.

It is through social interactions and society's belief systems that we gender our bodies. Girls' bodies are designated female in part because of their experience of menstruation. Boys' bodies are designated male in the absence of the experience of menstruation. Menstruation is a gendered phenomenon: as teens understand and interpret menstruation, so do they understand and interpret gender and gender expectations.

The two approaches to gender I follow, gender as process ("doing gender") and gender as a social institution with role expectations, are particularly relevant when looking at how boys talk about menstruation and how their talk differs from girls' talk. As we will see in the next two chapters, boys negotiate their own gender and girls' gender through social interaction, as girls experience menstruation and they do not. By talking about menstruation, they identify themselves as boys, as nonmenstruants. At the same time, because girls menstruate, boys have particular expectations for girls' behavior.

LIVING IN OUR BODIES

In addition to understanding gender, it is important to understand approaches to the body in explaining power in menstrual interactions among teens. We experience our bodies in a fundamentally social way and we experience our worlds through our bodies. For example, when our bodies are sick, our social worlds and social interactions are subsequently altered and transformed. Any changes in our bodies can affect how we interact with others. If we have a bruised arm, sore muscles, or are menstruating, it may affect the types of activities we do and our feelings and mood on that day. When something changes about our bodies, it changes the way we interact with it; thus, we reconceptualize the body itself.[20] Particularly for teens, who are finishing the massive bodily changes of puberty, the status of the body is important. We present ourselves in everyday life with a conscious, and sometimes subconscious, awareness of our bodies. We are all embodied beings.

There are three approaches that have been developed to understand the body and body-based gender differences, such as menstruation. Throughout the boys' and girls' interviews, the teens expressed a tension between essentializing girls to their bodies and understanding all individuals' lives as embodied. Without careful attention, discussing menstruation and the body can easily lead to essentialist arguments about the nature of broader gender differences.

The first approach, essentialism, or biological reductionism, posits that differences between women and men can be reduced to the physical differences in their bodies. This follows theories from biology and evolutionary psychology, which assume that individuals are hard-wired through evolution to do things one way or another. Essentialist explanations of gender often rely on binary notions where there are clear boundaries and oppositions between men and women, such as men are competitive and hierarchical while women are cooperative and interdependent. Essentialist arguments restrict both women and men to the perceived limitations of their bodies, define women and men by their bodies, and cannot account for changes in gender experiences over time or across cultures.

In contrast, a second approach is pure social constructionist theory, based in symbolic interactionism. This theory posits that we learn about and interpret gender through social interaction, socialization, and culture. Rather than attributing gender differences to biology, gender differences are seen as entirely socially constructed. This means that there is no objective reality; rather, we understand our realities and our experiences through talking with others. We define our experiences through social interaction. For example, a girl "throws like a girl" because she was taught to throw that way, rather than having some innate arm-shoulder musculature that makes her throw that way. We can identify what "throwing like a girl" looks like because others have told us what it looks like. Our experiences and assumptions about gender come from gender role expectations and gender norms.

A variant of this second approach, the gender fluidity perspective, suggests that women and men can be simultaneously masculine and feminine and that their expressions of masculinity and femininity depend on the situation.[21] The emphasis here is on exploring the differences among people, rather than the differences between genders. In terms of gender inequality, it is not essential difference that stratifies women and men, but our interpretation of our experience of that difference in social interaction. "Throwing like a girl," for example, is defined as undesirable and is used as an insult. Social constructionism and gender fluidity also take into account the complexity of gendered experience that includes intersections of race, ethnicity, class, geography, and sexuality. These perspectives allow for change and diversity as the meanings of gender are never fixed, but are situated in time, space, and place.

In the girls' and boys' interviews, the teens said that girls' experiences of menstruation do indeed make girls' everyday lives different from boys' everyday lives. However, they focused on the girls' shared experiences as a result of their experiences of menstruation. Menstruation is not simply an individual bodily phenomenon, but it is shaped by cultural contexts. Thus, I argue that a combination of gender essentialism and social constructionism is appropriate in understanding what the girls and boys said. Biology and the body are not irrelevant, but biology and the body do not exist outside of culture. The focus is not essential differences between girls and boys; rather, the focus is on how girls and boys construct a bodily process that is experienced by girls.

Embodiment is a third approach to understanding gender that focuses on the body as the site for social experience.[22] Embodiment focuses on the "lived body" (a concept from phenomenology[23]) rather than only the physical body. It is a way of reconciling both the classic Cartesian dichotomous split between the mind and the body and the split between social constructionism and essentialism. In embodiment, the mind works through the body. The "lived body" is how we experience our world through our bodies. Our realities are indeed socially mediated, but we experience reality by living in and through our physical bodies, which are divided into notions of men, women, masculinity, and femininity. We feel and interpret our bodily sensations and those sensations affect our social lives. For example, when our bodies are sick, our social worlds and social interactions are subsequently altered and transformed. The condition of our bodies affects our ability to stomach a long car trip or do all the sit-ups in gym class. If we have a headache or a cold, we might easily become irritable and grumpy. The body not only affects social life, but is affected by social life. The body not only shapes human experience, the social environment reciprocally affects the body.

Additionally, our views on our own bodies may affect our interactions with others and how we understand and interpret those interactions.[24] For example, any changes in our bodies can affect how we interact with others. If we have a bruised arm, sore muscles, or are menstruating, it may affect the types of activities we do and our feelings and mood that day. Embodiment also allows for shifting and changing identities. We express our identities through our bodies with piercings, tattooing, clothes, and style. As I will show, embodiment also allows for an understanding of the body as a site of power, which can be used in social talk to assert or resist power. Thus, the body is a social creation dependent on the social, discursive, and physical context in which it resides. Embodiment is thus a way of reconciling the material body (essentialism) with the socially constructed body (social constructionism).

Children, in particular, are defined by their bodies and experience the world in an embodied fashion. For example, they are labeled based on their age and the abilities of their bodies, such as the terms "baby," "toddler," or "adolescent." Adolescence is classified by pubertal changes in the body, including secondary sex characteristics such as facial and public hair and primary sex characteristics such as menstruation.

In her research, Pia Christensen (2000) learned that children experience their bodies in terms of the social consequences the body has on their lives. In describing their bodily functions, children emphasize their own actions and their interactions with others, rather than simply talking about their bodies as isolated entities. Children think of illness, such as catching a cold, not as simply a bodily phenomenon, but rather as a disruption to their everyday social activities and routines. Recovery and feeling better are also expressed in terms of the social. For example, one of Christensen's participants, a seven-year-old, said that recovering meant a resumption of her daily activities: "to do as I usually do." She frames her recovery in terms of social interaction, not how her body is feeling.

For these teen girls, the material body is the menstruating body. This has deep implications for their social interactions, how they envision their femininity, and how they manage their everyday lives. Girls' menstruating bodies also affect boys' social interactions with girls and with other boys. It affects how often they need to go to the bathroom at school, if they feel up to participating in gym class, and if they are in the mood to put up with boys' joking. Menstruation is one concrete point at which girls' experiences are distinguished from boys' experiences. The focus in the girls' and boys' talk is not on the body itself, but on how the body affects their daily experiences and influences their social interactions. The girls and boys socially construct the meanings of menstruation and the body, but they also use the physical body as a source of power in their social interactions. For some of the girls interviewed, menstruation is key to both the girls' sense of femaleness and to their identity as women and as gendered beings. By discussing and interpreting menstruation with others, the girls are developing their identities as women. Boys, at the same time, are developing their identities as men, as nonmenstruants. Their continual same-sex and cross-sex interactions contribute to their social construction of menstruation, femininity, and the body. Children and adolescents are embodied beings.

FIVE

Girls in Power

As shown in the previous chapters, the girls and boys show negative and ambivalent interpretations of menstruation where girls lack power in body issues. These interpretations are in line with the current models for thinking about menstruation. Much of the prior research is from psychological and developmental perspectives, rather than from sociological perspectives that focus on social interaction. A fair amount of research examines girls' attitudes towards menarche and menstruation and the psychological impact and meanings of menarche and menstruation. Much of this is negative.

However, these current models are inadequate for understanding the depths and complexities of today's teens and their experiences. Even though the previous literature and our cultural history of menstruation and the body predict that girls would have less power in interactions due to ambivalent and negative attitudes towards menstruation, this does not always happen. Upon deeper examination of the girls' and boys' talk, we can see that there is a lot more going on than simple expressions of secrecy and shame. At the same time as girls express negative and ambivalent views of menstruation, many girls use menstruation as a source of power. Even while boys tease and embarrass girls, some girls resist this and use their unique bodily experiences of menstruation to wield their own power. Menstruation does not correspond wholly with decreases in self-esteem and self-efficacy. Rather, girls can use menstruation as a source of their own unique specialness that they share with other girls and women. Boys, although seen as physically and sexually stronger, do not have all the body-based power. Girls can use their embodied selves to gain the upper hand in social interactions. Girls can use menstruation as a source of power. As we will explore in the next two chapters, this power may be because in menstruation, a social event that is now out in the open, so much of the negativity that is based in secrecy is no longer applicable as it was even ten years ago.

AGENCY AND POWER

Women's bodies are often culturally portrayed as passive and are devalued; this is evident in the girls' and boys' discussions of the body and menstruation. Much of the feminist literature on the body focuses on women's bodies as passive, as the objects of male sexual gazes.[1] As with childhood researchers, many feminist researchers are concerned about these passive and negative constructions of female bodies and seek out places of girls' and women's power in their lives.[2] Rather than focusing on the passive body, researchers should ask: How do girls and women actively define their lives? How do they wield power in their daily lives and social interactions? Additionally, how do girls and women use their bodies as sources of power?

Agency and power are based in language and social interaction. It is through interacting with others that we can assert power and agency. Following Michel Foucault (1977), power is a fundamental aspect of all social interaction and is primarily based in the body because it is through the body that we experience the world. Power is dependent on language because language not only gives meaning to the world, but also allows us to know the world, interact with others, and accommodate or resist the larger social institutions. Power is shown in relationships, language, and everyday practices rather than being an essential element that a person, group, or gender does or does not possess. Living in society, we individuals are constrained by society's norms, culture, and structure. But we are also agents with power to resist, change, and influence the circumstances of our lives. A task of postmodern feminism, based in the work of Foucault, is to uncover how power, knowledge, and resistance work in the everyday interactional experiences of individuals.[3] It is in these micropractices that girls and boys work to accommodate, resist, and redefine the gendered social order of their lives.

Power makes up agency. Agency is when embodied individuals act upon their circumstances and do not simply accept what the structure, or society, offers them. In this case, structure can be thought of in terms of the gendered interactional order, cultural norms, and the adult-based institutions, such as schooling and media, that organize children's lives. However, this structure cannot account for all of the girls' and boys' unique individual and peer-based responses to menstruation. Rather, girls can draw on their bodies in creative ways in their social interactions, providing evidence for agency. Agency is evident in both individual and collective strategies, and all these strategies are manifested in social interaction. Viewing and understanding children as agents is key to new approaches in the sociology of childhood.

Following poststructuralist and symbolic interactionist thought, agency, like power, is not an essential property of an individual or body. Rather, agency is fluid and dynamic, produced in social interaction, and is based in language.[4] Poststructuralism, in particular, gives primacy to how the structures of language and ideology construct the human actor. Language is inherently social and collective; it is what gives meaning to our world. Language shapes our understanding of reality. For example, without the language to describe menstruation, how can we understand what menstruation is? Language also enables us as actors in social interactions to both resist and accommodate. However, poststructuralism has been criticized as viewing the body as only discursively produced, rather than also capable of action.[5]

R. W. Connell (1995) contends that bodies themselves can be used in an agentic manner as they shape the course of social interactions. His term "body-reflexive practices" theorizes the body as both an object *and* an agent in social processes. As such, the body is a location for the negotiation of power. This embodied agency is flexible and can be used in many different ways by different people. Agency is a characteristic of embodied individuals as we each experience the world and act upon the world through our bodies.

I explore how girls can use their bodily experience as a source of and opportunity for agency. Prout (2000) finds that, although there is empirical work on children's agency, few researchers take this work beyond the level of description. In particular, there are few empirical examples in the literature on children (or adults) that draw on the body as a source of agency in everyday life.[6]

CREATIVELY RESPONDING TO DOMINANT SOCIAL NORMS

Much of the discourse surrounding menstruation in our culture and among the boys and girls interviewed is negative, including worries about leaking, exaggerated views of the emotional effects of menstruation on girls, or seeing menstruation as gross. However, in our interviews, the discourse surrounding menstruation was not *all* negative. Some of the girls, and even some of the boys, had positive views of menstruation, claiming menstruation as good, feminine, and as an integral part of the female experience (see also Fingerson 2005a). Teens do not merely integrate dominant norms from the larger social institutions they interact with (the teens' cultural contexts) such as schools, media, and the health and medical fields, into their peer cultures, but respond creatively to these norms and generate their own views.

Although only some of the girls described menstruation in positive terms, it was particularly salient to those who discussed it. I did not ask about non-negative views directly; rather, the teens brought them up themselves. These girls developed their language and views from alternate sources rather than accepting negative views from the dominant culture. For example, Sylvia said that menstruation is a "cleansing process" and that the purpose of menstruation is "to keep you healthy." Cindy said that menstruation is "our body's way of cleaning itself out" and that "it's just like taking a bath." Greta said that menstruation is an "annoyance that can be so wonderful also" because it allows women to be able to bear children.

Often, teens embedded these positive views in their negative descriptions, showing the complexity of their interpretations. Being positive about menstruation and the body does not mean that the girls are not still negative, but that they can think both positively and negatively about menstruation at the same time.[7] There is a tension for these girls between their positive and negative views. For example, Katie described menstrual blood as "nice mushy blood-rich stuff" but then later said that menstruation "sucks" because "you bleed a lot and it's really unpleasant." Many of the other girls and boys talked about menstruation negatively, but positive language also emerged in their discussions.

Katie, in her group interview, recognized that people's understandings of menstruation are based on culture, and if she could, she would change those attitudes to be more positive:

KATIE (14): I'd make people, like, not think it was so gross. It's like, I mean, even I think that to a certain extent, it's like, ughh, yuck, it's just so gross. But then it's like, one of those things that it's not gonna change. It's like, I don't know, it just—

JENNIFER (14): —it's like this is dead stuff on your head

KATIE: Exactly. Like—

JENNIFER: You—you—you don't consider it 'ooh, it's gross, it's hair,' you know. I mean people still like, pick up wads of hair that someone left behind and be like, 'ooh' you know. But I think menstruation has to be— it happens, to every girl!

KATIE: Yeah

JENNIFER: Well, most girls at least.

LAURA: So do you think the attitudes are kind of fine the way they are or just?

JENNIFER: They could be a little more understanding

KATIE: Yeah, more understanding and less like, less like, it makes you dirty when you're having your period or whatever.

It is interesting in this segment how Jennifer compares blood with hair. On the body, hair is okay. Inside the body, blood is okay. But once those items leave the body, they are constructed as gross, even though it happens to everyone. Jennifer has an astute understanding of how Mary Douglas (1966) defines "dirt," which is matter out of place. The matter itself is not the problem; it is the location of that matter.

In her individual interview, Jennifer first talked about menstruation's role in reproduction, but also said that menstruation offers her a different and unique perspective on the world:

LAURA: *What's the point of menstruation? Why do girls menstruate?*

JENNIFER (14): To have kids.

LAURA: *Yeah*

JENNIFER: Reproduce

LAURA: *So that's the primary point of it? To reproduce and have kids?*

JENNIFER: Mhm. It could probably also add some insight on the way the world works, and stuff.

LAURA: *What do you mean?*

JENNIFER: I mean, by having to go through something like, it takes pain to be good or whatever, you know, all that stuff. I mean, you have to be able to, to accept it, and say that you can get some good out of it and be—I don't want to get pregnant right now, so obviously it's not doing me much good, but it—it kind of makes me feel a little less, like, I'm not living a perfect life so I can look at the world with more perspective.

Jennifer feels that menstruation offers her something unique. She describes the challenge of menstruation as giving her a fuller perspective on life. This positive description is couched in somewhat negative terms, such as when she describes the pain of menstruation. However, Jennifer resists the cultural expectation of negative pain and gains something positive from the experience. This is similar to many of the other girls who, as we will see, see menstruation as something that gives them a responsibility and maturity that boys do not have. Jennifer finds something unique and special about her menstrual experiences.

FORGING CONNECTIONS

In the individual interviews, I asked the girls, "Can you tell if someone is menstruating?" This evoked many responses describing a community of women. Many girls responded with different ways they interact with their friends depending on if their friends are menstruating or not. These girls are not only aware of their own cycles, symptoms, and mood changes, but also have knowledge about their friends' experiences. Some girls are very forthcoming with their menstrual status and share it with those around them. Ally said that she can tell when some girls are menstruating because "some people announce it, and that's kind of obvious. . . . They'll just come and they'll be talking and they'll be like, you know, 'I hate being on my period, I am right now, and it's driving me nuts.'"

As an adult woman with more years of menstrual experience, these discussions were particularly revealing of the different embodied worlds teen girls inhabit. I generally have no idea when my friends and co-workers are menstruating, what their symptoms are, and we generally do not share our everyday menstrual status. Yet these girls are highly in tune with not only their friends' cycle timing, but also their friends' symptoms and management strategies. For them, menstruation is new, salient, and important in their everyday lives.

Many of the girls notice when their friends have their periods because of changes in their emotions and moods. For example, Sandra said her friends act differently when they have their periods. "There are ones that are grumpy, and Kasey [another research participant], she always wants chocolate, and so that's how I know." Linda and Cindy shared in their separate individual interviews that they know when some of their friends are menstruating because their personalities and moods change. Andrea can tell when her close friends are menstruating because of their mood swings. Andrea is on the volleyball team and she notices that after playing all season together, they are "all on the same cycle." Andrea also said that she is "always in a bad mood like a few days before I start my period, but I don't like notice it until someone says something and then I'm like, 'oh yeah, wow.'" For Andrea, it is her friends' recognition of her cycle that gives her notice of her body and its changes. Sylvia "can always tell" when her mother is on her period because "her temper, it gets shorter." Also, Sylvia said that she and her mom and her sister are usually on their periods at the same time. Greta can tell when her mom is menstruating because "she's a little more fatigued" and "she doesn't eat as much." By knowing these details about others' lives, the girls have the power of information in social interactions.

A couple girls in my interviews shared their experiences with "menstrual synchrony." Biological scientists hypothesize that "women who live in close quarters convey some as yet mysterious signal to one another—an odorless, volatilized chemical called a pheromone—that ends up harmonizing the timing of women's cycles" (Angier 1999:185). Although there is debate about the truth of menstrual synchrony, Natalie Angier reports data from women's colleges, family members, and lesbian partners that have all recorded menstrual synchrony. Angier describes this phenomenon as "a sisterhood in the blood." Two of the girls I interviewed believe they have experienced menstrual synchrony. This was a salient issue for them as it was not in response to one of my questions and the two girls are in different groups. In her individual interview, Andrea said that during volleyball season, the teammates are together all of the time and they all get on the same cycle. Rebecca brought up menstrual synchrony during her individual interview and said that she and her mom are currently on the same cycle. Also, she said that she has experienced synchrony during church camp and in her sports team. Regardless of the truth or falsity of this phenomenon, the importance of the girls' menstrual synchrony discussions is that they believe it and that it shows they discuss the timing of their menstrual cycles with other girls and women in their social groups.

Menstrual synchrony came up in one of the boys' group interviews. Jim said, "From what I noticed, the majority of [girls] are sequenced, I guess. When you get a group, from what I heard, when you get a group of girls that are close, best friends and all that, they tend to synchronize. And then they can all relate as a group and then that's like ten times worse as having one around, I guess." Matt added, "Yeah, because if there's just one, they usually don't talk about it much." Although the girls share menstrual talk with one another regardless of whether they are menstruating at that time or not, Jim and Matt saw an increase in girls' sharing of their experiences as evidence that they experience menstruation together. Jim also hinted at his feelings about menstruating girls when he said it is "worse" to have more menstruants around him. For Jim, menstruation is important in how it might affect his own life and social interactions.

For some girls, menstruating signifies that they are part of a larger group of women and they can now participate in this women's social discourse. Although not all women menstruate, it is an experience that most women share and that men cannot share. Menstruation is a coming-of-age process that can remind girls that they are connected to the world around them and to other girls and women. Alyssa, a Korean immigrant, said that menstruation is "one of the steps to being a woman, like, a lady." Kassie said that when she got her first period, she thought "I'm a woman now." She believes that menstruation is a "rite of passage" and would not want to give up menstruation if offered the chance to never menstruate again, but still have children. She feels her life would somehow be diminished if she did not menstruate. The teen girls are developing their identities as women.

For these girls, who have not given birth and are not experienced in sex, menstruation is how they define the female body. Without menstruation, then, they feel not as feminine, not as womanly. Breast development and secondary sex characteristics also play a large role in how girls (and boys) define the female body; but in our interviews, the girls and boys point to menstruation. Their feminine identity is dependent on this menstrual experience, and menstruating becomes even more important to maintaining that feminine identity.

As we age, we derive our identities as women and men from different sources. According to Jean Elson (2004), older women define the feminine body in terms of hormonal balance, sex drives, and the ability to display appropriate sexual attractiveness. Elson did research among older women who have gone through hysterectomies (removal of the uterus). Those who kept their ovaries, or at least parts of their ovaries, were pleased and relieved that they still had their hormonal cycles, including symptoms of PMS, so they could affirm their status as women. One woman said that by continuing her cycle, she can still identify with other women and she can "still be part of the conversation." This is similar to the connection our teen girls made between menstruation and their own identities.

Ally said that when she got her first period, "I felt all grown up and stuff, 'cause, like, I still remember, in junior high, we'd hear, like, the eighth-grade girls, and they were so cool, 'cause they were in eighth grade, and they'd talk, and all complain about having to go change their pad at lunch, and ne-ne-neh." When Ally got her period, she felt a part of this grown-up group, was able to participate in conversations about menstruating, and did not feel like a "little seventh grader" anymore. Being welcomed as a member of a group provides a power in social interaction, as anyone who has been excluded knows. Note the importance of shared social interaction in Ally's response as well as in Jean Elson's findings among older women. Similarly, Cindy looked forward to menarche so she could share in the menstrual discourse of her older sisters. "I was 12," Cindy said, "and I was excited at first, heh heh, 'cause both my older sisters had already started their periods and they were always, like, talking about it. And I was like, well, we can't wait 'til I'm big enough to have my period, and you know. And then I started it and I was like really excited." Although Katie said she is frustrated with the work of menstruation, she added that menstruation "is part of my body" and "part of my femininity." "It's like—it's something that I can like relate to in other women and it like connects me to the whole like—girl thing."

Interestingly, Klara provided a negative case as she feels that menstruation does not fit in with her overall conception of her body. She said, "I don't think of myself as being incredibly feminine. Like, I'm not all into the whole, make-up and, whatever stuff. I'm just like, whatever, so, it [menstruation] doesn't really fit my personality." Klara thinks that menstruation is a part of femininity and the community of women, and she does not feel like she is a part of this image.

"I DON'T THINK BOYS COULD HANDLE IT"

In my interviews, the responsibility for managing menstruation and the unique experiences that girls and women go through because they menstruate is used as a source of pride for the girls. Many girls said that menstruation teaches them how to handle their bodies, how to learn to deal with pain, and how to plan ahead and have menstrual supplies with them. It is through menarche and menstruation that women assume responsibility for their bodies.[8] It is this challenge that can empower girls, both for themselves and in their interactions with boys.

In both their group and individual interviews, many girls discussed the belief that boys could not handle menstruation, indicating that this is a widely shared perception. The girls expressed pride at having the responsibility of menstruation. For example, best friends Sylvia and Andrea shared their thoughts in their group interview:

LAURA: *How would you guys feel about it if men could menstruate and women couldn't?*

SYLVIA (18): I wouldn't like it.

ANDREA (17): I don't know.

LAURA: *You wouldn't like it?*

SYLVIA: No. I don't think that—

ANDREA: I think it would be weird.

SYLVIA: I think that we deserve it, you know.

ANDREA: I don't think they could handle it. Seriously, I don't think that they could do it.

SYLVIA: They might be able to learn to, but—

ANDREA: Yeah. But as it is now, I don't think that they could do it.

LAURA: *What did you mean when you said that, like, 'we deserve it'?*

SYLVIA: Like, I think that, I mean, I'm not thrilled by having my period or whatever, but I think that, I mean, we've dealt with it for this long. I mean, it is a privilege to be able to carry a child and, you know. And I think that, I mean, we've dealt with it for this long, we might as well keep it forever, because we can handle it well. I mean, obviously, the population's rising, so we're doing a good job.

Although Sylvia said that menstruation is not the most thrilling thing, she claims superiority over boys because she can deal with it. Earlier in their interview Sylvia and Andrea laughed about how "guys complain about everything" and "guys are so sensitive to seeing blood." They get a blister or a tiny scratch and "they make a huge deal about it." Sylvia said, "I think guys get grossed out really easily by little things." Both girls think that boys are not mature enough to handle bodily issues. They are proud to menstruate.

In another group interview, Linda said that "guys can't deal with it so, the woman has to take the responsibility" and so it is women who menstruate. Ally said that if men menstruated, "they'd complain about it a lot more" than women do because they could not handle it as well. These girls think that boys are babies, complainers, and whiners. In another group interview, Nancy agreed:

LAURA: *What differences would there be if men could menstruate and women couldn't?*

. . .

NANCY (17): Maybe they'd mature faster.

LAURA: *Men would mature faster?*

NANCY: Of course, how else would you be able to handle a responsibility that comes once a month, and you have to take care of it, and nobody else will take care of it for you but you.

LAURA: *Heh heh.*

NANCY: It's not like, and then your mom goes, 'Are you having your period today? Okay, let's just stick this up in there.'

Nancy said that boys would need their mothers to take care of them. Greta, in her individual interview, noted that when fifth graders learn about menstruation in health class, she does not think the boys are mature enough to handle the knowledge of menstruation. They were very uncomfortable with the topic, she remembers. Krissy agreed and said that her male cousin is not mature enough to handle the knowledge of menstruation, even now at age fifteen. Kassie relied on an entirely essentialist gendered argument, female superiority, and said "only girls can have it since we're the upper sex," the "better sex."

Further illustrating the prevalence of this attitude, in yet another group interview, the girls again contended that men would not be able to handle menstruation:

LAURA: *[What] if men could menstruate and women couldn't*—

. . .

LESLIE (16): They couldn't. They wouldn't handle it.

LACEY (16): I know.

REBECCA (15): Uh-huh.

LACEY: They'd get their first cramp and just fall down and cry.

ERICA (15): Yeah, guys are such wimps, and they, like, they tell you that you shouldn't be all—

GRETA (15): 'Suck it up'

ERICA: —upset that you have your period, and 'Suck it up,' or whatever. That's when I'm like, 'Yeah, right.' 'Cause, like, my dad does that all the time, if he gets sick, and he's like, [makes pathetic sounds].

LACEY: They're the biggest babies.

REBECCA: Yeah.

LESLIE: Yeah.

In this sequence, the girls develop their perceptions through collaborative talk that guys could not handle menstruation. Using sentence completions, such as when Greta inserts "suck it up," and agreements, such as when Erica says "yeah" and expands on Lacey's thought, the girls form a supportive sequence of collaborative talk. This example in particular shows how adolescents develop their views through social interaction. All of these girls show a very gendered perspective where girls and women, in terms of health and body issues, are competent and responsible, whereas boys (and men by extension, as shown by their discussions of male teachers and menstruation) are incompetent, irresponsible, and immature.

The girls expressed mixed feelings about menstruation as they do not like the pain and annoyance, but still derive satisfaction from the challenge. Menstruation provides an opportunity to learn how to handle discomfort and pain in a way not available to boys. Even as they talk negatively about it, the girls interpret menstruation and their bodies in an agentic way. Rather than being exclusively discouraged by the stigma and pressures to conceal their bodies, these girls draw on their ability to respond to and manage the symptoms and bleeding as a source of pride. Many of the girls use these skills to feel superior and privileged and to put boys down by calling them wimps. This use of menstruation also shows how the girls have found one way, although limited, that they can use their bodies to feel superior to boys, even though boys are generally stronger, larger, and physically more powerful than girls are.

In sum, these girls show not only how menstruation and the body enter into their social interactions, but also how they interpret menstruation as a positive and empowering experience, even as menstruation can be embedded in negativity. The teens are not "cultural dopes"[9] in terms of their attitudes on their bodies, only accepting the dominant culture's negative attitudes about menstruation. These girls draw on the resources of their bodies and their experiences of menstruation as a way of building a sense of their femininity and connecting to other girls and women. These connections can place them in power over boys, who do not "get it." Following theories of third wave feminism and embodiment, the body becomes a source of resistance to the dominant negative cultural constructions of menstruation, femininity, and girls' bodies. These girls are using their experiences of their bodies as a source of agency in their lives. By connecting with their own bodily rhythms and identifying with other women, the girls create a safe space in which their experiences and knowledge are not only valued, but are the key to desired group membership and valuable social relationships.

MENSTRUATION IS SOCIAL

Sharon Thompson (1995) writes that, in her interviews with girls about romance, sexuality, and relationships, the narratives the girls told sounded almost rehearsed. As Thompson finds, this is because they *are* rehearsed, in a sense, because they are told over and over again in groups of their friends. In the girls' group interviews, their talk about menstruation was comfortable and it is clear that this talk was not unique to the group interview setting, but that the girls are used to sharing these same stories recurrently within their peer cultures.

In our culture, menstruation has traditionally been seen as a private event not to be talked about in public. Yet, for the mostly white girls and boys Paul and I interviewed in Indiana, menstruation is not simply a private bodily event. Rather, they use menstruation as a resource in social interaction: for telling stories and for making connections with others through shared experience.

How do girls learn about menstruation? How do girls learn how tampons work? Teens learn this by hanging out with their friends and talking about it. Just as teens learn norms of dating, working, and schooling by talking about these activities with peers, older friends, and family, so too do they learn about menstruation. By telling stories about menstruation, the girls nurture their peer cultures, generate social bonds with one another, and develop their identities.

We explore many examples in this book, but here are a few topics the teens covered. One girl shared her frustrations with being splashed and getting wet at the pool during her period. Another talked about how she had cramps during sports practice and the difficulty she had explaining it to her male coach. Girls also shared physical details of their menstrual experiences, such as how heavy or light their flow is. Several girls shared their menarche stories, which were often quite embarrassing at the time, in the group interviews. Older teens often laugh about these narratives as they remember when they were more inexperienced and unsure. In their interviews, many of the girls talked about how, at menarche, they told only one or two people about their periods, but now are very forthcoming with their experiences among groups of friends.

In their interviews, the teens did not focus on the biological process of menstruation, but rather on the social and personal experiences of menstruation. The social aspect of menstruation is important for the girls. For example, in their individual interviews, two girls separately noted how excited they were to get their periods because then they could participate in the menstrual discourse that the older girls share. Another girl said that she would be happy if she never had to menstruate again, but also thinks that she would "lose something." She enjoys teasing her guy friends about menstruation and she enjoys the funny social interaction that accompanies the experience. Because menstruation has entered into the social realm, it thus enters into power relations in both single- and mixed-gender groups, as power is a characteristic of all social interactions.

Paul and I were continually impressed with how comfortable the teens were in sharing their menstrual experiences in their group interviews. By high school, menstruation has moved beyond individual embarrassment. One of the girls said that she is much more open about menstruation now than when she was in the sixth grade, when getting her period was still so new and uncomfortable. Another girl shared this feeling and said that if I had come to interview her and her group one or two years earlier, the girls would have been much quieter and not nearly as talkative, especially during the group interview. The boys also noted the difference in comfort level. One boy said that girls talk about menstruation "more so now than middle school cause they were still a bit ashamed of it, I guess. But now in theater, or not theater, but around the halls they'll be like 'damn it, not again!' and I'll see just people like bend over in the halls and be like, 'oh shit.' I find it kind of amusing."

GETTING "IT"

Natalie Angier (1999:105) contends that menarche is the clearest rite of passage from girlhood into womanhood and is thus an experience indelibly marked on the memories of girls: "what a woman really remembers is her first period; now there's a memory seared into the brain with the blowtorch of high emotion." Among the girls interviewed, menarche marks a significant change in the way girls experience and understand their bodies. Although not all experiences of menarche the girls share are joyful, menarche certainly is shared as a defining and important experience in these girls' lives.

Just as in *Are You There, God? It's Me, Margaret* (1970), many girls reported that they talked with their friends about menstruation before they reached menarche or at menarche. They learned from their friends' experiences and they would share their knowledge with each other to anticipate what would happen to their own bodies. Greta talked with her friend about it and said, "if this happened to her, then it's going to happen to me, like, any time now." Leslie got her period first, so her friends asked her for advice. She stated, "one of my friends called me and was like, 'I think I started my period, what do I do?' And I was like, 'Put on a pad!'" Friends are support networks that help girls learn about and deal with menarche and menstruation.

Kassie, age 16, was an outgoing leader full of comments and stories in the group interactions. She was quieter in the individual interview when her friends were not around. In her individual interview, she related her experience of reaching menarche during a sleepover with a friend:

LAURA: *What happened when you got your first period? Do you remember?*

KASSIE (16): Oh, here's a story. Um, my friend Tara, actually, was spending the night and we were in my bed, and, it was I—I was only in fifth grade, and so, and we get up the next morning, and there's, like, blood, on the bed, and we were like, well, we knew, in fact, what it was, so we wer—we both, like, raced to the bathroom,

LAURA: *You both went?*

KASSIE: Yeah, we both, and I was, like, 'Oh, it's me!' And I was, I was like 'Mom!' I was really excited about this, 'cause I like, 'Man, I'm a woman now,' but then, like, the cramps kicked in, like, an hour or two later, and I was like, 'Oh god.' Heh heh. Yeah, I was like, 'I want to be normal again,' it was weird, but, yeah, it was interesting.

LAURA: *So you called your mom, and you asked your mom about it?*

KASSIE: Yeah, and she was all happy and excited, and she called all her friends.

LAURA: *She did not!*

KASSIE: She did, too. She was like, 'Guess what?'

LAURA: *She called her friend and told them you got your period?*

KASSIE: Yeah.

LAURA: *Oh, my God, that is so amazing. Did it embarrass you?*

KASSIE: Yeah, it did, I was like, 'Mom!' [exasperated tone] heh heh, but yeah, yeah, I think it's funny.

Kassie's menarche is not an individually experienced event; rather, it is shared with different levels of interacting women: her own peers, her mother, and even her mothers' peers. Menstruation and menarche, for Kassie, are socially constructed as exciting, positive, and something to be shared and celebrated through this variety of social interactions. She was embarrassed and says it was "weird," but she was happy to be the center of attention. In addition, this example illustrates how Kassie defines a "normal" body. At menarche, not menstruating is normal and menstruating is initially abnormal.

In one of the group interviews, the girls each described their menstrual symptoms to each other. This was a particularly interesting moment because this sequence of talk was not in response to any of my questions; rather, it emerged out of their own discussion. This reflects what is most salient to them. This group (Kassie's group) was one of the most energetic and talkative of the girls' groups I interviewed. The talk was lively and peppered with interruptions, corrections, storytelling, laughter, and teasing. There were nine members of the group and the majority had been members of the group since early elementary school. They knew each other well, had grown up and experienced puberty together, and were very comfortable talking about the body and menstruation.

KORRINE (15): No one knows when I'm on my period. It doesn't affect me at all.

GRETA (15): No one knows unless I tell them.

KASSIE (16): I'm just not comfortable while I am.

KORRINE: Yeah.

KRISSY (16): I get hungry.

KASSIE: So, the only thing tha—

LACEY (16): I don't eat during my period.

GRETA: Neither do I. I'm not hungry at all.

KORRINE: I lay on floor and cry when I have mine.

LACEY: I get sore.

LESLIE (16): I've got some cramps badly.

Collective talk is when two or more individuals participate in a conversation. Collaborative talk, however, is a cultural routine where the participants build upon and support each other's contributions to the conversation. It reinforces the group's cohesion and solidarity through the sharing and receiving of views, opinions, and knowledge and through the attempt to reach a shared understanding of a phenomenon.[10] Collaborative talk is not always harmonious and disagreements and power are continually negotiated. In order to have successful collaborative talk, individuals must have shared experiences that, in this case, are their experiences with menstruation and body issues.

This is a nice example of collaborative talk where the girls build on each other's contributions. As the talk progresses, the symptoms the girls report feeling escalate in severity, as if the girls are engaging in "one-upmanship" in cataloguing their list of symptoms. Interestingly, Korrine initially said that her period "doesn't affect me at all" but then, in order to take part in this "one-upmanship," she later said that she lays on the floor in tears when she menstruates. This is supportive of the other girls' talk, but also adds a competitive element. This parallels an experience that Katie shared in her individual interview when she said she and her friends tell the equivalent of fishing stories, vying for the honor of having the worst symptoms. Katie said she and her friends "exchange—it's like fishing stories like, who has the bigger fish, it's like, who has the worst cramps and who bleeds the most. Heh heh. Like, proving your womanhood through menstruation." As the girls continued their talk beyond the transcript reported here, they try to decide who has had the longest period. Several lines of research, stemming from Carol Gilligan's (1982) book In a Different Voice, have shown that girls are cooperative and consensus builders in their interactions together. I find a more complex interaction here. At the same time as they collaboratively agree on shared experiences, they engage in a competition and develop a hierarchy. The girls continually negotiate power with one another in their talk.

STORIES AND SUPPORTIVE TALK

In the interviews, the girls' menstrual talk primarily takes the form of story-telling. The girls talk about their experiences getting their first period, managing menstruation, defining what is "normal," and dealing with menstrual products. The girls share a wide variety of stories as they learn from each other and experience menstruation as a social event. By sharing their experiences with friends, girls can feel reassured about their own experiences and know that they are not alone. They are able to commiserate together about their experiences through their storytelling. In childhood and adolescence in particular, group belonging is very important. Kids want to discuss in-group experiences with each other, as this helps to more firmly establish their shared bond.

When I present these data and analyses to groups of adults, both academic and nonacademic, they first ask routine questions about my data, methods, and analyses. Then, in almost all cases, both the women and the men start telling their own menstrual stories. They are eager to share these stories and the conversation often gets carried away with these interesting, humorous, and often embarrassing narratives. Many audience members are from older generations and had not told these stories before to any audience, much less a mixed audience.

Telling stories is a central element of understanding peer culture, as we can see which stories are told, accepted, built upon, and laughed about in social interaction. These menstrual stories help develop teens' own unique peer cultures, particularly as adults do not have this type of menstrual talk in their adult peer cultures.

Ken Plummer (1995) develops a "sociology of stories" in which he investigates the structures and formats of telling stories. He argues that stories are not simply texts, rather, they are "social actions embedded in social worlds" (p. 17). We use stories to illustrate the meanings and understandings of our lives. When examining stories, Plummer asks why people tell the stories, why they do not tell them, how they select language to articulate their experiences, how they find and assert their voices, and how the listener hears and interprets the story. He is concerned not only with what the teller is saying, but also with the social processes involved in the telling. Stories are produced in distinct social contexts by the teller, who is a real person experiencing his or her everyday life. For Plummer, stories are both symbolic interactions and political processes because they show power dynamics in the tellers' lives. The listeners are the interpretive community for the story and they construct their understandings of the story collectively with the teller.

In their interviews, both individually and collaboratively, girls shared elaborate stories with each other and with me. The girls' stories addressed two issues derived from Plummer's sociology of stories. First, what are the social processes for producing and listening to stories, how do people tell their stories, why do people tell the stories, and how are the listeners interpreting those stories? Second, what are the social roles that stories play, how do the stories affect the lives of people, and how do they both conserve and resist structures in society? Girls share with each other their stories of menarche, other menstrual experiences, embarrassing moments, and strategies for managing menstruation. They share these stories in collective and often collaborative talk. The girls tell their stories to offer emotional support, affirm other girls' experiences, and to share practical strategies for dealing with menstruation.

Through telling these stories, the girls build understandings and interpretations of menstruation both in the telling of the story and the reactions of others to the story. The girls build a community of shared experience through sharing their narratives. Plummer (1995:174) contends, "stories need communities to be heard, but communities themselves are also built through story tellings. *Stories gather people around them*: they have to attract audiences, and these audiences may then start to build a common perception, a common language, a commonality" (italics original). Kathleen O'Grady and Paula Wansbrough (1997:61) agree and say this holds true as well for women's experiences with menstruation, "*Together*—telling our stories, listening and learning—this is how we women come to understand the secrets of our bodies" (italics original).

The girls I interviewed form supportive communities by talking about their menstrual experiences. They build a safe space removed from gendered power relations where they can talk about their bodies. There are still power negotiations in terms of competition and hierarchy in this space among the girls (e.g., who bleeds the most or who uses tampons), but the girls know they can share their experiences with others who understand menstruation and its social implications. The results of telling stories for these girls include generating social bonds with one another, developing their identities, and nurturing their peer cultures.

WHAT'S NORMAL

The most common discussions among the girls about menstruation focused on what is normal and what has been most embarrassing. Beyond the initial experience of menarche, girls continue to share their menstrual experiences with each other. They tell stories about their own experiences and learn of their peers' experiences. This talk helps the girls understand menstruation and be reassured that their experiences are "normal" and shared by others their age. Of course, this could be a source of misinformation and anxiety, especially around tampon use, which can be a tricky aspect of managing menstruation because of the intimate nature of using tampons. Nevertheless, for the most part, the girls in the interviews talked about accurate and helpful information they learned from their peers.

In the previous example, the girls shared a supportive style of talk as evidenced by the repetitions, agreements, and expanded remarks. Throughout
the interviews, much of the menstrual talk shared by girls is based in such
supportive talk. Through repetition, Greta affirmed Korrine's statement that
"no one knows" when they are on their periods. Korrine and Greta both
showed agreement through Korrine's "Yeah" and Greta's "Neither do I" statements. Finally, Lacey and Leslie both expanded on Korrine's statement of her
painful symptoms in the last three lines with "I get sore" and "I've got some
cramps badly." The girls, in this sequence in particular, use their talk to support each other and affirm each other's beliefs.

Some girls focused on how they feel during their periods. Katie, a shy,
thin, tall blond girl who really enjoyed talking in the interviews about her
ideas on the body and menstruation, said in her individual interview:

> KATIE (14): Um, ((pause)) I don't kn—like, when I talk about it with my
> friends, one of the things we always talk about is like, how like self con-
> scious you are and how it's always like—whenever you menstruate you
> feel like icky, you know? Not all the time when you are menstruating, but
> like, certain—at certain times you realize you're on your period and you
> feel kind of gross, you know? And like, it just—heh heh, my friend and
> I we always talk about this, 'it smells so bad!' you know? Heh heh.

Through this talk, these girls learn about the variety of ways menstruation, a
physiological phenomenon they share, manifests itself in different girls' bodies and is experienced differentially by the girls. They reconfirm that their
own experiences are "normal" because others in the group share them. By
telling stories about shared experiences, they connect to the larger group of
menstruating women and develop their identities as women.

In one group, the girls collaboratively talked about tampons, problems
they have had, and what girls should and should not do when using tampons.
In the following sequence, the girls shared not only their own stories with
each other, but also those stories they heard from their peers and family.

> KASSIE (16): I remember the first time I actually got one [a tampon] in
> right, and, like, I fol—it was a really painful experience. I was like, 'Ah.'
> [noise like in pain] It really hurt a lot.
>
> ERICA (15): One of my mom's friends, when she was younger—Anyway,
> one of my mom's friends was, like, after she hadn't been on her period,
> like, very long, she put in a tampon, she was like 12, she put in a tampon
> and forgot it was in there, and then later, she put in another one.—
>
> LESLIE (16): —another one.
>
> ERICA: Yeah.

LACEY (16): I've heard about that.

LAURA: *Who?*

ERICA: And, like, she was, one of my mom's friends, and she, like, forgot about it, and then, like, after a couple days, like after two or three days, it really started to hurt, and she went to the doctor to see what was wrong—

LESLIE: How could you forget?

ERICA: —and they had to, like, surgically remove it.

KASSIE: Oh.

GRETA (15): She had two tampons in there, and she forgot about both of them?

ERICA: No, one. She put one in, forgot it was there—

LACEY: —Put the other one in—

ERICA: —and put the other one in, another one over it.

LINDA (16): Well, people on my soccer team last year used to put two in at the same time, just because

KASSIE: Just because it would work.

LACEY: Oh my God. Really?

ERICA: Oh my God, are you kidding me.

LESLIE: Oh my gosh.

LAURA: *What happened, what?*

LINDA: People, like, on my soccer team used to put two in at the same time, just because.

LAURA: *Ow.*

KASSIE: Because when you're running around—

LINDA: —Right.—

KASSIE: —it can—it starts to come out.

LINDA: When you play soccer and, like—

LAURA: *The tampon starts to come out?*

KASSIE: Yeah, it's weird, it's gross. And you're just like, 'Shit.' Yeah, I know a lot of people that did that.

GRETA: Two in, that's bad.

LAURA: *No, I don't even—*

KASSIE: Yeah, because you can't use the big ones when you play soccer, it's just uncomfortable. You have to use the little ones.

GRETA: There's, uh, uncomfortable normal.

KASSIE: I don't think I have that much room up there.

In this sequence, responses such as Lacey's "oh my God, really?" and Leslie's "How could you forget?" indicate that the story being told is something new that the girls learn about and to which they actively respond. Also, the girls share several narratives in this sequence, with one story reminding another girl of a story and so forth. The girls support each other through sentence completions and expansions. The girls in this sequence told stories that, in terms of content, share strategies for managing menstruation, and, in terms of structure, form supportive collaborative talk.

The collaborative stories provide practical information on tampon use, experiences of what is normal, and emotional support for issues with menstruation. Together through their talk, the girls define their views on tampons and what happens when girls use tampons. They negotiate what works and what does not work when wearing tampons. In their talk, they show the process of their learning and understanding of tampon use. In addition, they establish what is "normal" by starting the talk with a scary story and ending it with the wearing of two tampons at once, which they define as "normal."

Menstrual information is most effectively passed among peers. There is no broader cultural acceptance of such talk in public, so these girls have developed their own cultural norms to pass on such important information. This is similar to other information on women's experiences not as valued or accepted by the dominant (male) culture, such as women's experiences of childbirth and menopause. These are becoming more accepted in the public discourse, but such change is driven from below by communities of women (such as the Boston Women's Health Collective [1998]).

HOW EMBARRASSING!

Many girls enjoy telling stories about moments that, at the time, were very embarrassing, but now seem humorous because the girls are wiser and more experienced with menstruation and their bodies. They laugh at their experiences from when they were younger and were less sure of the process and management of menstruation. By telling embarrassing stories and laughing together over shared experiences, the girls generate and strengthen their social bonds with one another.

In one of the girls' groups, the girls have an extended discussion on tampon use and how when they were younger they did not know how to use tampons. Kassie told an embarrassing story about how, in school, she did not know how to put a tampon in, but she did not want to appear "uncool" in front of her friend; so she pretended to know. Right away, Leslie indicated with "Ooh" that she empathized with the potential embarrassment of this story:

KASSIE (16): I had never put in a tampon before. I didn't know how.

LESLIE (16): Ooh.

KASSIE: I wasn't sure. It was a big one. No, no listen to this, it was Julie—do you guys remember her? Julie Weerd.

LESLIE: Oh, Ward.

KASSIE: And I didn't want her to know that I didn't know how to put a tampon in, because I didn't want to, you know, seem uncool. So, I was like, 'You can do this.' I pulled the thing, like, I took the plastic part off, and I was like [makes confused face]. [Group laughs] And so, then, I pulled the tampon part out, and I was like, 'What is this for?' Like—[makes motion as if tossing tampon] [Group laughs] And it went out and on the floor. And I just, like, I did, and so I take it and I'm like, 'Okay,' you know. And like, that much [with index and thumb close together] of it goes in. I'm like, 'This feels kind of weird.' And, like, it really starts to hurt later. And, like, and, like, I'm walking like this ( ) in pain, 'cause like I—

LAURA: *You put this much of a tampon in?*

KASSIE: Yeah. And like, when I go to sit down, I'm like ( ). Awful. It was horrible. And, so, like, and then I'm like in giant pain, and I'm just like, 'Something is seriously wrong.' I didn't want to, like, tell anybody. And I had Mr. Kabel for English.

LESLIE: Oh. [Group laughs]

KASSIE: And he was like, 'You okay?' And I was like, 'Can I use the phone?'

KORRINE (15): He's a really weird guy.

KASSIE: Anyway, so I'm like, 'I need to use the phone.' So, I call my mom, and my mom was at her office, and I'm talking to her. I'm like, 'There's something seriously wrong.' She was like, 'What's wrong?' And I was like, 'I put a tampon in and something's bad.' And, so—and my mom was, like, in Indy [Indianapolis], so she comes to the school. Like, my mom's like ( ) and, like, brings me clothes, thinking that I had, like, spilled blood all over me, and, like, I had to tell her it was just-

LAURA: *Oh.*

KASSIE: She was like, 'What?' [in screeching voice]

The other girls collectively laughed and commiserated with Kassie as she shared this embarrassing early moment. This was embarrassing for Kassie on multiple levels. First, she did not want to admit she did not know how to use a tampon. Second, she was in pain in a public space, school, and wanted to hide her pain and the reason for the pain from her teacher, friends, and peers. She turned to her mother, a "safe" resource, for help. Now, as evidenced by Kassie's comfort with menstrual talk in her interviews and how she shared this story, Kassie is more comfortable with menstruation and is not embarrassed by it. Menstruation and concealment do not hold the power over her that they once did.

In her group interview, Kasey shared two stories about her mom, aunts, uncle, and grandma and their embarrassing experiences. The first was when her youngest aunt got her period and did not know anything about menstruation and the second was about when her uncle had to buy pads for his sister. Sandra introduced the story, but Kasey interjected and said that she would tell the story. Then, Sandra and Anne added their own knowledge about the incident and the family relationships. The four girls in this group are from a rural area and three of them are related to one another. Because the two stories were known by three members of the group, it is clear that the stories have been passed down into the girls' peer culture from the mother, aunts, and grandmother to the younger generation because of the entertaining and embarrassing nature of the events. By sharing the stories, the girls strengthen their social bonds and affirm their shared identities as women. These two stories are particularly salient to this group of girls because they are relatives and have shared family experiences. Interestingly, the stories were not shared when their aunts were young. As indicated in the first story, the youngest aunt did not know what menstruation was when she reached menarche. Now, these same women who did not discuss menstruation in their generation share the stories with their daughters and nieces. When Sandra said, "we could go on for hours," she suggests that there are even more menstrual stories from this family that have been shared. The teens are not only sharing stories amongst each other, which was the focus of my interviews, but it is clear that such stories are also entering into family conversations in a way they were not in earlier generations. I believe that because menstruation is now more in the open, there are opportunities for girls to use menstruation as a source of power and agency.

BUT ADULTS DON'T TALK THIS WAY!

In the group and individual interviews, the girls were comfortable with this very intimate level of menstrual talk. Even the boys often laughed and joked about their female friends' experiences and about their own experiences dealing with their female friends' mood swings. Although the boys were not as comfortable talking about the details of menstruation, they did share their social experiences related to menstruation with each other in the interviews.

The teens often share others' stories in the group interviews, which shows that they talk about the body and menstruation in everyday "natural" conversations. Otherwise, they would not know others' stories. Similar to their own stories, many girls share stories of *peers'* first menstruations, their cramping experiences, and their embarrassing moments. For example, in one group interview, one of the girls shared her friend's experience with an ovarian cyst and how this affected her menstrual cycle and symptoms. In another group interview, two friends collaboratively told a story about a girl they knew at school who had to wear a long coat inside all day because she started her period and worried about leaking. They were all in fifth grade and the menstruant was not only unpopular, but was an early maturer, developing breasts, hips, and starting her period well before her peers.[11] Her classmates did not know much about menstruation and were nervous about pubertal changes. The girls remember that "everyone sort of, like, avoided her because they thought it was contagious or something."

Adults with whom I talk about my research are often surprised at the content and comfort in the teens' talk. Things are different in the current generation of teens. The teens that participated in our research were born in the early 1980s. Gloria Steinem's "If Men Could Menstruate" (1978) was written before they were born and is now a part of their culture. Some teens even mentioned they read it for a school class. They can see (and some have seen) an annual production of Eve Ensler's *The Vagina Monologues* at the nearby university campus. When *The Curse: A Cultural History of Menstruation* was published in 1976, it was the first book to bring menstruation into mainstream popular culture, and it made such a large splash that the authors did talk shows and interviews all over the country. It was published almost ten years before these teens were born. In their preface, the authors talk about how journalists and fellow scholars were often hostile to them and their book. For example, Mary Jane Lupton was speaking at a psychiatric association meeting where several male psychiatrists said that when they treated female patients for fluctuations of mood and behavior, they did not consider menstruation as a factor. During her talk, Lupton mentioned that she was menstruating and said that menstruation "accounted for her easy flow of words and casual manner." She recalls that, "No one laughed." The audience was appalled that she "revealed herself." One man said, "Why, my own wife doesn't tell me when she is menstruating."[12]

The teens in our interviews are living in a different world, a world that is more comfortable with menstruation and sex than most adults experienced when they were teens. There is an openness in our culture today that was not there even in the late-1970s or 1980s, only 15 to 25 years ago. Many of the older people that I share my findings with are surprised that teens today are so forthright and open in their menstrual talk. These adults would not be able to use menstruation as a source of power in their social interactions. They tell me that when they were teens, they never would have talked about menstruation in public. Why might teens be more comfortable now?

First, the prevalence of mass media exposes teens to a much larger cultural world than they used to be. No longer are teens' social interactions limited to people they can talk to in person in their communities. Teens can follow along with the lives and conversations of characters in numerous television shows, movies, and real life celebrities. Further, there is a sensationalism and intense competition in the mass media where every show has to be more daring and more explicit than the last show. Issues of sex, violence, and the body that were once taboo are now talked about routinely, all day and on network television, not just in the evening hours or on cable. This casualness of media talk filters into children's and adolescents' lives and influences their peer cultures.

Second, as Jane Brody (2003) of the *New York Times* explains, the AIDS epidemic has changed the way the body and sexuality are talked about in the media and in everyday life. In order to talk about AIDS transmission and prevention, doctors, journalists, and health writers learned to discuss explicit sexual activities without being embarrassed or prudish. Our interviews were conducted shortly after the Clinton-Lewinsky affair when the blue dress and the sexual details were plastered over the daily news. Similarly, with the bulk of the U.S. population, the baby boomers, moving into old age, increasing attention is given to disease and illnesses such as breast cancer, impotence, and menopause. Infertility is also increasingly common and discussed on the national scene. Brody recalls that when she started reporting on health issues in 1966, editorial policy severely limited her ability to describe any sex-related issue in a meaningful, forthright manner. This has changed significantly.

Third, connecting both increased media prevalence and more open talk about body and sexuality, is the effect of third wave feminism on adolescent culture. Third wave feminism is the current feminist movement primarily driven by younger women. Among the priorities of third wavers (I discuss third wave feminism in more detail in chapter 6) are women's rights to sexual pleasure and women's rights to use and display their bodies as they choose. For example, girls and women feel that they have control and power over their own bodies and body expression, so they dress as sexily as they please for their own pleasure. They argue that this is not for the pleasure or objectification of boys and men. By dressing sexily, these third wavers claim power over their surroundings and over their appearance and thus that they control their effects on boys and men. This is shown by media icons such as Madonna and Brittany Spears and any walk through a local school as girls, even in elementary schools, wear outfits baring their midriffs. Third wavers' constructions of the body and sexuality have benefited from the second wave feminist movement, such as the publication of *Our Bodies, Ourselves* (Boston Women's Health Collective, original publication date 1976), which is credited with launching the women's health movement.

These issues have changed what is okay to talk about, discuss, and debate in public space. The teens I interviewed were born between 1981 and 1987. They do not remember Reagan's presidency. Girls have always been welcome and involved in school sports. Former U.S. Senator Bob Dole is best known for talking about impotency, not running for president. Most of them know someone who was born with the help of infertility science. The technology for genetic testing, DNA analysis, and MRIs have always been available.[13] In our interviews, the teens showed a remarkable candor and comfort in discussing menstruation. They are generally not embarrassed about it and do not use the types of linguistic strategies to maintain menstrual secrecy in their talk that adults would typically expect.[14]

INTERVIEWING IN COMMUNITY GROUPS

Additionally, the comfort displayed by these teens might be because they are being interviewed within their existing social groups. These transcripts nicely show how comfortable the girls are with each other in their talk and how much they have to say about menstruation and the body both to each other and to me as the interviewer. Most research on children is limited to settings of the school and the home. In contrast, my research participants were recruited from peer-based youth organizations in central and southern Indiana.

I find that using youth clubs is a good way to approach youth in a fun, group-oriented setting away from the restrictions and confines of the adult-run school and home. These organizations are youth-centered places where youth feel empowered, where they are primarily connected to other youth rather than adults, and where they are responsible for playing a variety of roles to keep the group functioning. The teens had more interactional power in the research setting, as Paul and I were entering *their* world, rather than bringing them into *our* world. This existing comfort and ability to speak freely in the setting is important in establishing rapport in the research interview.

Most importantly, these groups are ongoing communities. Many of the kids have participated in their groups for extended periods of time, have developed relationships with each other, have a shared history and culture, and are comfortable in the setting.[15] These relationships are invaluable in the group interviews as there is an existing community of talk that Paul and I were able to enter. The participants often referred to shared moments, as we have just seen, giving evidence of their shared history. Also, although group talk might inhibit individuals from sharing certain personal things, the interaction in group interviews can elicit more accurate accounts as participants must defend their statements to their peers with whom they interact on a daily basis.

ISN'T MENSTRUATION A PERSONAL EVENT?

The focus of this book is on how girls can use menstruation and the body as sources of power in their social interactions and how boys respond to this power. However, menstruation, we would think, is a personal and private experience. Girls may share that experience with others and talk about menstruation and menarche in terms of their *social* experiences, but it is still a *personal* event. Given this, we might predict that girls would also talk about menstruation in their individual interviews in terms of their private experiences.

Some of the girls' talk does focus on personal experiences. For example, the experience of menstruation gives girls an opportunity to pay attention to their cycles and the changes their bodies go through each cycle. Some girls are aware of the physical changes their bodies go through as they menstruate. For example, Jane said that during menstruation she eats less. "I'll eat a lot, like, right before, and then I'll eat less, and then I'll just start eating normal." Anne also finds that she is not nearly as hungry during her period as at other times in the month. Kasey craves chocolate during her period, just as she says her mom does. In fact, pointing to the social importance of menstruation, her friends, in their individual interviews, mentioned Kasey's cravings as indications that Kasey has her period. Katie and Kasey separately noted that during their periods they are more lazy and sleepy. Leslie said that "I can tell when I'm starting my period 'cause my waist expands and like my boobs get tender and I'm a little more agitated and I'm always more hungry." Although these girls may feel negatively about their periods, such as Jane who described it as "something to make your life miserable," they take the opportunity menstruation provides as a way of increasing body awareness.

Other girls were even more aware of their bodily rhythms and see the creative peaks in their cycles. Greta said that menstruation is "a cycle that I feel in my body." She notes that menstruation affects her mood, her complexion, and her attitude in general. Jennifer gets migraines during her period. In response, she drinks a lot of caffeine, which she believes increases her blood flow and helps her muscles relax. However, she therefore sleeps less and uses that time to paint and be creative. In many cultures, creativity is thought to be at its highest during the menstrual period.[16] Although an isolated example in our interviews, Jennifer's claim of creativity is similar to these views, not to those of the dominant U.S. culture.

The individual experiences most girls focused on in their individual interviews were their menstrual symptoms. Jennifer, for example, talked about her cramping and the migraines that she gets during her period. She shared her personal experiences with menstruation and did not talk about her symptoms in terms of social interactions. However, in the group interviews, discussions of symptoms were frequent. The girls talked about their symptoms as they experience them personally, but use this talk to engage in a sort of power competition for the worst symptoms and to share their symptoms and learn what is "normal." Thus, we learn that the girls discuss and interpret even their individual experiences of menstruation in terms of their social lives.

As Kathleen O'Grady and Paula Wansbrough (1997) write, "During so much of our daily schedules, we often forget that we have bodies and spend too much time inside of our heads. Periods have a way of reminding us that our brain and our body are connected. When we remember this connection, the feeling of wholeness that we experience gives us a new and special way of looking at the world" (p. 44). Menstruation can remind girls that they are embodied actors.

Even with these comments about girls' individual bodily experiences, in our interviews most girls discussed even their individual experiences with menstruation in terms of the social. For example, when many of the girls described menarche, they talked not about the specifics of how it felt or how they felt, but rather about what social resources they drew on to manage the bleeding. Katie said, "I went into the bathroom and there was blood on my underwear. And my mom came home from work and I was like 'I think I'm starting my period.' And she's like, 'oh I'm so proud of you.'" Her first sentence describes the individual act of finding blood on her underwear. Then, rather than continuing with her individual experience, such as how she may have felt, what she did herself to manage the blood, or what her individual reactions were, Katie instead talked about telling her mom that she had gotten her first period. Katie indicated that time passed between when she went to the bathroom and when her mom came home from work, yet she does not discuss what she did during this time. Katie focused on the social, not her individual or personal experiences.

In sum, because menstruation is in the social realm, it is thus a source of power as all social interaction is imbued with power negotiations. When it was silenced, shameful, and only in the private realm, there was no way for girls to assert any sort of power.

"WE SHOULD JUST CREATE A WOMEN'S STORE"

Some girls want even more power when it comes to their bodies and menstruation. When talking about what would make it easier for a girl to menstruate, some girls responded with ways of lessening the burden of management. Katie and Jennifer, in their group interview, suggested time off from school.

KATIE (14): Well, in a perfect world, we would have like, at least two days where we could stay home, like, whenever we wanted to during our period. 'Cause like, when you're on your period you're really lethargic, and it's like, 'I just don't wanna go to school today.' So like, have two

days during your period when you were allowed to stay home. So not
necessarily during the whole—whole thing, but just like, days when you
could like, take time off, read books, eat chocolate. Heh heh.

JENNIFER (14): Yeah, my friend always has to stay home sick when she
starts her period 'cause she gets migraines and cramps and everything and
she's just like, sometimes she starts throwing up and, so for her, it's just
like, nasty nasty time of the month!

This talk indicates a desire for greater agency. They want more control
over not only their bodies but also in their social situations and over the
social structure and social institutions. Some of the girls provided recommendations for coping with this system. Their recommendations are limited
to working within the dominant school and cultural systems, but still express
girls' desires for greater control. They want more control of their bodies and
their social situations.

To sum, in their narratives and group discussions, the girls and boys view
menstruation and girls' bodies in a medicalized, passive, and negative way.
However, further analysis indicates that girls can also use their bodies as a
source of power. They use their experiences of menstruation to develop a positive identity as women, to creatively respond to dominant social norms, to
forge connections with other women, and to share in something that is
unique to girls that boys do not experience. The girls in my interviews bring
menstruation out of a secret and shameful realm, where it has historically
been placed, into the open where it challenges dominant norms of what is
valuable knowledge, where the female body should be placed in discourse,
and the power of women's communities. Thus, girls' bodies can be sources of
both disempowerment *and* agency.

SIX

Boys' Responses

Because menstruation is a social event, it is embedded in power relations. Because menstruation is talked about in the social realm, it also enters into boys' everyday lives. How do boys respond to this power that girls can have? Boys do not experience menstruation. They do not understand what menstruating and managing menstruation is like. They know less about menstruation than girls do, which puts them at an interactional disadvantage. They are thus uncomfortable in such situations and find various ways of responding to these situations.

KNOWLEDGE IS POWER

Girls can use their bodies as power resources because of their knowledge about the experience of menstruation. This is knowledge that boys do not share and thus it places boys in a more threatened position in social interactions. (This type of knowledge is about the experience of menstruation, not the biological knowledge about girls' reproductive systems.) The boys and girls we interviewed learned about menstruation in fifth-grade health class, from their families, from snatches of conversations with friends, and from media advertisements. Initially, before they are formally told about menstruation, both boys and girls have a kind of "half-knowing."

According to Shirley Prendergast (2000), "this half-knowing had been in place by the time they were six or seven years old, and had come about as a result of seeing, overhearing or being told odd and inexplicable things: about 'blood'; what girls could or could not do when they were bigger; about being careful; about secrets that they should not tell" (p. 108). Some girls do not remember where they specifically learned about menstruation, just that they "kind of" knew about it. Anne remembers that she "just kind of caught on" when she first learned about menstruation. Erica remembers, "kind of always knowing" that menstruation is something that would happen when she got older. Premenarcheal girls have incomplete knowledge about menstruation, which includes not only ignorance but also misconceptions.[1]

By the time they reach high school, the age of our research participants, girls have their own experiences menstruating and they learn about menstruation from their own experiences and, importantly, from sharing those experiences openly with their mothers and friends. The boys, although interested in learning about it, are generally still dependent on these not-so-reliable sources, their incomplete knowledge and misconceptions, and their "half-knowing."

Brian, a quiet, skinny, dark-haired boy of 14, learned about menstruation "at lunch." He said, "In seventh grade I'd always eat lunch with four girls, maybe like five or six girls, and that's what they talk about at lunch sometimes. So I just kinda listened to that." Brian did not question the girls about menstruation or engage in the discussion with them; he just listened quietly. Boys are indeed interested in learning about menstruation and do so in both their cross-gender and single-gender interactions.

When discussing menstrual products, many boys talked about learning about them from the media, particularly advertisements. Walter said he learned about menstruation from "whatever was in magazines or TV." As mentioned in chapter 3, Don said, "I know about the little thing like this and how it has the wings that flap with the blue background so it looks like it's flying, yeah." This is a reference to an advertisement for menstrual pads with "wings" to prevent the blood from leaking over the side of the pad onto a woman's underwear. Dave also attributed some of his menstrual knowledge to advertisements. "Commercials are like, 'get the Tampax multipak' with, you know, the heavy days, and then you have the light days."

In their interviews with Paul, all the boys were unclear about the details of menstruation. This shows the unreliability of their sources. A few boys think PMS is "post" menstrual syndrome rather than "pre" menstrual syndrome. Some are not sure of the difference between "PMS" and actual menstruation. One boy was not sure if yeast infections, which he sees in commercials, and knows that "it deals with down there," have anything to do with menstruation, another "down there" issue for women. Also, some boys were not sure about the difference between a tampon (inserted inside the vagina to absorb the blood) and a pad (which is placed in underwear to catch the blood). They hear about both on television advertisements but it is never clear what the differences are. Brian tried to explain the products in his individual interview:

PAUL: *What do you know about different menstrual products?*

BRIAN (14): I know there are some pills for it and then like tampons and pads.

PAUL: *Okay. Um let's take it to where you said pills. What would the pills be for?*

BRIAN: For like um bloating and headaches and stuff. But mostly from like commercials where they talk about it—how they say Tylenol is not enough and stuff.

PAUL: *Gotcha. Okay. And what was the second thing you said—tampons?—*

BRIAN: —yeah. Stuff like that.

PAUL: *As far as you understand, what are those for?*

BRIAN: Mm, to like stop blood—like collect it all in this little bag thing.

In the following individual interview, it is painfully clear that Derek is not sure what menstruation is. However, he does not admit his lack of knowledge, but instead stutters his way through his narrative, explaining his difficulty with "it's hard to describe" and ends his discomfort with "I usually don't discuss it."

PAUL: *What is the point of menstruation? Why do girls menstruate?*

DEREK (19): Umm ((pause)) um ((pause)) whew uhh I don't know, it's hard to describe um.

PAUL: *Tell me whatever you think.*

DEREK: Whatever I think. Whew ((pause)) um ((pause)) umm I I wanna say it but I just, it's just hard to come out and say um ((pause)) Ahhh, whew ((pause)) I don't know, cleaning of the body or I don't know, something, that case I don't know it's, I don't usually discuss it.

Later, Derek admitted to Paul that other boys just do not know much about menstruation, "Some kids think they know it all but they don't. It's like, you don't even know what you're talkin' about, you know you hear 'em over discussing with another guy, and you're like, you don't even know what you're talkin' about." However, he never admits his own lack of knowledge. This would acknowledge that girls know more about something than he does, which is a major faux pas in teen culture. Instead, he said, "I don't usually discuss it" and "it's just hard to come out and say." His uses of the phrase "I don't know" in the transcript above are fillers, rather than an honest acknowledgement that he does not know.

Further complicating the issue and hindering any possible learning, most boys do not want to admit that they do not know about menstruation. Thus, they are uncomfortable in situations where menstruation is the topic of conversation. After the tape recorder was turned off at the end of the interviews, Paul asked each boy if he wanted an explanation of menstruation and menstrual products. Only one took him up on his offer. Additionally, only one boy admitted during the interview that he did not know what menstruation does. In the dominant culture, it is not a "masculine" quality to ask for help or to ask for things to be explained. This can be a sign of weakness. In our culture, males are associated with the mind and with knowledge, as evidenced by the common stereotype that men never stop for directions. As Derek explained, "we don't wanna make an ass out of ourself in front of the class." Menstruation is a place where males do not have the experience and the boys do not understand what is happening, so they are in a threatened position. It is the girls, in this case, who have the power.

Some boys also limit their learning and exploration because they think that menstruation and menstrual products are "gross." Jim said that "even in the wrapper, it's just like 'ughh,' it grosses them [boys] out or something." Additionally, knowledge specific to girls' and women's issues, particularly the body and menstruation, is devalued in the U.S. dominant cultural discourse.[2] By not learning about menstruation or showing interest in menstruation, boys perpetuate this devaluation.

Some boys are aware of the power the girls have because girls know more than they do, and the boys admit to leaving the area when menstruation comes up in conversation. This can prevent the girls from acting on this power. This could also be seen as the boys acknowledging the girls' greater power and, in a sense, forfeiting the power play "game."

> MATT (17): I was there when her mom was asking her [about her period]. Heh heh.
>
> DEREK (19): I'll be leaving now.
>
> MATT: That's right, I was like I'll see you later, I'm going to go to work now.
>
> JIM (18): I'd leave the door the first syllable that cames out for "per-." Heh heh.
>
> MATT: I was, I was like 'I'm going to go to work, I'll talk to you later.'

Matt, Derek, and Jim collaboratively agreed that if the topic of menstruation comes up, they leave the area. For Jim, if the first syllable of "period" is spoken, he said that he would be out the door. Interestingly, by acknowledging this power girls can have, the boys agree with the interpretation of girls' bodies as agentic. The boys discussed a way of subverting this power by physically leaving the interaction.

The following is from Paul's individual interview with Matt where Matt expresses awareness of the power of this talk:

> MATT (17): (somebody) talks about it and I like disappear
>
> PAUL: *Really, why, I mean, oh like groups of friends or something?*

MATT: Yeah

PAUL: *So they bring it up and you just—*

MATT: They just bring it up and we all just like scatter away from him

PAUL: *Oh. Who's we?*

MATT: My friends

PAUL: *So, what, if a guy brings it up, or if a girl brings it up?*

MATT: Really doesn't matter, we still like scatter, heh heh

PAUL: *No matter who—as long as it's brought up everybody takes off*

MATT: Yeah, pretty much

PAUL: *Why—Why do you think that is?*

MATT: They just don't want to hear about

PAUL: *Yeah, because it's something they don't want to know about, or they just*

MATT: Some of us think it's disgusting, and some of us just don't want to hear about it

PAUL: *Okay*

MATT: I just don't want to hear about it!

PAUL: *You don't want to hear about it. Just don't care to or?*

MATT: I just don't care to

PAUL: *Yeah*

MATT: Now, if I'm stuck in a car with her, yeah, maybe I have to listen to it. I turn the stereo up, she turns it back down, so there's no point.

Matt is uncomfortable with the topic because of his lack of knowledge and understanding. He has little to offer the conversation, no shared experiences or knowledge, and thus does not want to participate in the talk. He also wants to preserve his masculinity by avoiding and separating himself from the feminine. This is similar to how boys and men behave in other areas of life as they define masculinity as anything that is not feminine.[3]

BLAMING MENSTRUATION

Since they do not menstruate, boys' experiences with and understandings of menstruation are primarily based on their social interactions with girls and women (in addition to health class and what they view in the media). From these interactions, some boys talk about learning that menstruation can be painful for girls. Also, as shown in the following group interview, many boys learn that girls can get emotional, sensitive, and angry:

PAUL: *What's the first word or phrase you think of when I say menstruation?*

JIM (18): Period, heh heh.

DEREK (19): Yeh.

DAVE (15): Girls getting pissy.

PAUL: *What did you say?*

DAVE: Girls getting pissy.

JIM: PMS.

DAVE: They're always pissed about something no matter what you do. You can be as nice as you want to them and they'll [be] pissed at you.

JIM: Uh. That pretty much I think sums it up.

Through agreement statements, the boys affirm their views on menstruation and define girls' menstruation as frustrating for boys because of girls' behavior. Jim ends the discussion by saying that Dave's comment "sums it up." In saying this, Jim indicates that he does not want to engage further in this particular talk sequence. The boys' group discussions about menstruation are much shorter and less rich than the girls' talk, possibly because they have more limited knowledge and experience with menstruation.

In response to the question, "why do girls menstruate?" Matt answered, "Just to be real bitches I guess, heh heh." Curt said he can tell when girls and women are menstruating because, "sometimes they get, you know, they're real touchy, you know, they're just, they like to argue sometimes if you, if you, you know, make them mad or something, they'll really go off on you and I've noticed that about my mom a lot." The female in the interaction may or may not in fact be menstruating, but the boys define irritability and emotionality as period-induced. When asked how he would explain menstruation to a young boy, Brian said that "it's when girls get really mean and they bleed everywhere." Not only does he refer to the physical process of menstruation, the bleeding, but also to how girls handle social interactions during menstruation. Dave takes a similar approach and would tell a young boy, "It's a time when they get bitchy, you better deal with it." He said that understanding girls' moods is all young boys "really need to know."

Jim agreed but thinks that boys also need to learn about the symptoms of menstruation and what girls "go through." Later in Dave's individual interview, he said that when his friends have their periods, he feels the "best policy" is to stay out of their way. Curt said that when women around him are menstruating, "I uh try to be nice and try to leave them alone as much as possible." Although the boys in these examples respond to direct interviewer questions, many boys mention girls' symptoms in other places in their individual and group interviews as well, which shows the salience of this negative definition in boys' lives. These boys are from all the different groups and represent a wide range of ages.

Brian, age 14, recalled in his individual interview that when he was younger, his older male friends warned him about PMS and said to "stay away" from girls who have PMS. He was unaware of what PMS or menstruation was, but learned that "it is some bad thing that makes the girls really mean." Brian was exposed to a negative orientation to menstruation from his male peers before he acquired more detailed knowledge about menstruation. Dave first learned about menstruation in health class, but then in middle school he reported that he started "hearing girls bitch about it." Boys learn negative imagery of menstruation from both other boys and girls. This indicates that boys do not simply define menstruation as negative on their own, but that the girls' "bitching" promotes this negative view. Later in his individual interview, Dave said that he understands that girls get bitchy because of their cramping and other physical menstrual symptoms.

Even though many boys take their cues about menstruation from girls, it frustrates the girls that boys blame girls' menstrual status for their "bitchy" social behavior. In their group interview, Lacey and Kassie agreed that many boys are uncomfortable with menstruation and that these boys blame girls' mood swings and certain social behaviors on their periods. Lacey said that when girls act a certain way, boys react with "God you're stupid, you're on your period." Kassie added that boys also say, "You on the rag? You're kind of bitchy today."

The girls are not given permission to be "bitchy" in their "normal" everyday interactions; rather, the boys blame their periods for any nonfeminine behaviors. This can be disempowering for girls because the boys essentialize, or reduce, them to their bodies. Girls' feelings are attributed to their bodies and hormones, rather than to their own unique experiences. Girls are not simply controlled by their bodies; they have their own agency in interactions. It bothers Rebecca that boys attribute any mood change to menstruation. In her individual interview, Rebecca said, "I don't understand why girls have to [menstruate] and guys don't." She explained, "Because I mean, guys are like, they're like I hate how they're just like, yeah, are you going to be in a bad mood now, daddadadada, or you're in a bad mood, PMS dadadadada. And I'm like, actually no, maybe I'm in a bad mood 'cause you're bugging me about it." Rebecca is annoyed that the boys around her do not understand menstruation and only "bug" her about it rather than understand and support her, as girls do.

Kathleen O'Grady and Paula Wansbrough (1997) write:

Both names—"on the rag" and "the curse"—are sometimes used as put-downs when a woman is moody, angry or assertive by people who have the confused idea that menstruation makes women go crazy. These people think

women should always be sweet, quiet and meek. When a woman doesn't act
the way they think she should, they believe something is wrong with her
and place the blame on the very thing that makes her most womanly—the
fact that she can bleed and have babies. (pp. 25–26)

When women speak or act in ways that others find threatening, the others
may not only blame PMS or menstruation for women's actions but may also
dismiss women's views as the result of symptoms, not as legitimate statements.[4] Since menstruation cannot be seen by outward appearance, this
blaming and dismissing of women's views can happen whether women are
menstruating or not.

In our interviews, many boys seemed to respond to girls based on the idea
that women should be a certain way ("sweet, quiet and meek") and when
they are not, these boys blame menstruation and PMS. Girls are not encouraged to display other types of behaviors; rather, they are supposed to be pleas-
ant and "feminine" in their social interactions. Later in this same group interview, the girls collaboratively said that if boys could menstruate, they would
lose the power to blame girls' emotional responses on their periods. Linda said
that boys would stop "blaming everything" on menstruation if a girl is "whiny
or moody," or, as Kassie added, "upset." This blaming also supports the boys'
and girls' medicalized definition of menstruation. Girls' behavior is attributed
to a physiological condition of illness and thus girls can be seen as exempt
from responsibility for their behavior.[5] Several boys see menstruation as a
chronic medical problem, an illness that affects girls once a month emotionally, psychologically, and physically.

However, some girls agreed with the boys' assessment of girls' moods and
reactions during their periods. There is a tension between those girls who do
not want their menstrual status to define them and other girls who think that
it should be recognized as a potentially problematic condition. Kasey would
tell a young boy that during menstruation, "this is the week that you leave the
girl alone, don't say anything to her, she is having personal problems." Sylvia
would tell a young boy to be particularly careful around young menstruating
girls because "girls often times don't feel very secure about it." Greta also
would give young boys "a little bit of a warning" on how to interact with menstruating girls. She would say, "You respect a girl when they tell you that
they're having a problem, any problems at all, you better be respectful and just,
it's really none of your business." She added that maybe "boys should just steer
clear" of menstruating girls to avoid any confrontations. Rebecca is concerned
that boys will be mean to girls during their periods and would tell a boy, "don't
ever tease a woman about it, don't make rude comments about it, 'cause it's
not that big of a deal." In yet another individual interview, Nancy would tell
a boy how to interact with menstruants, "it's not your fault if she bites your
head off, although you just want to stay away from her or be really nice."

It is particularly interesting that Jane discusses the effects of menstruation on boys when she responded to the question, "what is the point of menstruation?" in her individual interview. She said that menstruation is "something to make guys miserable . . . 'cause they have to put up with the whole PMS and all that." Jane sees menstruation in terms of its social effects on boys, not just the effect on her own body. Interestingly, Jane said she knows when girls around her are menstruating because "you like look at them wrong, and they fly off their handle or something." She attributes their responses to menstruation and hormones, similar to how the boys place blame on menstruation. In a sense, these girls buy into the idea that there are certain appropriate emotions and social behaviors for women to have, and that being irritable, moody, and upset are not included in "feminine behavior." At the same time, this can be an empowering line of talk for girls, as menstruation provides them with a way of directly affecting and influencing boys.

The boys' talk promotes exaggerated views of menstruation. As in the examples above, many boys talked about PMS and other menstrual symptoms in exaggerated terms, stressing how "bitchy" girls get and blaming menstruation for any moodiness or unfeminine behavior displayed by girls. This exaggeration is understandable because boys do not experience menstruation themselves. Rather, they listen in on girls' stories and learn through social interaction how menstruation can affect girls.

This fear of emotional upset stems from our cultural views on menstruation. In a 1984 *Mademoiselle* article, Aimee Lee Ball wrote that menstruation "can reduce us to tears, make us fat, make us sweat, make us mean and it can turn a perfectly reasonable 120-pound person into a crazed one-woman potato-chip destroyer" (p. 212). Ball believes that during menstruation, girls and women undergo a sort of altered emotional state filled with tension, unreasonableness, and irritation. Historically, early and mid-twentieth-century advice books passed along this idea of the overly emotional menstruant. For example, Lawton and Archer (1951), both medical doctors, told their readers that during menstruation girls may experience irritability and depression. Although positive mood changes associated with menstruation have been reported, they are not focused on in the everyday dominant culture or in social and medical research.[6]

"GROSSING THEM OUT"

Many boys think menstruation is "gross" and some boys engage in gross joking. This contrasts with many girls who see menstruation as "not a big deal" and do not dwell on any grossness they might feel. The girls can recognize boys' menstrual talk compared to girls' because of its gross and nasty nature. For example, Jennifer said that when boys talk about menstruation, it is when they are "making gross jokes." Katie told a particularly nasty joke she heard at summer camp from a guy. In another group interview, Briana said that boys think menstruation is gross so they have gross jokes, while girls are more interested in telling menstrual stories. Sylvia recognized a joke as having been told by a male because it is so gross. Boys have only their limited information and experience with menstruation to draw from. Because boys do not experience menstruation on an everyday level, their incomplete information can be exaggerated through jokes and talk.

Most of the girls interviewed did not describe menstruation in either jokes or stories as "gross" or "dirty" or say that it makes them feel "unclean." For example, in one of the girls' group interviews, they talked about how they do not like society's secretive and dirty attitudes towards menstruation:

> KASSIE (16): I wish we weren't so hush-hush about it.
>
> LESLIE (16): Or about—or like it's dirty.
>
> KASSIE: Yeah, like it's some dirty thing. Like, what's that book? What is it? 'Carrie?' 'Carrie.'

Kassie refers to the Stephen King short story and film *Carrie*, which describes Carrie's menarche and how Carrie's mother defines it as dirty, gross, sexual, and, as Linda later offers, "against their religion." Many girls do not see menstruation as dirty or unclean and wish society felt differently about menstruation.

This is in contrast to other research that has found that girls and women find menstruation to be dirty and smelly and that this discourse is transmitted in adolescent culture through the social interaction girls have with each other, parents, siblings, advertising, and boys.[7] According to Mary Douglas (1966), menstrual blood is defined as dirty because it is matter not in its proper place. Blood belongs inside our bodies or on Band-Aids covering scrapes and cuts. This, I contend, is a masculinist interpretation, because menstrual blood in women's vaginas is indeed matter *in* its proper place. However, the girls interviewed recognize that boys think of menstruation as "gross," but the girls see it as something normal and as a part of their bodies that they are used to, like urinating or defecating. This could be because the girls interviewed have experienced menstruation for at least one or two years. Younger girls, at or near menarche, and boys who do not have menstrual experiences may be much more likely to think of menstrual blood as "dirty." They are not used to the experience and management of menstruation.

MENSTRUATION AS A SEXUAL ISSUE

Unlike for girls, for whom menstruation is a hygienic, management, and womanhood-sisterhood issue, in their narratives, some of the boys categorize menstruation as a sexual issue. Don said that when he first learned about menstruation, he looked up "the sex stuff" in encyclopedias in the library. Don explained that "the reason [girls] menstruate is because a boy hasn't had sex with them." When he thinks about how to explain menstruation to a young boy, he couches it in terms of explaining sex and reproduction. Menstruation for him is the lack of pregnancy. Don might be thinking of stories (in the media or among people he knows) where a girl has had sex and is either anxiously awaiting her period or hoping for pregnancy. Later in his interview he was even more explicit and said that he does not want to think about his mother or sister menstruating because menstruation is "something sexual that your sister is dealing with." He avoids it because "like if you're a girl, you don't want to talk about your brother's erection." When Don talked about joking about menstruation, he again equated menstruation with erections and said that it is just like when boys joke together about "when you wake up in the morning and you've really got, a big deal erection for no apparent reason."

Dave agrees with Don in that he also sees menstruation as an issue his mother deals with that he does not want to know about. As he said, thinking about his mother menstruating is "the same that—thinking about, like, you know, your parents are doing it. You just don't wanna know about it." When asked how he would explain menstruation to a young girl, Jack said that if he did explain it, her "parents probably would be—get pretty mad." He sees such a discussion as inappropriate coming from a guy because it is a sexual topic.

For boys, the vagina indicates sexual access. Some even think about girls in general in terms of access to sexual intercourse. It makes sense that boys would think about menstruation as related to sexual intercourse because they not only "officially" learn about it in the medicalized context of health class during the sexual education section, but most importantly, menstruation deals with girls' sexual and reproductive organs. This might be a way of regaining the interactional power because sexual issues are a place where boys tend to have the power.

Many of the girls and boys talk about menstruation in terms of reproduction, but do not directly relate it to sexual intercourse and sexuality. But, as Karin Martin (1996) learned in her interviews with teens, puberty in general is intimately connected to sexuality. Teachers connect puberty to sexual intercourse in health classes, and it is at puberty that parents begin to talk with their children about sexual issues. Menarche and menstruation are markers indicating that girls are sexually mature. This sexualization implies, in the dominant U.S. culture, heterosexualization. Janet Lee and Jennifer Sasser-Coen (1996a) argue that heterosexualization means that women are sexual objects for men's pleasure.[8] This heterosexualization inserts girls and women into the gendered (and unequal) social order. In our interviews, boys tied menstruation to sexual issues much more than girls did. For boys, the vagina indicates sexual access. For example, as we saw earlier, some of the boys' menstrual terminology relates more to sex than to the experience of menstruation, which the girls focus on (e.g., "take the dirt road" compared to "I'm flooded"). By couching menstruation in the sexual, boys' lack of knowledge is emotionally charged because dominant norms of masculinity, especially for adolescents, hold that boys should know more about sex than girls should. Interestingly, neither the boys nor the girls in these interviews discussed other aspects of puberty, such as breast development or public hair, in relation to menstruation. They did not even say things like, "I heard that you couldn't get pregnant while having your period."

The girls do not sexualize menstruation to the extent that the boys do. In my interviews, Klara (age 16) is the only girl who directly discussed menstruation in terms of a connection to sexual intercourse and reproduction. When she thinks about how she would explain menstruation to a young girl, she would first start with sex and "when babies are made." Then, she would describe how the extra tissue that is built up is shed "when your body realizes that there isn't going to be a baby." When I asked Klara when she first learned about menstruation, she responded with "I learned about sex when I was really young." She does not respond with a discussion of menstruation, but continues her narrative by describing learning about the broader topic of sex.

One of the rare times girls mentioned sex in relation to menstruation was when I asked about menstrual jokes. In fact, this happened in Klara's group interview. In general, both sexual-related talk and joking are boys' ways of talking about menstruation, and girls recognize this talk as boy-generated. However, in Klara's group interview, the girls told two jokes that emphasized how having sex while menstruating would be gross. In the first, Nancy told a joke about three nuns (nuns are required to be celibate) who go to a morgue because "they want to know what it's like to have sex before they die." The nuns "figure if they have sex with a dead guy, it's not quite as bad as if it was a real guy." The guy wakes up because of the "blood transfusions." Her friend, Klara, and I thought the joke was "really bad!" Klara then responded with another sexual joke about menstruation where a prostitute who has her period has sex with a customer. Surprisingly, Klara is pretty sure that it was a girl who told her this joke. Given the focus on sex and how menstruation is defined as gross, it was surprising that girls shared these two jokes. Most of the girls interviewed did not see menstruation as gross and did not define menstruation as sexual to the extent that boys did.

None of the other girls couched their descriptions of menstruation in terms of sex as Klara and the boys above did. This could be because, for girls, menstruation is an everyday occurrence that has nothing to do with the sex act, an act that is not "everyday" in these particular teen girls' lives. Similarly, in the early- and mid-twentieth-century advice literature written for girls, sexuality is rarely mentioned. In my analysis, I found only one text that mentioned sexuality directly with menstruation. Grace Elliot (1930) states at the beginning of her discussion that menstruation and "sex desire" are intricately related. However, she does not further develop this idea.

BOYS' JOKES

It is important to explore the language the teens use in their talk because people assign meaning to their worlds through language. Language use can also help us understand power relations. In her group interview, Jennifer said that when guys talk about menstruation, they joke about how gross and nasty it is:

LAURA: *So what do you think about when people talk about menstruation?*

JENNIFER (14): Well, I mean, if guys are talking about it, they're normally joking around and making gross jokes, you know. But, heh heh.

LAURA: *Like what?*

JENNIFER: Anything, like, if someone says something that they think is a touchy subject, they'll turn it into a nasty joke.

For Jennifer, boys are immature about any sensitive or "touchy" issue. Rather than talking about it, the boys have to be "nasty" about it. Jennifer positions herself above this juvenile behavior.

Later in this same group interview, Katie told the group about a joke a boy told her at summer camp. This illustrates the types of jokes boys tell about menstruation.

LAURA: *Have you heard any jokes about menstruation? Like you mentioned how the guys tell jokes. Do you guys know any jokes? Heh heh. You know one! Okay, let's hear it!*

KATIE (14): Heh heh. Okay, it's really gross, and it's really, really gross. Heh heh. Okay.

LAURA: *But we're already laughing, so it's gotta be funny*

KATIE: No, heh heh. It's so gross that is goes beyond being funny, OK, I heard it at summer camp from a guy

LAURA: *From a guy?*

KATIE: Yes. OK. So there's this girl and this guy calls her up and he's like, say—so 'baby you wanna have sex tonight?' and she's like, 'I'm on my period.' But he's like, 'Okay, whatever, I'm coming over anyway.' And she's like, 'whatever if you want to.' So they're like, having sex or whatever and somebody comes to the door. So he gets up and answers the door and he has like, blood on his finger and his friend's like, 'so what are you doing?' and the guy's like, oh, eating pizza and the guys li—and the guy's like well what's on your finger and he's like, 'spaghetti sauce' and he licks his finger'

JENNIFER (14): Heh heh. Oh gosh. Heh heh

KATIE: I told you it was gross.

This particular joke references the old menstrual taboo on intercourse during menstruation, which in contemporary culture is a common practice, but not regulated by taboos. As Janice Delaney, Mary Jane Lupton, and Emily Toth (1988) find, the main reason for rules against intercourse during menstruation (going back at least to Leviticus 15:19 in the Bible) is fear of the blood itself. For the male, this blood signifies pain, death, injury, battle, and castration. Officially, however, the reasons given for the intercourse taboo range from keeping holy to keeping hygienic, as men, of course, should not be afraid of women. Just as with other menstrual taboos and practices, women, both in antiquity and today, can turn this into a source of power. If a woman does not want to have sex, she can have a "legitimate" reason not to by saying she is menstruating. Today, Delaney, Lupton, and Toth find, abstaining from sex during menstruation is found among people from all classes and all cultures. However, it is primarily a matter of taste, not taboo.

Katie and Jennifer agreed that boys tell jokes about menstruation, not girls. Jennifer said that girls do not tell jokes; instead, they tell stories because "they know the pain, and they're like, 'it's not something to joke about! It's for the rest of my life!'" Understanding boys' misunderstandings about menstruation, Jennifer said the reason boys tell jokes is because "they're uncomfortable" with the topic. This highlights the complex power relationships involved in adolescent menstrual discourse. Generally, jokes are told by those in power, with the target someone with less social power (such as women, racial and ethnic minorities, or sexual minorities). However, the menstruation joking here is more complex. Boys *joke* about menstruation because of their lack of knowledge and experience, not only because they are being sexist or trying to exert power over girls. Derek explained, "because everybody's, like, kinda weirded out a little bit so they just make a lot of jokes." Girls tell *stories* about menstruation based in their extensive experience with menstruation. This pattern might hold true for sexual jokes as well. Those with less sexual experience might joke while those with more experience might tell stories.

When I asked one group of girls if they knew any jokes about menstruation, they emphasized that guys tell jokes:

LAURA: *Do you guys hear any jokes about menstruation? Like jokes?*

BRIANA (16): From a guy's point of view yes.

LAURA: *What have you heard? Like give me a good joke.*

MARCIA (19): Well, I heard a blond joke that has something to do with it.

LAURA: *Let's hear it.*

MARCIA: How do you know when a blond's having a bad day? Her tampon's behind her ear and she can't find her pencil.

ERIN (18): Heh heh. That's gross.

This same joke was told in two separate group interviews, illustrating its prevalence. In another group interview, one of the girls shared a joke that "had to be from a boy, because it was really gross." After hearing the joke, her friend Andrea agreed saying, "A girl wouldn't, like, wouldn't say that."

The jokes told by the boys to the girls focus on the "gross" and the "nasty" about menstruation and menstrual blood. Sylvia and Andrea said in their group interview, "boys think it's gross" but "girls don't think it's that gross, because they deal with it all the time." Sylvia told a joke in the group interview and, similar to the girls in the group above, said that she thinks the joke "had to be from a boy, because it was really gross." Sylvia identified the joke as male-driven specifically because it was "gross."

Interestingly, the boys Paul interviewed did not share many jokes or stories about menstruation in their group discussions or in their individual interviews. This may be because the boys were uncomfortable sharing jokes in front of Paul, an adult, or because there are norms against telling menstrual jokes in their peer culture. They might not know enough about menstruation to feel comfortable joking about it. Paul asked the boys directly if they wanted to share any stories or jokes about menstruation. In many of the girls' groups, this question solicited several storytelling sessions, both collaborative and individual. However, the boys gave short responses and did not engage in the same type of extended collective talk. The following is from one of the boys' group interviews:

PAUL: *Do you have any stories about menstruation? Things that happened at school? At sporting events?*

JIM (18): No.

PAUL: *Umm, anything you heard in the halls?*

DAVE (15): Emily Ross fell over once. She doubled up and then like dove over.

PAUL: *Dove over?*

DAVE: She's like 'Oh I fell over by accident.'

PAUL: *Why?*

DAVE: I don't know. [She] called it cramps. She bent over and fell over.

PAUL: *Gotcha ya. So no stories you've heard about at all?*

JIM: No.

PAUL: *No legends of sort.*

DEREK (19): Someone ran track last year, some girl, she like, she's like running the two mile. She's run like a couple laps and then she got out and coach like ran over and she's 'I'm sorry.' It wasn't like she was sore or anything, she just, she was on her period.

JIM: There's no like big story.

DEREK: Yeh, there are just little things.

PAUL: *No uh [our high school] legends about . . .*

JIM: No, I remember walking in Baxter Hall and it was a practical joke if you want something like that. Someone had a tampon on the wall with red ink on it.

PAUL: *Red Ink? Ugh, nice touch.*

JIM: Yeh, I thought so. I was really, not something I'd want to see, but that's the only thing I can think of.

Paul probed frequently, attempting to solicit responses from the boys in this group. Rather than the boys themselves showing interest and asking for clarifications in each others' stories, Paul was forced into this role to keep the conversation going. Many girls reported being teased about menstruation, but the boys, in their all-male group interviews, did not discuss this type of teasing or provide evidence that they joke about menstruation.

The boys might avoid menstrual talk because they perceive the girls as having the power in these cross-gender interactions. Rather than being in a low-power situation, the boys avoid menstruation. Later in this same group interview, Paul asked if there are "period" jokes that circulate among the boys. The boys said no. Jim said, "No, that's just a subject you don't really touch." Matt added, "or care about." However, the boys then said that they do not tell such jokes because they are afraid of girls' angry responses. Derek said, "There's too many girls at [our high school] that would probably get a hold of you and hurt you, heh heh." Matt added that girls would, "drag you out behind the weeds and beat you to death, throw you in the trash can." These boys would not only have less power, but they anticipate strong responses from girls should they tease the girls about menstruation.

In another boys' group interview, the boys admitted that they have heard "plenty" of jokes about menstruation. This contradicts the first group's statements that they do not share jokes. However, the boys in this second group still did not use the group interview as a joke-telling session, even when Paul initiated with a joke of his own. Larry offered one joke that he heard from his friend, "I don't trust anything that bleeds for three or four days and does not die." He admitted that he thought it was a funny joke and Walter, the other boy in the group interview, also thought it was funny. Larry said there are "plenty of jokes out there" but he does not remember them. However, he still agreed that guys generally tell the jokes, not girls. The boys, he reported, share jokes in male groups. Don, in his individual interview, said that when menstruation comes up and boys are present, they will "laugh and joke about it for a second and then move on, it's not anything that's ever really built upon." This may be why Paul's question did not initiate a joke-telling session, because boys see menstrual jokes as something to comment on briefly, not as a base for an extended discussion.

Some boys acknowledged telling gross jokes about menstruation and several girls reported hearing jokes from boys. Also, even though some girls reported being teased and embarrassed by the boys, the boys do not admit to this in their interviews. This may be because these are teasing events that the boys do not focus on or remember as menstrual-based. Rather, the teasing could just be a part of their cross-gender interactions because they try to embarrass girls about a number of things. Or, this could be because in our interview questions, we asked the boys about menstrual jokes, not about teasing girls in other ways. The girls were more forthcoming with elaborate menstrual talk while the boys were quieter and did not develop long sequences of talk about menstruation. The boys may not have volunteered the information if it was not asked about directly.

Girls tell stories about menstruation using a different language than they report the boys using because, for girls, menstruation is matter-of-fact because "they deal with it all the time." Erica said that if she had to explain menstruation to a girl who knew nothing about it, she would say, "it's a gross thing unless you know like why it's happening." She understands menstruation and deals with it in her everyday life so she does not think it is "gross." Other research also finds that boys' menstrual humor is derogatory and meant to tease and embarrass girls, while girls' humor is based in sharing their bodily functions and the inconveniences they experience.[9] The boys' humor asserts their power over the girls, while the girls' humor focuses on support and collective experience.

WHO HAS THE POWER?

Even though girls have more knowledge and experience with menstruation, boys can have more social power than girls when menstruation is defined as secretive and shameful in cross-gender interactions. This makes girls a ripe target for teasing and embarrassment. For example, Barrie Thorne (1994) finds that children use differences between their bodies as ways to tease the other sex and highlight the differences between the sexes. She contends that power differences between fourth- and fifth-grade boys and girls are communicated and learned through social interaction, which focuses on the body. She talks about "gender play," which is where children use the frame of "play" as a cover for serious, gender-based messages that their play conveys about sexuality and aggression. Examples of gender play include bra-snapping and "cooties" rituals. In cross-gender interactions, girls are more "polluting" than boys are. Girls give cooties more often to boys than boys give to girls. Also, the name "cooties" was frequently changed to "girl stain" or "girl touch." The most unpopular girls were sometimes called "cootie queens" or "cootie girls" and no such similar terms were used for unpopular boys. This shows that boys are more powerful; they are masculine and not stained by femininity.

Boys define themselves and their masculinity in opposition to femininity. For example, male athletes and coaches often use terms such as "girl" and "pussy" to insult those players who lack toughness.[10] It is important for boys to be tough and aggressive and at the same time, to belittle and separate themselves from anything that is weaker or feminine.[11] The girls' treatment as a source of contamination highlights the social power differences between superior boys and inferior girls. Boys and girls learn this difference through embodiment and body-based social interaction.

Menstruation is not simply a biological phenomenon; rather, it is a cultural event that is tied to larger questions of women's place in society. Gendered power relations are evident in and based on the body, specifically through menstruation.[12] For example, some theorists argue that our social rules about menstruation, such as keeping it a secret and hiding pads and tampons and other menstrual "evidence," are derived not from women's culture but from social etiquette controlled by men. This etiquette does not celebrate menstruation but holds that women should behave as if their monthly cycles are not occurring. Menstrual blood is seen as different from nongendered bodily fluid, such as snot, pus, or blood from a wound.[13] This difference stems from gender inequality. It is also seen as different from other biological female differences. For example, breasts, another characteristic that girls have that boys do not, are seen by the dominant culture as sexual objects for boys' visual and tactile pleasure, not as sources of food for babies. Menstruation, as shown by boys' gross joking, contaminates and pollutes sex; it does not enhance it and thus should be concealed and hidden.

EMBARRASSING AND TEASING GIRLS

Schools, in particular, are a place for cross-gender interactions between boys and girls about menstruation. Leslie, a cute, small pixielike girl, was embarrassed to leave her classroom to go to the bathroom because of the boys. She said, "When you leave class, like, in the middle of class to go to the bathroom to change your pad or tampon, and there happen to be immature guys in class and—like, 'Why are you leaving with your backpack on?' [in nasal voice]."

Leslie wants to turn the tables on the boy and respond with "Why do you have to be such an immature jerk?" In addition to the teasing, this example hints at the power complexity in menstrual interactions. Leslie sees this boy as immature for his sexist and ignorant remark and thus wants to place herself in a position of experience and increased power. But, at the same time, she wants to keep her menstrual identity private.

In my interview with Lacey, a blond 16-year-old whose mother leads her community group, Lacey said she wishes that guys could menstruate so they would understand the experience and then not pick on her. "I wish guys could go through it for a day . . . bleed through the day, get cramps for the day, be moody for the day, everything . . . and be like, 'okay, now you want to pick on me?'" This issue is particularly salient for Lacey because she added this comment at the end of the interview, not in response to any specific question I asked.

In one of the group interviews, the girls shared stories about how boys will rifle through the girls' school backpacks and embarrass girls about the menstrual products they find:

LESLIE (16): The funny thing is, they'll [boys] be going through your backpack or something, they'll be like, 'What's this? Oh my god!'

KASSIE (16): Yeah.

GRETA (15): Don't go there, especially when it's in a separate little part. Oh, [boys] persists to open [the little bags] up.

KASSIE: It's like there's a bigger world in there, and you're like, 'No, just pads and tampons.'

KORRINE (15): Elizabeth keeps hers in her purse.

LESLIE: Or there's, like, some little flowered little Clinique bag, and they know it's not your make-up bag. And they're like, 'So, is your make-up in here?' I was like, 'No.'

LACEY (16): 'No.'

LESLIE: It's like, 'Is there where you keep your pencils?' I have this small little pocket, inside at the bottom of my bag, you know. I'd stick in the front part, but, you know—

The boys are in a more powerful position as they violate the girls' personal space by rifling through the girls' backpacks. The boys know they might find menstrual supplies and can thus tease girls about them. Yet, Kassie works to diminish this power by saying menstruation is not a big deal. For Kassie, it is "just pads and tampons." Kassie masterfully regains control of the situation as the boys, then, lose the power to tease her. As we will explore in the next section, many girls know the boys are unsure about menstruation and girls can use this to their advantage.

In sum, in their menstrual talk, the boys in our interviews defined menstruation primarily in terms of how it affects their social interactions with girls. Not only do boys hear girls complain about menstruation and their symptoms, many boys attribute certain behaviors by girls to menstruation. When girls are irritable or "bitchy," these boys see this behavior as menstrually induced and blame menstruation, rather than the girl, for the behavior. Even when girls are not menstruating, their "nonfeminine" behavior is blamed on menstruation. Many boys exaggerate the symptoms and experience of menstruation in their talk and think it is gross. Because they do not experience menstruation themselves, they hear about it from others and develop their perceptions in their group talk. Finally, some boys relate menstruation to sexual intercourse. Since boys' access to heterosexual sex is "down there," it makes sense that they would think of menstruation, which also deals with girls' genitalia, as sexual. For many boys, the vagina is seen as only a sexual organ, not one that functions in other capacities.

GIRLS' ADVANTAGES

These power relations between girls and boys concerning menstruation are complex. Rather than the boys having the sole power in these interactions through gross and negative menstrual jokes, the girls also have power. At the same time that the boys use negative cultural imagines to gain power, the girls have exclusive access to menstrual experience. Thus, the girls can have power in mixed-gender interactions. The girls know the boys are unsure and the girls use this to their advantage.

For example, in one group interview, the girls talked about how their male teachers are "so scared of" menstruation. The girls find this funny as they derive power from their menstrual status in the face of a teacher, who is usually more powerful because he is adult, a teacher, and a male.

> LACEY (16): 'Yeah.' If I ever get to class, like, you know, late, and my teacher's, like, 'Where were you?' He doesn't li—he hates my guts, mostly—
>
> LINDA (16): Who?
>
> LACEY: Mr. Pease. I was like, 'I was at the nurse.' He was, like, 'Where's your purs—your pass?' I was like, 'I had to get something.' 'Oh, okay.'
>
> LESLIE (16): They're scared of it. It's so funny.
>
> KASSIE (16): Oh, I know. It's like your defense toward any male teacher.
>
> LESLIE: If they're like, 'Why did you skip class?' 'I lost the string.' [group laughs]
>
> KASSIE (16): Yeah. No, seriously, that's what Mr. Brinstein, I came in, like, 20 minutes late one day, and he was like, 'Where have you been?'

And he hated me, and I was just, like, 'I had a female problem.' He said, 'Okay.' [group laughs]

LESLIE: But one day, he was like, I was like, 'Can I go to the bathroom?' He was like, 'Why do you have to go to the bathroom?' I was like, 'Because I have to go to the bathroom.' He was like, 'Oh my gosh, okay,' and he, like, throws the pass at me, and he's like, 'Go, go.' [insistently]

KASSIE: When they know you're on your period, they're, like, afraid to make eye contact with you, like they're going to catch it or something.

KORRINE (15): It's contagious.

GRETA (15): Contagious PMS.

LACEY: This girl that sits behind me in journalism, she said that one of her teachers wouldn't let her go. She was like, 'If you don't let me go, I'll bleed all over your classroom.' [group laughs]

This example shows not only how male teachers respond negatively to menstruating girls, but how the girls use this negative response to gain interactional power. This points to the complexity of power in menstrual discourse and the power girls can develop because of menstruation. This also shows the fluidity and flexibility of power; as the teacher does not hold ultimate power, the girls can generate their own sources of privilege. They are comfortable expressing a public menstrual identity and using it to their advantage.

In another group interview, the girls acknowledged the power they have and noted that guys are very "uncomfortable" with the topic of menstruation. In another group interview, the girls talked about teasing their dads and brothers with discussions about menstruation because of their obvious discomfort. Briana said that her dad "just doesn't like to hear" about menstruation and will go to the store for pads, but that is it. Erin said that, "We always tease dad. We're like 'Dad don't you hate it for us when we get that string just hanging out?' and he's like 'Don't. Just stop.' We just go on further about that. He's like 'I don't want to hear about this.' And mom will get in on it too. Mom will start doing it to dad, too." In an individual interview, Lacey also talked about how she enjoys teasing her guy friends about menstruation because they are uncomfortable with the topic. This active use of this power, however, is reserved for girls who are comfortable talking about menstruation in mixed-gender spaces. In our interviews, either these girls tend to be older and thus more experienced with menstruation or they are in situations where the girls outnumber the boys.

Boys and men do not know much about menstruation, do not experience menstruation, and many do not want to admit that they do not know much about menstruation. Thus, knowledge about menstruation is defined as not valuable in dominant culture. As discussed earlier, the female experience, particularly the reproductive experience, is not valued in our society's power structure. In one of the group interviews, the girls talked about how boys do not want to hear about menstruation and the boys try to silence the girls' discourse. But, the girls resist this:

LAURA: *What do guys say about it? Do they say anything?*

ERICA (15): They don't want to hear anything about it.

KASSIE (16): No.

LACEY (16): No.

ERICA: The other day, I was telling all my friends, they were like, 'Shut up. I don't want to hear anything else.' And then, it's really funny to keep going, and you're like, 'Yeah, I lost a little tissue, a little blood.'

LACEY: ( ) that tampon now.

KORRINE (15): They're like, 'We never asked to hear about any of this.'

KASSIE: No, but ( ).

LESLIE (16): The funny thing is, they'll be going through your backpack or something, they'll be like, 'What's this? Oh my God!'

The girls and boys are playing a game where each "team" takes turns annoying the other team. This example nicely illustrates the complex power relations between boys and girls in menstrual discourse. It is not just the girls or the boys who have the power; rather, the power is negotiated constantly in social interaction. First, the boys attempt to assert power where they try and silence menstrual talk even as they search through girls' bags for menstrual evidence. Then, rather than succumbing to this power, the girls respond by continuing their talk, thereby asserting their own power in the interaction.

EXPRESSING POWER:
SECOND AND THIRD WAVE FEMINISM

In several of the girls' stories and narratives, themes of self-identification and self-definition arose. These girls do not let boys get away with teasing them or blaming their moods on menstruation. They actively take on the identity of menstruant, use it as a way to assert power, and to prevent others from having the power to label them.

"First wave" feminism is widely regarded as the fight for women's suffrage in the nineteenth and early-twentieth centuries, culminating in the passage (1919) and ratification (1920) of the 19th Amendment to the Constitution. The main goal of the "second wave" feminist movement, which was most active in the 1960s and 1970s, was to change the structure of patriarchy,

which favors men in both private and public sectors. Gender inequality, second wavers argue, is a fundamental aspect of our society and it must be rooted
out at the structural level. Women and men are equal and the policies of government, organizations, family, and institutions should reflect that equality.
Accomplishments of the second wave movement included broadening affir-
mative action laws to include sex (1967); the Equal Pay Act of 1963; pro-
hibiting discrimination on the basis of sex in federally funded education programs in Title IX (1972); and the Equal Rights Amendment, which was
passed by Congress in 1972 but never took effect because it was not ratified
by enough states. The second wave feminist movement continues today, even
as it shares space with the burgeoning third wave.

The third wave is the current generation of feminists comprised of
women in their teens, twenties, and thirties.[14] The goals of third wave feminism are diverse and much more individualistic. Primarily, third wavers focus
on women's diverse identities (including race, ethnicity, class, and sexuality),
both embracing and critiquing women's consumer culture, women's right to
pleasure, women's safety, and women's right to use and display their bodies in
any way they want. It is third wavers' personal experiences that bring them
to feminism and it is their personal responses, they say, that make up their
political responses. Third wavers grew up being told and believing that they
can do anything. They grew up with the idea that women and men, girls and
boys, are equal. When they experience gender discrimination, rather than
marching or protesting, as with the first or second wavers, third wavers get
angry and write zines, websites, blogs, and music. They define this as feminist
activity because it makes public their personal experiences and feelings.
Third wave feminism is also fundamentally characterized by its diversity.
Rather than large all-encompassing organizations such as the second wave's
National Organization of Women, third wavers are involved in a host of
smaller organizations that form coalitions depending on the issue at hand.
These organizations are often based on identity, such as college-age women,
or a narrow political goal, such as reproductive choice.

The body, in particular, is central to third wave analysis and many invoke
the body in their interpretations of gender, partially basing their ideas on a
strain from the second wave, radical feminism, which emphasized sexuality
and celebrated bodily difference.[15] Third wavers show off their bodies and see
their bodies as a source of power, both sexual and social, that girls and women
control for themselves. For both third wavers and embodiment theorists, the
body is not static nor is it only for function. It is a site for girls and women to
express their own unique identities, feelings, and convictions in an increasingly visual culture. Clothing, style, tattoos, piercings, and midriffs are all
forms of girls' and women's self-expression. Girls and women assert power and
control in their worlds through their bodies, in a world where few of these
opportunities exist. For example, for third wavers, in order to be fully human,

women must claim their sexuality. Third wavers attempt to reclaim women's sexual power by not allowing men to dehumanize them, objectify them, or claim language about women's bodies. They believe in women's sexual agency. For example, rather than viewing sexual images (both pornography and erotica) as men objectifying women, some third wavers argue that women use these images to control the effects they have on men.

Reclaiming language is fundamental to third wave feminism, as shown in *Bust Magazine*, an example of a radical third wave feminist publication. On browsing the Spring 2001 issue, I found swear words, such as "fuck" and "shit," on most of the pages. The focus is on sex and showing pride in women's sexuality and the body. One reader wrote in the Letters section that *Bust* is for "young women who know where their pussies" are. These are "modern women who delight in their bodies and are proud of it." Another woman wrote that *Bust* gives off a "fuck-me-shoes feminist/am I sexy vibe." "Cunt" rather than "vagina" is the term of choice. These third wavers claim the language of their bodies that was once used to denigrate them. Ingia Muscio (1998), in her book *Cunt: A Declaration of Independence*, advocates starting a "Cuntfest," which is "not your mother's 'Vagina Monologues.'" Muscio works to remove the negative power from the word "cunt" by claiming the word and realigning its meaning with something that spiritually, emotionally, physically, psychologically, and financially benefits women, not men.

Some recent marketing programs for menstrual products follow this "in your face" strategy. For example, "Vinnie's Tampon Case," created in 1995, featured a drawing of Vinnie, a working-class-looking boy with an auto mechanic's baseball hat on and the large words "Vinnie's Tampon Case, One Size Fits All" prominently displayed on the canvas package. The case was so successful that the male designer, Vinnie D'Angelo, expanded his offerings to include a CD (Vinnie's Music for Menstruators) and bubble bath (Vinnie's Cramp Relieving Bubble Bath). D'Angelo says that he wants to help women take pride in their periods. "Nothing melts my heart more than getting Hello Kitty stationery from a young girl who hasn't gotten her period yet, but says she's excited now, and thankful."[16] For third wavers, language, body, actions, and identity expression work to empower girls and women.

In the girls' and boys' narratives, they often expressed opinions and feelings based in second wave feminism. For example, some girls talked about changing structural things such as including Midol in the nurse's office, having special locker compartments to conceal supplies, or getting days off from school. Some boys also acknowledged that girls are disadvantaged in society by things such as menstrual supplies that are made by men, rather than by women. Also, some of the girls are more in line with second wave cultural feminism, which celebrates womanhood, women-only spaces, and "essentialist" women's qualities such as nurturance, care, and empathy. The girls who are proud of their abilities to reproduce and who seek out a community of girls and women with which to share these feelings and talk are expressing this type of second wave feminist sentiment.

The teens in our interviews do not neatly fall on one side of feminism or the other, but expressed second wave views and third wave views simultaneously. However, more often, the girls in our interviews expressed feelings and attitudes in line with third wave feminist thinking. They are not ashamed of their bodies, use terms like "ragging" to describe menstruation, find it funny to confront boys and men openly about menstruation, and work to define their own bodies in their own terms. They use their bodies and menstruation as a source of open power, for example, when a girl tosses a tampon to a friend across the classroom, or when a girl tries to embarrass her male teacher by asking to go to the bathroom to change her pad. They do not see menstruation as directly related to procreation and do not feel a larger connection to "womanhood." Some of these girls also do not seek out a separate cultural space in which to experience menstruation, but talk about menstruation openly with boys. With the challenge of menstrual management for girls comes a feeling of responsibility and empowerment.

POTENTIAL FOR MANIPULATION

The girls use their knowledge about their bodies as a power resource in their interactions with boys and men. Girls are also able to use menstruation to manipulate male peers and teachers because males do not have the expertise and knowledge about menstruation that females have and are thus in a disadvantaged position. For example, some boys talk about girls using menstruation and menstrual symptoms as an excuse to avoid certain activities. This is one result for the medicalization of menstruation and PMS, where menstruation is seen as a chronic medical condition with symptoms. Menstruation indeed has concrete physiological symptoms, such as pain and nausea, which the girls must manage. These boys resent this potentially manipulative power girls have.

Derek gets frustrated with girls because he sees them using menstruation as an "excuse to get pissed." He argued "some girls that doesn't know how to cope with it yet," and they say, "'I'm I'm hurtin', I'm, I can't do this, and I don't feel like doin' this, and I'm going just lay down' or you know it's like, 'you big wuss' (laughter)." Later, when asked what he thought life would be like if girls did not menstruate but could still have children, Derek wondered what then "would be their new excuse" for not wanting to do things and to get out of things. Derek does not think the girls are really experiencing pain. For Derek, girls are the ones who are complainers and whiners. This contrasts with our earlier discussion where girls expressed that boys are "babies" and would not be able to handle menstruation. Here, Derek thinks girls complain because they have, in fact, *not* learned how to cope with menstruation.

Some girls do not see menstruation as an "excuse" to get out of things, but rather as a legitimate physiological complaint. They use the biomedical construction of menstruation to receive special attention and treatment.[17] In her individual interview, Ally affirmed the boys' attitudes and related a story about a boy in school who "was mad, because he was like, 'How come girls always get out of gym class, just because they're on their period?'" This made Ally and other girls in the classroom angry because the boys do not acknowledge or understand their pain. Ally said, "we tried to describe it for the boys" and some of the boys then responded positively and then understood the girls' perspective.

Jane, a wiry cross-country runner, also does not see menstruation as simply an excuse. Her cramps legitimately impede her sports performance, as she described in her individual interview:

JANE (14): It's hard, like, if you're running, 'cause if you get cramps and stuff, you can't run that great.

LAURA: *Mhm.*

JANE: It's hard to explain to your coach why.

LAURA: *Do you have a male coach?*

JANE: Yeah.

LAURA: *What do you say to him?*

JANE: It's like, 'Well, I have cramps,' and he's like, 'Oh, you can take it easy.' 'Well, these cramps don't go away for about a week.' But our coach has, like, all girls, and a wife, and, so, he tries to understand.

On the other hand, some girls agreed with the boys and do not like it when they see girls using menstruation as an excuse. Sylvia and Andrea both said "I don't use it as an excuse." Sylvia said, "And I hate it when people, whenever girls are like, 'I can't run, because I'm on my period,' I'm like, 'That's bullcrap.'" She finished with, "I might be on mine, too. I mean, deal with it." Sylvia and Andrea see these girls as using menstruation as a source of power to avoid activity, but in an inappropriate fashion, as a way of "manipulating people." Earlier, Sylvia and Andrea discussed how boys would not be able to handle menstruation. They positioned themselves as superior to boys because they can manage it. However, girls who complain about menstruation and use it to avoid activities work against Sylvia and Andrea's interpretation of women as powerful. They resent this manipulation and the message it sends to others about girls.

At the same time, Sylvia and Andrea may not experience the pain of menstruation as other girls do. They may misperceive other girls' experiences and define them as manipulation. The potential for manipulation is certainly there, but both girls and boys who do not understand the full extent of menstrual symptoms may misperceive it. Girls have a variety of menstrual experiences and not all girls experience the same levels of pain. Dave insightfully stated this when he talked about whether or not he can tell when those around him are menstruating. His girlfriend "doesn't get bad cramps and so nothing's really that, hurting that badly. Whereas, like, when they're cramping, they're just pissed off and they snap back at you for no reason." Although he did not address manipulation in his narrative, he showed an understanding that girls' social interactions and moods are dependent upon their unique symptoms, not just on the fact that they are menstruating.

In sum, both girls and boys recognize that some girls use their symptoms to manipulate and intimidate boys and male teachers who are not going to question the girls' menstrual status. These girls assert power over males, adults, and even the school structure. Menstruation is a place where males do not have the experience or understanding so they are in a disadvantaged position. Using this knowledge does not change the macro structure of power relations between boys and girls, but in moments such as this, however small, the girls can draw on their bodies to empower themselves in their social interactions with boys. Additionally, the power shown here is language-based and collective. The girls talk about menstruation, a taboo topic, in single and mixed-gender groups. They form a community of support through their shared experiences of menstruation. In the dominant culture, menstruation is not publicly acknowledged. In a third wave manner, these girls resist this and report talking about menstruation out loud in their single and cross-gender interactions. Rather than being silenced by the boys' misunderstandings and discomfort, the girls use this topic as a source of power in gendered interactions.[18] However, other girls disagree with this manipulation. Collectively, the girls know and understand menstruation, but they disagree on how to use the power that comes with this knowledge.

ALTERNATE RESPONSES BY BOYS

Not all boys feel negatively about menstruation, try to avoid menstruation, engage in gross and nasty joking, or engage in power plays surrounding menstruation. Don, a thoughtful 18-year-old who frequently paralleled menstruation with his diabetes, said in his individual interview:

DON (18): Well, it's like, everyone, you know, stigmatizes, you know, menstruation with it's 'that time of month' uh, whole,—it—post menstrual syndrome or whatever that a women gets, you know, crabby. I've heard about, like, cramps and st—and stuff. Uh, and you take Midol for cramps I know. And, uh, and uh, but I haven't—I haven't ever detected any noticeable change in a women's, you know, uh, personality because

of men—I've always wondered how it—it—it—it's been even stigmatized the term PMS and the whole crabbiness that comes along with it,
because I haven't noticeably detected it in anyone, any girl I've, I've ever
known, you know. I don't know, I mean, maybe it's there. It had to come
from somewhere I figure.

Don is confused as to why people's reactions to menstruating girls are so
strong because he does not see the changes in girls' personalities. He does not
see the stereotypes in his own experiences with girls and women. This confusion shows not only in the text of this transcript, but also in his difficulty
in putting his words together.

Jim, age 18, is a boy of average height who for years was skinny and is
happy to now have finally reached his desired weight. He sees the differences
in girls' emotions and actions, but does not focus on the negative aspects as
other boys do. Rather, he said that during his female friends' periods, they
have "the abnormal mood swings" but, "they don't like, turn it into, like,
what most people think is like a rage or anything." For Jim, girls are more
moody but it is not in a socially detrimental way. Later, when he talked about
describing menstruation to a young boy, Jim said that he would explain menstrual symptoms. He thinks that boys and men should be aware of the symptoms and the frustrations that girls go through, such as "the cramping, uh,
breast enlarged, like, the hurt, the tenderness of the breast" and "headaches."
Jim himself is sensitive to his girlfriend's and mother's feelings during their
period and said that during their periods, he does not "roughhouse" with his
mom or "wrestle around" with his girlfriend. Jim in particular, unlike the
other boys, tries to understand the symptoms of menstruation rather than
simply dismissing any mood swing as hormonal. This could be due to age.
Both Don and Jim are 18 years old and have more experience with girls and
menstruation. They may not be as nervous or as susceptible to other boys'
locker room talk about it. Don also has the added experience of diabetes,
which heightens his understanding of embodiment, or how the body is an
important factor in everyday life and social interaction. The management of
diabetes can create an increased empathy for the chronicity of girls' menstrual experience and management.

As discussed earlier, not all boys think that menstruation is a big deal.
Four of the boys discussed how menstruation is not problematic or unusual,
and they do not understand why others think it is such a gross thing. Like the
girls who view menstruation as not a big deal, these boys resist the power that
menstruation holds over their lives. They do not engage in the power plays
surrounding menstruation. As with girls, this attitude among boys could be
due to their age and their increased experience with menstruation with sisters, mothers, or girlfriends. These teens may be more comfortable with their
matured bodies, as adults are.

Some of the boys even expressed positive views on menstruation, similar to those the girls expressed. Jack sees menstruation as something girls complain about, but he also believes that menstruation is cleansing and healthy for girls. Larry is quite unusual in his understanding of general power relations in society as well as the specifics of menstruation. He said that the point of menstruation is it gives girls a "chance to renew their body, and kind of like cleans out the old lining, gives them a change to have a rebirth sort of thing." Larry learned about menstruation from his mom, who is a public school teacher (married to his dad, a psychologist), and this is where many of his positive views come from. Yet, he couched his discussion in terms of girls having to "deal with" menstruation and the frustrations of menstruation. He said that girls "complain about stuff" and they say "'Well you don't have to go through this.'" From these discussions with girls, he is glad he does not have to menstruate. In his group interview, Larry further displayed his maturity and positive conceptions of menstruation by saying that if women had a celebration for menstruation, "I think it'd be pretty cool, you know. I guess it's kind of, like, their celebration time to be a woman, you know. I think it's kind of cool."

"MY FRIEND KRISTIN EXPLAINED . . ."

Even as many boys blame menstruation for girls' behavior, see it as gross and as sexual, or do not see it as a big deal, they are very interested in learning about menstruation. The boys in the following group interview said they try to stay away from the subject by leaving the area or trying to change the topic of conversation when it comes up. Yet, at the same time, they said that they learn about menstruation and menstrual products from their female friends. This can be valuable information, although, as Dave said, the information is often more than the boys want to know:

DAVE (15): People at school sometimes are very open.

CURT (15): A little too open.

JIM (18): Detailed.

PAUL: *More than you want to know?*

DAVE: Yeh, pretty much, heh heh.

PAUL: *Well you said, actually we were talking about, you said the ones [tampons] at school suck because your girlfriend told you?*

DAVE: Yeh, she says they're made out of cardboard.

JIM: Yeh they are. I know the nurse personally and she tells me all this stuff when I'm in the office. So she like 'oh yeh they stink.' I'm like didn't want to know that but all right.

DAVE: My friend Kristin explained how to put on, put in a tampon, heh heh. She's like this is the hole; this is the tampon; and it goes in like this.

JIM: And you pull the string. Push it through, push it in like that and it stays up there and you pull the applicator out, heh heh. Don't ask me how I know, I just know, heh heh. Trust me I just know.

Although the boys first said that the girls are "a little too open" about menstruation in their conversations in school, the boys clearly pay attention to them and learn about menstrual products from these interactions. Even though they do not admit it, the boys must have asked questions or otherwise engaged in a two-way conversation in order to get such detailed information. They then shared this rather detailed knowledge in the group interview. These boys construct this knowledge as important enough to share with one another.

The boys asked each other questions about menstruation in the group interview so each could share the information he has learned from girls and women. At the end of the interview, Paul asked the group if they had any questions about menstruation, the body, or any of the topics they talked about during the discussion. In his group, Jim asked the first question:

JIM (18): What's with the chocolate thing? That's always . . . Is it a craving?

PAUL: *That's actually, it's actually, I think it's mainly the sugar.*

JIM: It's the sugar need? So you can give Skittles and they'll be fine? Heh heh

PAUL: *Probably yeh.*

MATT (17): Here's some Skittles, I hope you're fine in a couple of hours, heh heh.

PAUL: *You never know, maybe there's just something special about chocolate.*

JIM: I don't know. It's just—

PAUL: *—I know what you mean.—*

JIM: —I've been around like my aunts and girlfriend and friends of hers and people I know saying I need some chocolate and I'm like 'No, no. Go away. I don't want to talk to you now because you're going to bring up something about something that happened.'

PAUL: *Oh, so you're assume if they're asking for chocolate.*

JIM: Well, not necessarily. I'm just saying, I can just hearing it coming before it even starts out. And some of them will be like 'Man I need some chocolate, I have that craving because it's that time.' I'm like okay here's my candy bar, leave.

MATT: Here's your candy bar, get away from me.

DEREK (19): Bill Hackey gives it away because he's talking about 'I want some chocolate.' Sitting in class. I was laughing.

JIM: What you talking about Bill. He's a big guy. He works with me. We deliver pizzas.

DAVE (15): Is it true that like mothers make fun of their like daughters when they first have their periods?

PAUL: *They (make) fun of them?*

DAVE: Yeh, 'cause I saw this play called the Vagina Monologues (heh heh).

PAUL: *The Vagina Monologues? Where was this?*

DAVE: The Union.

PAUL: *Oh, okay.*

DAVE: This big poster that says—

PAUL: *—It was here?—*

DAVE: —Yeh. They had a big poster that said 'vagina friendly is here.' But, like, 'When I was 12 my mother slapped me because I was bleeding everywhere.' heh heh.

PAUL: *Well, I guess the only safe answer to that would be that different moms react differently.*

MATT: Uh, most mothers know when their daughters are going to go on their period and if they're late, they're like 'Are you pregnant?'

PAUL: *You think they keep tabs?*

MATT: What?

PAUL: *You think they keep tabs?*

MATT: My girlfriend's mom, she's like, my girlfriend was like a couple of days late, her mom's like 'Are you pregnant?,' she's like 'No.'

The boys in this group, including Paul, collaboratively tried to increase their information about menstruation and understand why girls respond to menstruation and symptoms in the ways that they do. They all pulled together and shared what they have learned from girls.

Interestingly, Dave had even seen the play, *The Vagina Monologues*, at the local university campus. This play, by Eve Ensler, is about women's experiences with their vaginas. The play made an impression on Dave, as he remembers some of the lines and tries to understand them. The particular line he quotes (about being slapped) is confusing to him because he is a child of the 1990s, not of an earlier time when slapping was indeed common practice among some ethnic groups in the United States and elsewhere (slapping was to warn girls about the dangers of sex and pregnancy).

Later in the group interview, the boys said that they are curious about menstruation but feel that it is a "taboo" topic. Jim said, "It's like taboo. It's like Area 51. I mean, we know about it, we're curious about it, but we don't know." (Area 51 is a highly classified military base in Nevada, subject of many rumors and conspiracy theories.) Jim further added that boys "have the right to talk about it, but we can't talk about it because we don't go through it, so we don't know." The other boys in the group agreed with Jim and offered this as the main reason they say they do not ask about menstruation or tease girls about menstruation (although the girls report they are being teased in school). In another boys group interview, Larry expressed a similar sentiment, saying that menstruation "doesn't apply to me, so I'm not that interested." These boys also recognize, as the girls do above, that they have difficulties interacting with other girls and boys about menstruation because they do not experience it themselves. According to these boys, the girls have more power in interactions dealing with menstruation.

BEEF JERKY

Finally, as embarrassed and as unknowledgeable as boys might be about menstruation, some are still able to joke about menstruation in a non-negative way. The following is from a group interview with boys:

PAUL: *What if men could menstruate and woman, women couldn't? What differences might there be? And how would you feel about it?*

. . .

JIM (18): There'd be manly names for the tampax, tampons or whatever.
DAVE (15): Iron pads, heh heh.

. . .

JACK (17): It'd smell like beef jerky instead of flowers, heh heh.

Not only is this one of the more humorous statements the boys made in their discussions about menstruation, it illustrates nicely how the dominant negative and embarrassing constructions are not the only interpretation of menstruation the boys have. This example shows the collective humor that boys engage in around a sensitive topic. It shows that the media and product advertisements are one area where knowledge about menstruation is accessible to boys. Additionally, thinking back to gendered norms, this example shows how the boys define "feminine" products versus "masculine" products. This example shows how the teens themselves recognize how gendered language and experience can be. They are not "cultural dopes," but are highly aware of the larger gendered social structure.

Methodologically, this example in particular shows the usefulness of group interviews, not only for exploring issues infrequently talked about in front of field researchers, but also for the value of asking "what if" questions. By asking, for example, "what if boys could menstruate and girls could not," respondents are empowered to imagine a different type of world. The teens thus do not simply focus on what is wrong or negative about the current situation, but can imagine what they might like to do differently and how they might react to different circumstances. These types of questions drew powerful comments from the girls and boys, as shown in the data, such as the comments from some girls that boys could not "handle" menstruation.

SEVEN

Conclusion

Bodies in Interaction

―――――――――――

THE TEENS' CONCLUDING THOUGHTS

At the end of the interviews, Paul and I asked the teens if they had any further comments about menstruation and the body or if they had any questions for Paul and me about menstruation and the body. Many of the girls and boys were interested in why Paul and I were doing the interviews. A couple teens were excited to appear in a book. Several understood that it was for my dissertation. (Linda, who had looked at her mom's dissertation, said, "oh no, poor girl, she has to do this!") In one of the boys' group interviews, Dave was jokingly unsure of Paul's knowledge and asked, "Could you answer any of them [our questions] if we did?" Paul said, "Sure" and added humorously that, "For the most part, I guess. I paid attention in health class."

A few of the girls thought about their future adult lives and wondered how adults view menstruation and the body. Ellen asked me, "What do you think people your age feel about it? I don't know, feel about body and stuff like that? Do you think they have a different outlook on it? Or?" Ellen is interested in how older women feel about their weight. Possibly, Ellen is seeking some reassurance that the teen obsession with weight and body might get better as she grows older. At the end of one of the group interviews, Jane asked me, "Does it get any better as you get older?" She was referring to the hassles of menstruation in the hopes that older women did not have to deal with the frustrating management issues that teens do.

Greta was focused on the more immediate term. She asked me, after a pause, "Was there anything that you did that made, made anything easier for you, like, other than just the regular?" Greta wanted advice from an older woman about any tricks I knew of that made menstruation easier for me. She later said that, "you really have to plan ahead for it" indicating that her biggest concern is managing menstruation so she does not have "a really bad experience." Similarly, Anne asked me, at the end of her individual interview, how I felt about menstruation. Sandra, at the end of her group interview, asked the same thing. Dave asked a similar question at the end of his individual interview when he asked Paul, "How do you feel about *your* body?" (Recall that half of our questions were about the body, although these data are not analyzed in this book).

The teens' questions can be interpreted in two ways. First, they could be wondering how adults feel about menstruation and the body. Or, they could be turning the tables and gaining interactional power in the interview by asking us the type of questions that we had been peppering them with for the previous half hour or so. The person who asks a question and successfully receives a response has the power at that moment in the interaction, such as in a doctor's or accountant's office. The client/responder does not have the interactional power in such a setting to ask the doctor what her blood pressure is or the accountant what his salary is. The teens had been so generous with their responses that both Paul and I answered their questions without hesitation.

Three of the girls offered concluding thoughts at the end of their interviews that reflected much of what went on in the girls' interviews. Katie said that, "I don't really mind it [menstruation] but I think it's kind of weird. Like, there's gotta be a better way to do this somehow." She added that it could be worse, explaining that "before pads and stuff, people had to like use rags. And they'd like wash them and stuff. And I can't even imagine." She focuses on the management of menstruation and the annoyances that are involved. This implies issues of concealment, hygiene, embarrassment, and frustration. Recall, for example, that Katie was one of the girls who was most intimidated by tampon use.

When I asked at the end of Ally's group interview if anyone had any questions or comments, Ally said, "I'd like to know why people never talk about it . . . It's like—it's part of life. What's the big deal? I don't get it." This is a fairly mature attitude, much more like that of an adult woman who is used to menstruating rather than a teen for whom menstruation is relatively new. It also reflects several of the teens' attitudes that menstruation is in fact not a big deal yet is treated as a very big deal by their teen peer culture. These teens feel they have moved beyond the cross- and within-gender power plays involved in menstruation and are used to their embodied experiences.

Briana concluded her individual interview by adding the comment, "I just wish men would have periods and that's all I care about it." She continued, "We have to, like, go through birth. We have to have our periods, and what do they get? They don't have to do anything? They've been given the good life, throughout centuries and millenniums. That's all I have to say about it." She had a focus similar to Katie's on the annoyances of managing menstruation, but she also focused on the gendered power differences that menstruation brings about.

DIFFERENT INTERPRETATIONS

In their menstrual talk, the girls and boys showed how they experience and define menstruation differently in their peer social interactions. The social power between boys and girls in menstrual talk is based in these differential understandings of menstruation and, most interestingly, is constantly negoti-ated and shifting in different social situations and contexts. The teens inter-pret menstruation based on their experiences and use these interpretations in their group talk, thereby reproducing them in their teen cultures. Following Corsaro's (1997) interpretive reproduction, these menstrual constructions can be affected by the wider world, such as from discussions with adults, other family members, and talk in school, but the interpretations are created and negotiated by the teens themselves within their peer cultures and group talk. Girls and boys use different strategies and approaches in telling their men-strual stories that reflect the different goals and the roles the stories play in their social interactions. As they share their menstrual stories and strategies using a supportive talk structure, the girls form a community of mutual under-standing and experience. Girls told menstrual stories about getting their first period, embarrassing moments, and how to use menstrual products and man-age menstruation. When girls tell menstrual stories, they affirm themselves as girls, as women, as female. They reaffirm their gender identities because they discuss a set of experiences they share because they are women. It is not a shared body, but the shared experience that stems from the body around which they form a community. Additionally, in their menstrual stories, girls use code words to communicate about menstruation, and both boys and girls use alternate words for "menstruation," which to them sounds adultlike and formal. They use words that better reflect their feelings about menstruation and their teen-language patterns.

Boys create their identities in part through sharing menstrual experiences. Recall that gender is produced and reproduced in social interaction. The boys continually affirm their gender by defining girls in social interactions as men-struants and themselves as nonmenstruants. Boys tell stories to each other to tease girls about menstruation and to share strategies for handling girls who are experiencing symptoms such as mood swings or cramps. The boys tell stories and jokes in a complaining manner as they label menstruation as annoying, bad, and frustrating. When girls do not act "feminine," many boys blame it on menstruation, a medicalized condition that girls are not held responsible for. They affirm their gendered identities as men, as nonmenstruants, and as those who must respond to and interact with women who undergo a physical process that is not entirely clear to them. Because of this, the boys' talk is different in its language and tone. The boys' talk is much less developed and is often ended by a speaker before it can progress to the full extent that we see in the girls' talk.

In their individual and group interviews, the boys did not tell elaborate stories like the girls did. Although boys used menstruation and their experiences with menstruating girls as resources in their talk, this talk is more brief, less rich, and not as deeply expanded on or explored as the girls' talk. This is because menstruation is experienced directly by girls and only indirectly through social interaction by boys, so boys do not have as much experience or as much personal and emotional investment in menstruation. Also, following the "boy code" means that boys discuss personal and emotional matters with each other much less than girls do.[1] Karin Martin (1996) found a similar difference in her interviews with girls and boys about general issues of puberty and sexuality, which affect boys just as much as girls. Even though the boys in her interviews were dealing with issues very close to their own personal and emotional experiences, they were still less reflective and talkative than the girls were.

SOCIAL INTERACTIONS AND GENDERED POWER

Teens use menstruation and the body as resources in their everyday social interactions. For adolescents, menstruation in particular is one way of highlighting the fact that we are each embodied. Our bodies are social actors and influence our social interactions. The body is a gendered *social* phenomenon as it is discussed, interpreted, and lived in *embodied* social interaction. Menstruation, in particular, is not merely a physical process that girls experience individually. Rather, these girls are embodied beings as they use menstruation as a social event and discuss menstruation in their talk through sharing experiences, strategies, and support. Additionally, menstruation is not just a "woman's issue." Menstruation enters boys' social lives through talk with other boys and in their social interactions with girls. We have also seen the importance of the bodily experience as teens experience the world through their bodies. A girl's menstrual status and experience can be an important focus of her everyday interactions. This is different from most adults' experiences, where menstruation is not as salient to their lives as it is to the lives of adolescents.

This complexity in the power dynamics among girls and boys is one of the most striking findings of my research and these themes weave throughout this book. Following symbolic interactionism, the constructions of menstruation and girls' bodies are constantly negotiated, shifting, and emerge through social interactions. Within these social interactions, teens develop and react to power relations and resistances to that power. Resistance and power are intricately tied together and researchers can use evidence of resistance as a means to understand power relations. I find that, in the teens' menstrual talk, the girls and boys display a continual negotiation of power and resistance.

For many girls, menstruation is something that is embarrassing and shameful and the boys can use this definition to tease and embarrass girls. Many girls are affected by this teasing and embarrassment and, in a sense, accommodate these negative discourses. However, the power relationships are more complex. The boys also see that the girls' exclusive access to the knowledge and experience of menstruation gives the girls power in their interactions. Girls resist these discourses by using their bodies as sources of agency in their everyday lives and social interactions. For example, although the boys attempt to silence menstrual talk and label menstruation as not a valued subject of discussion, the girls resist this silencing and continue their menstrual talk. Boys must respond to this reversal of gendered power. At the same time, many teens feel that menstruation is simply "not a big deal." The girls both accommodate the dominant culture's constructions of menstruation as gross and medicalized and resist them by providing their own constructions of menstruation as "not a big deal."

There are many dualisms, contradictions, and tensions in these views. There is no single negative or positive model the girls and boys follow in their interpretations of menstruation. Menstruation can be (a) disempowering; many also say menstruation is (b) "not a big deal;" yet, at the same time, menstruation can be (c) empowering for girls as girls generate agency through their bodies and menstruation. This agency can be both collective and individual and is based in the girls' senses of responsibility and the management of menstruation, their knowledge of menstruation, and their positive views about menstruation. They can use menstruation as an opportunity to exert power over their social worlds and to resist the negative cultural definitions of women's bodies and menstruation. The girls and boys also construct their own interpretations of menstruation and exert agency in their lives, while, at the same time, they are influenced and affected by the larger social institutions in society such as cultural history, school, health and medicine, and the media. The tensions in the teens' constructions of menstruation and uses of girls' bodies in social interaction are theoretically fascinating and add complexity to our understandings of embodiment, agency, and adolescence.

Most research finds that much of the talk surrounding menstruation is negative. However, I find that, although there is some negativity, girls and boys both construct menstruation in neutral and even positive terms. In some cases, the girls are aware of the power inequities they are resisting, such as when they acknowledge that if men menstruated, society would treat menstruation in a much different and more accepting way. Another example is when one of the girls tossed a pad to her friend in the classroom, intentionally violating the teenage norm of concealment and announcing her menstrual identity publicly. In other cases, the girls do not explicitly discuss the power relations and how they resist them. Rather, I interpret their acts as forms of resistance. For example, I contend that, when girls use terms such as "ragging" or "bleeding" instead of "menstruation" they resist the medicalized and adult terminology to describe their bodies' natural process. They claim menstruation as their own and use their own language to discuss and describe it. Also, when the girls construct menstruation in a positive and healthful way, they resist the dominant and medicalized definitions of menstruation as a disease and gross.

In these interviews, the girls and boys construct menstruation as an important bodily difference that differentiates girls' experiences from boys' experiences. The girls in fact use this sexual difference itself as a source of power and resistance. In teens' social interactions, menstruation is a source of both power for boys and girls and agency for girls. The body itself is an actor in social life. There is a debate among social researchers about whether or not we should focus on gender difference or gender fluidity and whether there are "essential" differences between girls and boys.[2] I do not resort to essentialism in children's peer cultures because there is a large overlapping range of girls' and boys' experiences. But, following the embodiment approach, I find that menstruation, a biological difference that most girls experience, is important to teen culture, as it is used as a source of talk and interactions. We cannot forget that we are all embodied beings interacting in the social universe.

Further research in gender dynamics should explore this complexity in power relations and resistance in other realms of adolescent collective talk, particularly in terms of the body, but also in talk about school, family, the media, or any other topic shared in cross-gender interaction. As in menstrual talk, these other realms of talk can also show us how adolescents use talk to negotiate power relations and how they also use talk to resist power. It is not simply the boys who have the power; rather, the processes of power are much more complex and intricate in teen social interactions. In striving for gender equality, increased self-esteem, and a safe environment free of sexual and physical assault, it is important to understand how girls and boys learn and negotiate power and resistance. It is also important that adults interested in promoting sexual and general health among teens learn and use teens' own language of the body to most effectively communicate with them.

MENSTRUAL CELEBRATIONS

The teens in our research live embodied social lives, where the body and the state of the body affect their everyday social interactions. Treating the menstruating body with respect is one step in treating the entire female body with respect, particularly during adolescence when menstruation is prominent in girls' and boys' lives. This respect is vital for equalizing gender relations and empowering girls in their own physicality and sexuality. This empowerment boosts girls' self-confidence, such as in sport, academic, professional, and sexual contexts. As Owen (1998) contends, if women's femininity and womanhood were valued through puberty and into adulthood, many abuse and self-esteem problems in women and girls might be significantly lessened. As menstruation is one of the key modes of embodiment for teens, it is important that teens and adults foster positive views of the menstruating body.

How might we develop a conception of menstruation that highlights the positive and pro-social aspects of menstruation for teens? A conception that celebrates girls' bodies? A conception that fosters self-esteem for girls? A conception that recognizes that we are all embodied selves?

Recently, some writers have examined menstruation and highlighted positive constructions of menstruation and women's bodies, cycles, and lives from our culture's discourses.[3] Several authors have suggested new cultural traditions, such as puberty rituals, that would affirm menarche and menstruation to redefine the experience as a positive event. For example, upon menarche, we could give girls a material token, such as flowers, to show the girl that something wonderful and positive has happened. Such a token can be discreet, which would respect a girl's possible wishes to keep her reaction and the event a private yet celebrated moment in her life. Natalie Angier (1999) writes, "When your daughter or niece or younger sister runs to you and crows, 'It's here!' take her out for a bowl of ice cream or a piece of chocolate cake, and raise a glass of milk to the new life that begins with blood" (p. 119). (Such rituals could also extend to other female experiences, such as menopause or hysterectomy.[4])

Andrea, whose mom is a nurse, gave her a special present upon menarche. Andrea said that she "thought it was a little weird," but it was clear that getting the necklace and the positive feelings surrounding the gift were (and still are) important for Andrea. None of the other girls mentioned receiving a gift, but this could also be due to the fact that the interviews focused more on the current experiences of menstruation rather than on menarche. Other girls did mention how excited their moms were, such as Kassie, whose mom was so excited that she called a bunch of her own adult friends to tell them about Kassie's menarche.

At the end of our group interviews, we talked with the girls and boys about how they would feel about one type of menstrual celebration. We asked:

In some cultures, menstruation is celebrated as a positive event and a woman is considered to be at her most powerful, psychically and spiritually, when she is menstruating. Women would go into a moon-lodge and have a holiday or party with other women where they would play games, talk, and sit on special moss padding and give their blood back to the earth. It was a time of rest, relaxation, and for gathering wisdom. What would you think of a menstruation celebration like this?

Of the seven girls' groups interviews, five of the groups came to the consensus that such a "party" would be "cool" or "okay." For example:

KATIE (14): That'd be so cool!

JENNIFER (14): I'd make it a whole lot less, 'it's my—my time of the month, ughh.'

KATIE: Yeah, it'd make it more special instead of like, instead of it just being one of those things that you hate and you have to go through. It'd make it like, special.

In another group, Sylvia and Andrea thought that "it would be fun." Sylvia said that it would be a "binge-eating fest." Andrea agreed and said, "Exactly. Just, like, to hang out with, I don't know, like a bunch of girls, and just, like, talk." Although, both said that they could do without sitting on the moss padding. Ellen and Ally's group agreed. They said that they think it would be "cool," but without the moss. Ellen asked, "Isn't that a tad bit unsanitary, like you're sitting on the ground, right?" Ellen said later, "I would do it if we didn't have to do the moss." Ally added, "Yeah, it's like, minus the moss, and I'm cool."

Two of the seven girls' groups decided that such a celebration would be "too weird." Briana said in her group, "I just don't think any party could block out the pain." Erin added, "Just give me a robe and sit me on a couch." After more discussion, Marcia said that she "definitely" would not want to "celebrate" getting her period.

The second dissenting group was not as clear-cut in their objections. After I told the story, Kasey immediately said, "Can we say, 'Cuckoo!'?" Sandra said such a celebration would be "very, very weird." The discussion quickly turned to the moss. Kasey said, "It would stink" and "I think it would get really bloody." Yet, Sandra then said "the relaxing would be good" and Kasey added, "and get, like, away from the guys." So, for this second dissenting group, it appeared that the party in the hut sounded okay, but again, the moss was the problem. Had I known about the specific problems with the moss, I would have just asked about the seclusion in the moon-lodge.

Interestingly, in three of the seven girls' groups (the three groups representing both sides of the issue), the girls worried that putting hormonal women in a hut together would bring about fighting. For example, in one group that thought that sitting on moss would be "gross":

ERIN (18): Yeah. I see cat fight.

LAURA: *Really? Why?*

BRIANA (16): Okay, seriously though. You're kind of moody during that time. Maybe even before, usually for me before. It's like I don't want to deal with other people before that—

MARCIA (19): —when you get that many women with those many different opinions and that bad mood in a small, confined area—oh no.

LAURA: *Sitting on moss.*

BRIANA: Only one will come out alive.

MARCIA: Exactly. ((pause)) With a handful of hair.

These girls buy into the stereotype that premenstrual and menstruating women's hormones make them unable to control their impulses and more likely to get into fights. Some of this is based on their own realities, as they do not want to be with others during their periods (as Briana said), but much of it, I think, is due to dominant stereotypes of out-of-control menstruants. In general, most of the girls thought that having such a celebration would be a good thing, although they appreciate modern tampon and pad technology and could do without the moss.

We also asked the boys what they would think of such a celebration. Both of the boys' groups thought that it would be "pretty cool." In one group, the boys seemed to be astutely aware of the purpose of such a moon-lodge:

JIM (18): I think it's just to get away from the guys so they [the girls] don't make them [the guys] mad.

JACK (17): Sounds like a guys' poker night, heh heh.

MATT (17): Yeah, really.

JACK: Let's go do some hunting.

The boys understand that it is an opportunity for the girls to have time away from the boys, just as boys enjoy their stereotypical hunting excursions and poker nights. Larry, in the other boys' group, also expressed this sentiment and said, "I think it'd be pretty cool, you know. I guess it's kind of like, their celebration time to be a woman, you know. I think it's kind of cool." Yet, Jim, above, noted that the girls may be leaving so they do not make the boys mad. This hints at the conflicting reasons for seclusion in a moon-lodge. Is it because the women want to have a reason to seclude themselves from their everyday responsibilities and gather with other women? Or, is it because the men want to seclude the women away from the rest of the community because of the women's unpredictable hormonal status, which might make the men "mad"? Neither reason has been anthropologically nor historically confirmed.

REFLECTIONS ON RESEARCH METHODS

At the end of any research project, it is important to reflect on methodological decisions and what those decisions mean for future work. No other research has explored adolescent girls' *and* boys' collective talk about menstruation. Most research on menstruation uses only individual interviews and has adults as research respondents. No other research has explored the importance and significance of menstruation as a topic in teens' (or adults') social interactions. This research can help us learn how the gendered body has a role in peer culture and how individuals use the body in their power relations. This not only helps us understand teens' lives better on a micro level, but also connects what is going on in teen peer culture to broader work in understanding human social interaction.

In addition, norms surrounding menstruation and its place in public space are changing very quickly in our culture. In this research, I explore how teens today construct menstruation and how teens today use menstruation in their everyday talk. In future research, it would be interesting to explore how women and men of different ages experience and discuss menstruation and their embodied lives. When I present this data, older women and men are surprised at the candor of the teens and how comfortable they are talking about menstruation. With the increasing risk of sexually transmitted diseases, teens today need to know more about their bodies and be more comfortable in expressing their needs and desires. Norms of body talk have changed significantly in the past decades and it would be interesting to explore the contents and structures of such talk in older generations. It would be interesting to explore all different kinds of body talk among different ages and how women and men experience their embodied lives.

In this study, I use only single-gender groups. I believe that boys' discourses affect girls' discourses and vice versa. The interconnectedness between boys' and girls' talk and their beliefs about menstruation and the body are issues that need to be explored. Generally, boys' discourses can be structurally more powerful in mixed-gender interaction and girls may be silenced by their attitudes and talk during a mixed-gender discussion. However, as the stories told in our interviews showed, girls can have more interactional power on topics such as menstruation, where girls have the experience and boys do not. Adding additional complexity, boys and girls have different communication styles, which may conflict and be cause for frustrations and misunderstandings.[5] In future research, it would be interesting to conduct mixed-gender groups to compare to the findings of single-gender groups.

The findings in this book are based on mostly white adolescents, all living in southern Indiana. There is some variety in class and rural-urban residence, but, for the most part, the sample is quite homogenous. I did not find significant differences in the menstrual talk of working- and middle-class teens, or between rural and urban teens. I was unable to generate as much interest from boys and thus we were able to interview only half the number of boys as girls.

However, I do feel that the data are relevant to many teens' experiences and that many readers of this work, especially young adults and teens, will recognize themselves, their experiences, and their cultures in the data and analyses. The social processes of power relations, agency, constructions of menstruation and the body, storytelling, and social interaction these teens display are found in many social groups. Researching these processes expands our knowledge of teens. But, it can also inform studies of younger children, adults, different racial and ethnic groups, different regions of the country, and different countries. Future research might examine how these processes are evident and differentially manifested among these other groups of interacting individuals. By understanding the wide variety of interactions among people, we can better facilitate understanding, cooperation, and respect.

CONCLUSION

What does this research contribute to our understanding of social life? In this book, I have shown that teens use menstruation and the body as resources for talk, power, disempowerment, resistance, and agency in their social interactions. By exploring their menstrual talk, we can understand how their bodies are actors in their everyday lives. The primary theme weaving throughout the data and findings is the complexity of power dynamics among girls and boys. By looking at how both teen girls and boys talk about menstruation, I show how teens' interpretations of menstruation are negative, ambivalent, and based in our cultural history; how their interpretations are at the same time positive; how larger social institutions influence their peer cultures; and how they negotiate power and agency in their embodied social interactions. I find that the body, usually a source of disempowerment for girls, is also used as a source of power, in part because menstruation enters into everyday social interactions. I explore how girls use this power and how boys respond to this power. Most importantly, I contend that body process is vital in our understanding of children's unique cultures, their social interactions, and their power relations.

In the girls' and boys' individual and group interviews on menstruation, we can see how gendered power works in their social interactions and how this power is based in embodiment. These two theoretical threads weave throughout their interviews and my analyses. The embodiment approach to gender is a new approach in sociology and contrasts with essentialism and constructionism. I develop it here as I explore high school-age adolescents' social interactions and gendered power, which show how all of our social experiences are embodied.

What can we do with these findings? We can support teens by encouraging their explorations of their worlds, answering their questions about their bodies, and giving them space to be with other teens to develop their own understandings of social life. We can offer girls support of their bodies and their maturity by affirming menstruation and celebrating impending woman-hood. We can affirm that girls can have bodily power without having to be thin and beautiful. We can ensure that teens, particularly girls, have knowl-edge about their bodies to promote sexual agency. Without knowledge and language, teens cannot respond to sexual situations in the safest manner. An engaged and open understanding of the body is crucial to how teens respond to social situations and to their own emotions, psychology, and bodily needs.

APPENDIX A

Participants in Individual and Group Interviews

The following tables present demographic information on each research participant. The sample was a "convenience" sample, as I contacted community groups of teens living in my area and interviewed those that were interested and available. I initially attempted to recruit through the schools, but this proved unwieldy and technically unfeasible (e.g., in dealing with the many layers of school administration for noncurricular research). All the community groups I contacted were interested in participating, but some groups were less committed and we were only able to interview one or two teens from those groups. The teens were not paid for their participation, although I did provide sodas and snacks.

The teens are both from working- and middle-class backgrounds. I coded the teens' socioeconomic class status based on what they said their parents do for a living. Some of the teens would be considered upper-middle class or even upper class, but I coded them as middle class, as their experiences are based in the community's and groups' middle-class norms. The girls' groups were exclusively working or middle class and the boys' groups had some crossover, although most participants in each group were one class or the other. Examples of working-class professions include factory worker, bus driver, and maintenance worker (all were settled-living working class, as opposed to poorer and less financially stable hard-living working class[1]). Examples of middle-class professions include nurse practitioner, geologist, business owner, secretary, sales representative, and librarian.

In my analyses, I did not find differences by social class. I initially thought that it might be important since social class is often related to cultural and speech patterns. Geography, in this case, might have been more important than class. All the teens came from the same five-county area in southern Indiana. However, in understanding the context that each of these teens come from, it is important to keep in mind their class backgrounds.

GIRLS

Total girls: 26
Number of girls' group interviews: 7
Number of girls' individual interviews: 23

	Name	Age	Grade	Social Class
Group 1	Katie	14	9	middle
	Jennifer	14	10	middle
Group 2	Kasey	13	9	working
	Sandra	14	9	working
	Anne	14	8	working
	Jane	14	9	working
Group 3	Andrea	17	12	middle
	Sylvia	18	12	middle
Group 4	Ally	17	11	middle
	Ellen	17	11	middle
	Alyssa†	18	12	middle
Group 5	Lacey	16	10	middle
	Erica	15	10	middle
	Greta	15	10	middle
	Leslie	16	10	middle
	Krissy‡	16	11	middle
	Korrine	15	10	middle
	Kassie	16	10	middle
	Linda	16	10	middle
	Rebecca	15	10	middle
Group 6	Marcia	18	*	working
	Cindy	18	12	working
	Erin	18	*	working
	Briana	16	10	working
Group 7	Klara	16	10	middle
	Nancy	17	11	middle

* not currently in school
† Teen is Korean-American immigrant
‡ Teen is biracial (black and white)

BOYS

Total boys: 11
Number of boys' group interviews: 2
Number of boys' individual interviews: 11

	Name	Age	Grade	Social Class
Group 1	Derek	19	12	working
	Jim	18	12	working
	Matt	17	12	working
	Curt	15	9	working
	Dave	15	10	middle
	Jack	17	12	working
Group 2	Walter†	18	12	working
	Larry	18	12	middle
Individual Interview Only				
	Martin	16	10	middle
	Don	18	12	middle
	Brian	14	9	working

† Teen is biracial (black and white)

APPENDIX B

Interview Guides

The research participants in this study were high school-age teens ranging from age 14 to 19. I conducted twenty-six individual interviews and seven group interviews with girls. Paul conducted eleven individual interviews and two group interviews with boys. In three cases, only one boy participated from his community group so Paul was only able to conduct an individual interview. In addition, three girls were unable to participate in an individual interview, but completed the group interview.

There were significantly more girls than boys interviewed for two reasons. First, there are fewer community groups that are geared towards boys and there are fewer boys participating in mixed-sex groups. Second, I think that there was less interest among the boys to discuss issues of the body and menstruation than among the girls even though Paul, my male research assistant, was present at most of the introductions I gave for my research to all-male or mixed-gender groups. Although boys discuss these issues with their peers, I believe that girls are more interested in the opportunity to initiate such discussions, even with a relative stranger. Karin Martin (1996) also found that significantly more girls than boys were interested in participating in her research interviews on adolescent experiences of puberty and sexuality.

Prior to the individual and group interviews, Paul and I conducted pilot group interviews (one girls' group and one boys' group) to see how the teens would respond to the questions. After the pilots, I conducted a microanalysis of the interviews to develop a deeper understanding of the respondents' patterns of talk.[1] This analysis allowed me to reorganize and reword some of the questions and to add additional questions to better make use of the teens' own language structures and topics they brought up that I had not anticipated. The pilot runs were an invaluable experience and not only strengthened the interview guides but also gave us the confidence that the teens would respond to and be interested in our questions and the topics of menstruation and the body.

INDIVIDUAL INTERVIEWS

In the individual interview guide, we began with general questions about each teen's age, grade, family, school, and community group. By starting out with these nonspecific questions, the interviewer can develop rapport and comfort in the conversation with the participant (unlike in survey interviewing, where such "dull" questions are placed at the end of the questionnaire). Then we asked questions about the body (although we asked questions about the body in these interviews, in this book my focus is on menstruation). We explored issues of their feelings towards their own weight, athleticism, looks, and musculature. These first questions are identical in both the boys' and girls' interview guides. After the body questions, we asked the menstruation questions. In the girls' interviews, I let the girls know how excited I was about these questions because so many other people are asking about the body, but not many are asking teens about menstruation. I tried to build up enthusiasm about these questions to make the setting as comfortable and friendly as possible given a topic that is not always presented as such. The interview questions are nearly identical for the girls and the boys. The exceptions are cases where I would ask about the girls' personal experiences menstruating. For the boys, Paul instead asked about their experiences with their sisters, friends, or mothers.

INDIVIDUAL INTERVIEW GUIDE: GIRLS

- How old are you? What grade are you in?
- Who do you live with? (parents, siblings) How old are your siblings?
- What school do you go to?
- What have you found interesting in _____ [name of organization]? What do you do in _____ ? (Short questions here to get to know the teen better.)

BODY QUESTIONS

- Are you happy with your weight? Have you dieted in the past two weeks?
- Are you athletic?
- How do you feel about your body compared to those of your friends? [compared to what you see in the media?]
- If you could change one thing about your body, what would you change?

MENSTRUATION QUESTIONS

- Where did you learn about menstruation?
- What is the point of menstruation? Why do girls menstruate?
- Can you tell when someone is menstruating? How?

- How would you explain menstruation to a young girl who knew nothing about it? To a boy?
- How are things different for you when you are menstruating? Do you do anything different?
- How do you know about different menstrual products? What do you use?
- How would you react if you had the chance to never menstruate again, but could still have children?
- When did you begin your period? Can you tell me about your first period?
- Do you feel that menstruation relates to the rest of your body? Do you think it's a part of your body or is it something "extra"?
- Do you have any other comments about menstruation?
- Do you have any questions for me about the body or menstruation?

INDIVIDUAL INTERVIEW GUIDE: BOYS

- How old are you? What grade are you in?
- Who do you live with? (parents, siblings) How old are your siblings?
- What school do you go to?
- What have you found interesting in _____ [name of organization]? What do you do in _____ ? (Short questions here to get to know the teen better.)

BODY QUESTIONS

- Are you happy with your weight? Have you dieted in the past two weeks?
- Are you athletic?
- How do you feel about your body compared to those of your friends? [compared to what you see in the media?]
- If you could change one thing about your body, what would you change?

MENSTRUATION QUESTIONS

- Where did you learn about menstruation?
- What is the point of menstruation? Why do girls menstruate?
- Did you notice when your sisters or female friends started to menstruate? How?
- Can you tell when someone is menstruating? How?
- How would you explain menstruation to a young girl who knew nothing about it? To a boy?
- How are things different when your girl friends, sisters, or mothers are menstruating? Do they do anything different? Do you?
- What do you know about different menstrual products?
- How would you feel if girls never menstruated but could still have children?
- Do you have any other comments about menstruation?
- Do you have any questions for me about the body or menstruation?

GROUP INTERVIEWS

The group interview questions were designed to generate discussion and talk
among participants about issues on the body and menstruation. The group
interviews lasted from thirty minutes to over one hour. The individual interviews were sometimes conducted prior to the group interviews and sometimes
after, depending on the logistics of the setting and time constraints of the
group. When the individual interviews were completed after the group interviews, the teen would often reference topics covered in the group. These
teens were also sometimes more limited in their responses since they were
thinking only of the items brought up by the group. The topics had already
been framed by the group and they sometimes had a harder time bringing in
their own ideas.

In studies of youth, it is important to ask both directed and nondirected
questions. Directed questions, which are questions about specific experiences
and topics, help the adolescent think of specific answers rather than trying
immediately to formulate general analyses and opinions. Children are not
always as self-reflective as adults. Thus, in dealing with adolescent research
participants, I included specific questions that could either stand alone or be
used as a stepping-off point for more general reflective questions if the adolescent felt comfortable and capable. Nondirected questions provide more
opportunity for children to collaborate in their answers and expand on the
responses of others. This type of interaction is typical of the discussion styles
in many peer cultures and is reflective of their natural way of developing
shared meanings.

We began the group interviews with demographic questions and by asking how they all know each other. In order to understand the dynamics and
history of the group participants, it is important to know how long the members have been together in the group and if they know each other in other
contexts such as school. As with the individual interviews, we started with
questions on the body and then moved to menstruation. In the group interviews, we asked questions about teens in general rather than about the participants' specifically. I did not want any individual to feel pressured to share
something personal about herself or himself in the group setting, so we
actively encouraged the teens to talk in general terms.

At the end of each group interview, we asked the teens what they
thought about the research interviews and if they would have conversations
like this in their real lives. As the research setting is artificial, I wanted to
assess their comfort level with the interaction and see if they thought it was
in any way reflective of real life. Often, the teens would first say "no," they
would not have conversations like the interview. But then, most would
think back and say "yes," and remember specific instances when they had
discussed these very same issues recently with friends. The data transcripts

themselves can also attest to the adolescents' comfort and the naturalness of their talk during the interviews.

Overall, the teens seemed to enjoy participating in the research and enjoyed telling us their stories, both collectively in the group interviews and individually in the individual interviews. Other researchers have also found that youth participants enjoy being asked about their experiences and enjoy participating in social research.[2] I believe if the research participants are enjoying themselves in the interviews, they are much more likely to provide more valid and reliable responses. Also, the teens were very generous with their time and I wanted them to enjoy the time they donated to the project.

GROUP INTERVIEW GUIDE: GIRLS

- For the tape, say your name, age, grade, and school. [I initially thought to use an ice-breaker here, but most of the girls (and boys) were already so familiar with one another that this was unnecessary.]
- How do you all know each other? Are you in other activities together besides <<organization name>> ?

BODY QUESTIONS

- Do you think teens are happy with their bodies?
  — Their looks?
  — Their athleticism?
  — Their weights?
- Historically bodies have been seen in many different ways—sometimes the emphasis was on being heavier to show how wealthy they were because they had money to eat. This is how things were, what about today? Some people want to *change* something about their bodies, do you? Do you think other teens feel the same way?

MENSTRUATION QUESTIONS

- What's the first word or phrase you think of when I say "menstruation"?
- What do you think about when people talk about menstruation? Do you think boys think about it differently than girls? Do their guys' views influence you?
- What other words do you use for menstruation? What words do you use when you talk about it?
- Do you have any stories about menstruation? Things that happened in school? At sports?
- What do you know about menstrual products? Do you see advertisements on television? From your family? Why do you think there are so many?

- Have you heard any jokes about menstruation? [Tell hockey player joke to open up as a joke-telling session.]
- What if men could menstruate and women couldn't? What differences might there be? How would you feel about it?
- Is there anything you would change about our attitudes towards menstruation? Can you suggest any changes in the world that would make it easier to be a girl menstruating?
- In some cultures, menstruation is celebrated as a positive event and a woman is considered to be at her most powerful, psychically and spiritually, when she is menstruating. Women would go into a moon-lodge and have a holiday or party with other women where they would play games, talk, and sit on special moss padding and give their blood back to the earth. It was a time of rest, relaxation, and for gathering wisdom. What would you think of a menstruation celebration like this?
- Do *you* have any questions about menstruation, the body, anything we've talked about?
- What did you think of the focus group and the individual interviews?
- Would you have a conversation like this in real life? With your friends?

GROUP INTERVIEW GUIDE: BOYS

- For the tape, say your name, age, grade, school and your [most exciting place to live, favorite animal, etc.].
- How do you all know each other? Are you in other activities together besides <<organization name>> ?

BODY QUESTIONS

- Do you think teens are happy with their bodies?
  — Their looks?
  — Their athleticism?
  — Their weights?
- Historically bodies have been seen in many different ways—sometimes the emphasis was on being heavier to show how wealthy they were because they had money to eat. This is how things were, what about today? Some people want to *change* something about their bodies, do you? Do you think other teens feel the same way?

MENSTRUATION QUESTIONS

- What's the first word or phrase you think of when I say "menstruation"?
- What do you think about when people talk about menstruation? Do you think girls think about it differently than boys?

- What other words do you use for menstruation? What words do you use when you talk about it?
- Do you have any stories about menstruation? Things that happened in school? At sports?
- What do you know about menstrual products? Do you see advertisements on television? From your family? Why do you think there are so many?
- Have you heard any jokes about menstruation? [Tell hockey player joke to open up as a joke-telling session.]
- What if men could menstruate and women couldn't? What differences might there be? How would you feel about it?
- In some cultures, menstruation is celebrated as a positive event and a woman is considered to be at her most powerful, psychically and spiritually, when she is menstruating. Women would go into a moon-lodge and have a holiday or party with other women where they would play games, talk, and sit on special moss padding and give their blood back to the earth. It was a time of rest, relaxation, and for gathering wisdom. What would you think of a menstruation celebration like this?
- Do *you* have any questions about menstruation, the body, anything we've talked about?
- What did you think of the focus group and the individual interviews?
- Would you have a conversation like this in real life? With your friends?

Notes

CHAPTER ONE.
INTRODUCTION

1. See: Amann-Gainotti (1986); Beausang and Razor (2000); Blyth, Simmons, and Zakin (1985); Brooks-Gunn and Ruble (1982); Delaney, Lupton, and Toth (1988); Golub (1992); Grahn (1993); Greif and Ulman (1982); Houppert (1999); Hughes and Wolf (1997); Koff and Rierdan (1995a); Koff, Rierdan, and Jacobson (1981); Kowalski and Chapple (2000); Lee and Sasser-Coen (1996a); Logan, Calder, and Cohen (1980); Moore (1995); Owen (1998); Paige (1984); Rierdan, Koff, and Flaherty (1985); Usmiani and Daniluk (1997); and Whisnant and Zegans (1975).

2. According to *Publisher's Weekly*, at the end of 2001, *Are You There God? It's Me, Margaraet* was the eighth best-selling children's book of all time, selling almost 6.5 million paperback copies from publication by Dell in 1972 through December 2001. This list includes the first four enormously popular Harry Potter books by J. K. Rowling.

3. Such as Hughes and Wolf (1997) and Owen (1998).

4. Such as Delaney, Lupton, and Toth (1988); Laws (1990); E. Martin (1992); and Lee and Sasser-Coen (1996a).

5. Kissling (1996) is an exception, as she explores adolescents' accounts.

6. M. Fine (1992) and Thorne (1987).

7. Qvortrup (1994).

8. Corsaro (1997).

9. Exceptions include Amann-Gainotti (1986), who examines boys' reactions to menstruation; however, her questions are restricted to how they learned about menstruation. Lovering (1995) also spoke with boys about menstruation, but they were younger boys who had very limited experience with it. Other researchers, such as Lee (1994) and Lee and Sasser-Coen (1996a), restrict their observations to girls and only mention boys in terms of their changing relationships to girls at menarche because of the perceived increase in girls' sexuality.

10. Mead (1934); Blumer (1969).

11. Bordo (1993).

12. Foucault was also one of the first theorists to connect power to the body. However, in contrast to the embodiment perspective that I follow (explained in chapter 4), Foucault took a poststructuralist stance where the body is discursively produced—the body is constituted as text. Rather than being a material entity able to generate its own social action, the power of the body, for Foucault, is limited to how it is constructed through language.

13. Prout (2000); Williams and Bendelow (1998).

14. Such as Eder, Evans, and Parker (1995); Thorne (1994); and Willis (1981).

15. See Fingerson (2005b). In addition to menstruation and the body, such issues might include divorce, death, or sexuality.

16. Taylor and Rupp (1991).

17. See, e.g., Fingerson (1999).

18. "Menarche" (MEN-are-kee) refers to a girl's first period. This term is from the Greek words "men," which means "month," and "arche," which means "beginning."

19. Briggs (1986); DeVault (1999); and Zola (1991).

20. Eder and Fingerson (2002).

21. Grimshaw (2000).

22. For an exception, see Hoyle and Adger (1998).

23. Finegan (1998).

CHAPTER TWO.
NEGATIVE AND AMBIVALENT EXPERIENCES

1. James, Jenks, and Prout (1998).

2. Simpson (2000).

3. Transcribing conventions:

. . .	omitted text
—	word that was cut off by next speaker, latching, or overlapping speech
[word]	explanatory information for reader
( )	inaudible speech
(word)	barely audible speech with guessed word
((pause))	a noticeable pause in the speaker's speech

4. These interviews were conducted in early 2000, before the U.S. wars in Iraq and Afghanistan.

5. Baumgardner and Richards (2000).

6. Following Schwalbe et al. (2000).

7. See Messner (2000).

8. Also known as the Sapir-Whorf hypothesis after the two scholars who first developed the theory, Sapir (1963) and Whorf (1940).

9. Delaney, Lupton, and Toth (1988).

10. Kilbourne (1999).

11. Milow (1983).

12. McRobbie (1991); Tolman (1994).

13. Kissling (1996).

CHAPTER THREE.
CULTURAL CONTEXTS

1. E.g., Corsaro (1997) and Qvortrup (1994).

2. Amann-Gainotti (1986); Beausang and Razor (2000); Brooks-Gunn and Ruble (1982); Koff, Rierdan, and Jacobson (1981), Kowalski and Chapple (2000); Lee (1994); Lee and Sasser-Coen (1996b); Ruble and Brooks-Gunn (1982); and Stolzman (1986).

3. Lee (1994).

4. Amann-Gainotti (1986); Koff, Rierdan, and Jacobson (1981).

5. Kowalski and Chapple (2000).

6. Amann-Gainotti (1986); Ruble and Brooks-Gunn (1982).

7. Stoltzman (1986).

8. Amann-Gainotti (1986); Ruble and Brooks-Gunn (1982).

9. Brooks-Gunn and Ruble (1982); Lee and Sasser-Coen (1996b).

10. Brumberg (1997); Lee and Sasser-Coen (1996a).

11. Brumberg (1997).

12. Amann-Gainotti (1986).

13. Delaney, Lupton, and Toth (1988); Wasserfall (1999).

14. Grahn (1993).

15. Delaney, Lupton, and Toth (1988).

16. Mozes (1955).

17. Delaney, Lupton, and Toth (1988).

18. K. Martin (1996); O'Grady and Wansbrough (1997).

19. Golub (1992).

20. Ehrenreich and English (1987).

21. Verbrugge (2000).

22. Brumberg (1997).

23. Bullough and Voght (1973).

24. Brooks-Gunn and Ruble (1982).

25. K. Martin (1996) finds similar attitudes in her research, as some of the girls she interviewed did not make a big deal about their periods and said they "just started."

26. Delaney, Lupton, and Toth (1988); Brumberg (1997).

27. Delaney, Lupton, and Toth (1988).

CHAPTER FOUR.
MEDICALIZATION AND
GENDER POLITICS OF THE BODY

1. Brumberg (1997).

2. Verbrugge (2000).

3. Verbrugge (2000).

4. Emily Martin (1992) finds a similar pattern in her interviews with women; however she does not attribute this construction to teens' health education.

5. Angier (1999).

6. Angier (1999).

7. Lovering (1995).

8. Christensen (2000).

9. See also Karp (1996).

10. Figert (1996); Tavris (1992).

11. See, e.g., Elson (2002); Gladwell (2000); Kelley (2003); McCullough (2003); Rako (2003); and Tsao (2002).

12. See Gordon (1988) for a review

13. Boston Women's Health Book Collective (1998).

14. E. Martin (1992).

15. Simmons and Blyth (1987).

16. K. Martin (1996).

17. K. Martin (1996).

18. Corner (1951); Bullough and Voght (1973).

19. Laws (1990).

20. Nettleton and Watson (1998).

21. Heywood and Dworkin's (2003) analyses are a good example of gender fluidity, as they explore women and men in sport, particularly power lifting. Also, Messner (2000) advocates this perspective as he explores social interactions among girls and boys in youth soccer.

22. Williams and Bendelow (1998). Elson (2004) and Tolman (2002) each use the embodiment approach in their research analyses. For example, Tolman contends that sexual desire is socially constructed and cannot be understood in purely biological terms. Desire is a bodily process regulated by hormones, but our experience of sexual desire is shaped by our interpretations of desire, based in social interaction. Tolman finds that adolescent girls are denied feelings of sexual desire and have no language or experience in which to understand or interpret their desire.

23. The approach of phenomenology (based in the interpretive perspective) examines lived meanings and experiences. Here, I am interested in the lived experience of the body, or what is termed the phenomenology of the body. As Nettleton and Watson (1998) contend, phenomenology attempts to understand how people experience their bodies and how they articulate those experiences.

24. Nettleton and Watson (1998).

CHAPTER FIVE.
GIRLS IN POWER

1. For example, Bordo (1993) describes the body as a "politically inscribed entity," a passive construction based in poststructuralist thought.

2. E. Martin (1992).

3. Davis and Fisher (1993).

4. Emirbayer and Mische (1998); Davies (2000); and Weedon (1997).

5. Williams and Bendelow (1998).

6. Important exceptions in U.S. research include K. Martin's (1996) finding that adolescents use their bodies and their sexuality as sources of agency. Boys learn through puberty that their bodies are a source of power and control. Girls use sports and school participation to express control in their lives. Additionally, in her study of preschool children, K. Martin (1998) finds that children use their bodies to shape and construct their interactions, particularly in cross-gender situations (see also Thorne's [1994] research on elementary children). E. Martin (1992) explores menarche, menstruation, childbirth, and menopause and finds girls and women often resist the dominant negative and medicalized constructions of these physical processes. Bailey's (2001) work shows that women use lactation and pregnancy as sources of self-expression and empowerment, yet, at the same time, they can make women feel reduced to their biology and thereby operate as a form of social control.

7. See also Rierdan and Hastings (1990).

8. See Puri (1999).

9. Davis (1995).

10. Corsaro (1997); Eder (1988); Eder, Evans, and Parker (1995); and Fingerson (1999).

11. Early maturation has been found to be correlated with unpopularity. Girls who develop either early or late are found to have lower self-esteem and experience less social prestige with peers (Simmons and Blyth 1987; Thorne 1994).

12. Delaney, Lupton, and Toth (1988:xii–xiii).

13. These types of items are on the annual "Mindset List," updated annually and distributed by Beloit College to its faculty at the beginning of each academic year and can be found in news reports and on the Web. It describes the mindset of the incoming freshmen to help professors understand and relate to their new students, and highlights the large generation gaps that often exist. Other examples from the actual list for the freshmen class of 2006 (most born in 1984) include: there has always been a Diet Coke; cars have always had eye-level rear stop lights, CD players, and air bags; drug testing for athletes has always been routine; and Fox has always been a television network choice.

14. Kissling (1996) discusses these linguistic strategies.

15. For the importanace of ongoing groups to social research, see Heath (1998); James (1995); K. Martin (1996); McRobbie (1991); Tannock (1998); Tolman (1994); and Wulff (1988).

16. E. Martin (1992).

CHAPTER SIX.
BOYS' RESPONSES

1. Koff and Rierdan (1995b).

2. E. Martin (1992); Lee and Sasser-Coen (1996).

3. Eder, Evans, and Parker (1995); G. A. Fine (1987).

4. Weitz (1998).

5. Parsons from his 1951 work as cited in Riessman and Nathanson (1986). Although, increasingly, responsibility for being sick is being shifted to the individual (Gordon 1988), such as in the case of AIDS or lung cancer.

6. Lorber (1997); E. Martin (1992).

7. Amann-Gainotti (1986); Lee (1994); K. Martin (1996); and Prendergast (2000).

8. In our interviews, there were no indications of any other sexuality besides heterosexuality. We did not directly ask about sexual identification, but the teens all spoke and acted in-line with default heterosexuality. Following our Institutional Review Board (IRB) protocol for human subjects, we did not directly ask about any sexual issue. Had we asked about sexual issues, not only would the IRB have posed greater barriers to our research, but parents and community group leaders would also have been more hesitant to participate and our sample would not have been as strong.

9. Figert (1996); Laws (1990).

10. Eder, Evans, and Parker (1995).

11. G. A. Fine (1987).

12. Lander (1988); Laws (1990).

13. Houppert (1999).

14. For more detail on third wave feminism, see Baumgardner and Richards (2000).

15. Richards (1998). In contrast, following the lead of first wavers, many second wave liberal feminists hesitate to look to the body, but instead argue that women and men are equal and should be defined by their intellectual abilities, not their bodies. However, there have been a variety of responses to the body in second wave feminism, as evident in the many essays included in Price and Shildrick's (1999) volume that expressly focuses on second wave theorists and the body.

16. Beaudry (2002).

17. Many older women in fact report doing this in the workplace (Lorber 1997).

18. Michael Messner (2000) finds similar phenomena among four and five year old girls in the United States using their bodies and voices to celebrate their soccer team, called the "Barbie Girls." Although their male peers were chanting in opposition to the girls' celebration of Barbie, the girls were not silenced and instead chased the boys off.

CHAPTER SEVEN.
CONCLUSION: BODIES IN INTERACTION

1. Pollack (1998).

2. See, e.g., Messner (2000); Thorne (1994).

3. See Logan, Calder, and Cohen (1980); Delaney, Lupton, and Toth (1988); Martin (1992); Lee and Sasser-Coen (1996a); Hughes and Wolf (1997); and Owen (1998).

4. Owen (1998).

5. Scott (2000).

APPENDIX A

1. See Bettie's (2003) class distinctions.

APPENDIX B

1. This analysis follows Briggs's (1986) recommendations.

2. For example, K. Martin (1996); Taylor, Gilligan, and Sullivan (1995).

References

Amann-Gainotti, Merete. 1986. "Sexual Socialization during Early Adolescence: The Menarche." *Adolescence* 21:703–10.

Angier, Natalie. 1999. *Woman: An Intimate Geography*. New York: Random House.

Bailey, Lucy. 2001. "Gender Shows: First-Time Mothers and Embodied Selves." *Gender & Society* 15:110–29.

Ball, Aimee Lee. 1984. "I hate my period . . . period! With a friend like this, who needs enemies?" *Mademoiselle* 90:212–13.

Baumgardner, Jennifer and Amy Richards. 2000. *Manifesta: Young Women, Feminism, and the Future*. New York: Farrar, Straus and Giroux.

Beacher, Abraham I. 1955. "Your Daughter and Menstruation." *Sexology* 21: 696–700.

Beaudry, Kendall. 2002. "Marketing Menstruation." *Mother Jones*, July/August: 21.

Beausang, Carol C. and Anita G. Razor. 2000. "Young Western Women's Experiences of Menarche and Menstruation." *Health Care for Women International* 21:517–28.

Bettie, Julie. 2003. *Women Without Class: Girls, Race, and Identity*. Berkeley: University of California Press.

Blume, Judy. 1970. *Are You There God? It's Me, Margaret*. New York: Bantam Doubleday Dell.

Blumer, Herbert. 1969. *Symbolic Interactionism: Perspective and Method*. Berkeley: University of California Press.

Blyth, Dale A., Roberta G. Simmons, and David F. Zakin. 1985. "Satisfaction with Body Image for Early Adolescent Females: The Impact of Pubertal Timing with Different School Environments." *Journal of Youth and Adolescence* 14:207–25.

Bordo, Susan. 1993. *Unbearable Weight: Feminism, Western Culture, and the Body*. Berkeley: University of California Press.

Boston Women's Health Book Collective. 1998. *Our Bodies, Ourselves for the New Century: A Book By and For Women*. New York: Touchstone Books.

Briggs, Charles L. 1986. *Learning How To Ask: A Sociolinguistic Appraisal of the Role of the Interview in Social Science Research*, vol. 1. New York: Cambridge University Press.

Brody, Jane. 2003. "Trans Fats to Safe Sex: How Health Advice Has Changed." *New York Times*, November 11, 2003.

Brooks-Gunn, Jeanne and Diane N. Ruble. 1982. "The Development of Menstrual-Related Beliefs and Behaviors during Early Adolescence." *Child Development* 53:1567–77.

Brumberg, Joan Jacobs. 1997. *The Body Project: An Intimate History of American Girls.* New York: Vintage Books.

Bullough, Vern L. and Martha Voght. 1973. "Women, Menstruation, and Nineteenth-Century Medicine." *Bulletin of the History of Medicine* 47:66–82.

Charmaz, Kathy. 1991. *Good Days, Bad Days: The Self in Chronic Illness and Time.* New Brunswick, NJ: Rutgers University Press.

Christensen, Pia Haudrup. 2000. "Childhood and the Cultural Constitution of Vulnerable Bodies." Pp. 38–59 in *The Body, Childhood and Society*, edited by A. Prout. Houndmills, Great Britain: MacMillan Press.

Connell, R. W. 1995. *Masculinities.* Berkeley, CA: University of California Press.

Corner, George W. 1951. "Our Knowledge of the Menstrual Cycle, 1910–1950." *Lancet*: 919–34.

Corsaro, William A. 1997. *The Sociology of Childhood.* Edited by C. Ragin, W. Griswold, and L. Griffin. Thousand Oaks, CA: Pine Forge Press.

Coutinho, Elsimar M. and Sheldon J. Segal. 1999. *Is Menstruation Obsolete?* New York: Oxford University Press.

Davies, Bronwyn. 2000. *A Body of Writing: 1990–1999.* Walnut Creek, CA: Alta Mira Press.

Davis, Kathy. 1995. *Reshaping the Female Body: The Dilemma of Cosmetic Surgery.* New York: Routledge.

Davis, Kathy and Sue Fisher. 1993. "Power and the Female Subject." Pp. 3–20 in *Negotiating at the Margins: The Gendered Discourses of Power and Resistance*, edited by S. Fisher and K. Davis. New Brunswick, NJ: Rutgers University Press.

Delaney, Janice, Mary Jane Lupton, and Emily Toth. 1988. *The Curse: A Cultural History of Menstruation.* Chicago: University of Illinois Press.

DeVault, Marjorie L. 1999. *Liberating Method: Feminism and Social Research.* Philadelphia: Temple University Press.

DiFranco, Ani. 1993. "Blood in the Boardroom." in *Puddle Dive.* Buffalo, NY: Righteous Babe Music.

Douglas, Mary. 1966. *Purity and Danger: An Analysis of the Concepts of Pollution and Taboo.* London: Frederick A. Praeger.

Eder, Donna. 1988. "Building Cohesion Through Collaborative Narration." *Social Psychology Quarterly* 51:225–35.

Eder, Donna, Catherine Colleen Evans, and Stephen Parker. 1995. *School Talk: Gender and Adolescent Culture.* New Brunswick, NJ: Rutgers University Press.

Eder, Donna and Laura Fingerson. 2002. "Interviewing Children and Adolescents." Pp. 181–201 in *Handbook of Interview Research,* edited by J. F. Gubrium and J. A. Holstein. Thousand Oaks, CA: Sage Publications.

Ehrenreich, Barbara and Diedre English. 1978. *For Her Own Good: 150 Years of the Experts' Advice to Women.* Garden City, NY: Anchor Press/Doubleday.

Elliott, Grace Loucks. 1930. *Understanding the Adolescent Girl.* New York: Henry Holt and Company.

Elson, Jean. 2002. "Manipulating Menstruation Is Misguided." *Newsday.com,* October 31, 2002.

———. 2004. *Am I Still A Woman? Hysterectomy and Gender Identity.* Philadelphia: Temple University Press.

Emirbayer, Mustafa and Ann Mische. 1998. "What is Agency?" *American Journal of Sociology* 103:962–1023.

Faegre, Marion L. 1943. *Understanding Ourselves: A Discussion of Social Hygiene for Older Boys and Girls.* Minneapolis: The Minnesota Department of Health.

Figert, Anne E. 1996. *Women and the Ownership of PMS: The Structuring of a Psychiatric Disorder.* New York: Aldine de Gruyter.

Fine, Gary Alan. 1987. *With the boys: Little League Baseball and Preadolescent Culture.* Chicago: University of Chicago Press.

Fine, Michelle. 1992. "Disruptive Voices: The Possibilities of Feminist Research." *Critical Perspectives on Women and Gender.* Ann Arbor: University of Michigan Press.

Fingerson, Laura. 1999. "Active Viewing: Girls' Interpretations of Family Television Programs." *Journal of Contemporary Ethnography* 28:389–418.

———. 2005a. "Agency and the Body in Adolescent Menstrual Talk." *Childhood* 12:91–110.

———. 2005b. "'Yeah, Me Too!': Adolescent Talk Building in Group Interviews." *Sociological Studies of Children and Youth* 11:261–87.

Foucault, Michel. 1977. *Discipline and Punish: The Birth of the Prison.* New York: Vintage Books.

Gilligan, Carol. 1982. *In a Different Voice: Psychological Theory and Women's Development.* Cambridge: Harvard University Press.

Gladwell, Malcolm. 2000. "John Rock's Error: What the Co-Inventor of the Pill Didn't Know, Menstruation Can Endanger Women's Health." *New Yorker* 76:52–63.

Golub, Sharon. 1992. *Periods: From Menarche to Menopause.* Newbury Park, CA: Sage Publications.

Gordon, Deborah R. 1988. "Tenacious Assumptions in Western Medicine." Pp. 19–56 in *Biomedicine Examined,* edited by M. Lock and D. R. Gordon. Dorddrecht, The Netherlands: Kluwer Academic Publishers.

Grahn, Judy. 1993. *Blood, Bread, and Roses: How Menstruation Created the World.* Boston: Beacon Press.

Gravelle, Karen and Jennifer Gravelle. 1996. *The Period Book: Everything You Don't Want to Ask (But Need to Know).* New York: Walker and Company.

Greif, Esther Blank and Lathleen J. Ulman. 1982. "The Psychological Impact of Menarche on Early Adolescent Females: A Review of the Literature." *Child Development* 53:1413–30.

Grosser, Bridget. 1998. "Taking the Sh! Out of Menstruation." *New Moon Network* July/August:8–9.

Heath, Shirley Brice. 1998. "Working Through Language." Pp. 217–40 in *Kids Talk: Strategic Language Use in Later Childhood, Oxford Studies in Sociolinguistics,* edited by S. M. Hoyle and C. T. Adger. New York: Oxford University Press.

Heywood, Leslie and Shari L. Dworkin. 2003. *Built to Win: The Female Athlete as Cultural Icon.* Minneapolis: University of Minnesota Press.

Houppert, Karen. 1999. *The Curse: Confronting the Last Unmentionable Taboo, Menstruation.* New York: Farrar, Straus and Giroux.

Hughes, K. Wind and Linda Wolf. 1997. *Daughters of the Moon, Sisters of the Sun: Young Women and Mentors on the Transition to Womanhood.* Gabriola Island, British Columbia: New Society Publishers.

Ingersoll, A. J. 1974. *In Health.* Edited by C. Rosenberg and C. Smith-Rosenberg. New York: Arno Press.

James, Allison. 1995. "Talking of Children and Youth: Language, Socialization, and Culture." Pp. 43–62 in *Youth Cultures: A Cross-Cultural Perspective,* edited by V. Amit-Talai and H. Wulff. London: Routledge.

———. 2000. "Embodied Being(s): Understanding the Self and the Body in Childhood." Pp. 19–37 in *The Body, Childhood and Society,* edited by A. Prout. Houndmills, Great Britain: MacMillan Press.

James, Allison, Chris Jenks, and Alan Prout. 1998. *Theorizing Childhood.* New York: Teachers College Press.

Jefferis, B. G. and J. L. Nichols. 1894 (1967). *Light on Dark Corners: A Complete Sexual Science & Guide to Purity Containing Advice to Maiden, Wife & Mother.* New York: Grove Press.

Karnaky, Karl John. 1943. "Vaginal Tampons for Menstrual Hygiene." *Western Journal of Surgery, Obstetrics, and Gynecology* 51:150–52.

Kelley, Tina. 2003. "New Pill Fuels Debate Over Benefits of Fewer Periods." *New York Times,* October 14, 2003.

Kilbourne, Jean. 1999. *Deadly Persuasion: Why Women and Girls Must Fight the Addictive Power of Advertising.* New York: Free Press.

Kirkendall, Lester A. 1948. *Understanding Sex.* Chicago: Science Research Associates.

Kissling, Elizabeth Arveda. 1996. "'That's Just a Basic Teen-Age Rule': Girls' Linguistic Strategies For Managing the Menstrual Communication Taboo." *Journal of Applied Communication Research* 24:292–309.

Koff, Elissa and Jill Rierdan. 1995a. "Preparing Girls for Menstruation: Recommendations from Adolescent Girls." *Adolescence* 30:795–811.

Koff, Elissa and Jill Rierdan. 1995b. "Early Adolescent Girls' Understanding of Menstruation." *Women & Health* 22:1–19.

Koff, Elissa, Jill Rierdan, and Stacy Jacobson. 1981. "The Personal and Interpersonal Significance of Menarche." *Journal of the American Academy of Child Psychiatry* 20:148–58.

Kowalski, Robin M. and Tracy Chapple. 2000. "The Social Stigma of Menstruation: Fact or Fiction?" *Psychology of Women Quarterly* 24:74–80.

Lander, Louise. 1988. *Images of Bleeding: Menstruation as Ideology*. New York: Orlando Press.

Laws, Sophie. 1990. *Issues of Blood: Politics of Menstruation*. London: Macmillan Press.

Lawton, Shailer Upton and Jules Archer. 1951. *Sexual Conduct of the Teen-Ager*. New York: Greenberg.

Lee, Janet. 1994. "Menarche and the (Hetero)Sexualization of the Female Body." *Gender and Society* 8:343–62.

Lee, Janet and Jennifer Sasser-Coen. 1996a. *Blood Stories: Menarche and the Politics of the Female Body in Contemporary Society*. New York: Routledge.

———. 1996b. "Memories of Menarche: Older Women Remember Their First Period." *Journal of Aging Studies* 10:83–101.

Logan, Deana Dorman, Judith A. Calder, and Betty L. Cohen. 1980. "Toward a Contemporary Tradition for Menarche." *Journal of Youth and Adolescence* 9:263–69.

Lorber, Judith. 1994. *Paradoxes of Gender*. New Haven: Yale University Press.

———. 1997. *Gender and the Social Construction of Illness*. Thousand Oaks, CA: Sage Publications.

Lovering, Kathryn Matthews. 1995. "The Bleeding Body: Adolescents Talk about Menstruation." Pp. 10–31 in *Feminism and Discourse: Psychological Perspectives, Gender and Psychology*, edited by S. Wilkinson and C. Kitzinger. London: Sage Publications.

Maddux, Hilary C. 1975. *Menstruation*. New Canaan, CT: Tobey Publishing Co.

Martin, Emily. 1991. "The Egg and the Sperm: How Science Has Constructed a Romance Based on Stereotypical Male-Female Roles." *Signs: Journal of Women in Culture and Society* 16:485–501.

———. 1992. *The Woman in the Body*. Boston: Beacon Press.

Martin, Karin. 1996. *Puberty, Sexuality, and the Self: Girls and Boys at Adolescence*. New York: Routledge.

———. 1998. "Becoming a Gendered Body: Practices of Preschools." *American Sociological Review* 63:494–511.

Mayall, Berry. 2000. "Conversations With Children: Working with Generational Issues." Pp. 120–35 in *Research With Children: Perspectives and Practices*, edited by P. Christensen and A. James. London: Falmer Press.

McCullough, Marie. 2003. "Nature vs. Culture: Period-stalling Drug Raises Questions." *Philadelphia Inquirer*, September 15, 2003.

McRobbie, Angela. 1991. *Feminism and Youth Culture*. Boston: Unwin Hyman.

Mead, George Herbert. 1934. *Mind, Self and Society*. Chicago: University of Chicago Press.

Messner, Michael A. 2000. "Barbie Girls Versus Sea Monsters: Children Constructing Gender." *Gender & Society* 14:765–84.

Milow, Vera J. 1983. "Menstrual Education: Past, Present, and Future." Pp. 127–132 in *Menarche: The Transition from Girl to Woman*, edited by S. Golub. Lexington, MA: Lexington Books.

Moore, Susan M. 1995. "Girls' Understanding and Social Constructions of Menarche." *Journal of Adolescence* 18:87–104.

Mozes, Eugene B. 1955. "Superstitions about Menstruation." *Sexology* 22:236–41.

Muscio, Inga. 1998. *Cunt: Declaration of Independence*. Seattle, WA: Seal Press.

Nettleton, Sarah and Jonathan Watson. 1998. "The Body in Everyday Life: An Introduction." Pp. 1–24 in *The Body in Everyday Life*, edited by S. Nettleton and J. Watson. London: Routledge.

O'Grady, Kathleen and Paula Wansbrough. 1997. *Sweet Secrets: Stories of Menstruation*. Toronto: Second Story Press.

Owen, Lara. 1998. *Honoring Menstruation: A Time of Self-Renewal*. Freedom, CA: The Crossing Press.

Paige, Karen Ericksen. 1984. "Social Aspects of Menstruation." Pp. 123–44 in *Cultural Perspectives on Biological Knowledge*, edited by T. Dister and K. Garrett. Norwood, NJ: Ablex Publishing.

Parker, Valeria Hopkins. 1940. *For Daughters and Mothers*. Indianapolis, IN: Bobbs-Merrill Company.

Plummer, Ken. 1995. *Telling Sexual Stories: Power, Change and Social Worlds*. London: Routledge.

Prendergast, Shirley. 2000. "'To Become Dizzy in Our Turning': Girls, Body-Maps and Gender as Childhood Ends." Pp. 101–24 in *The Body, Childhood and Society*, edited by A. Prout. Houndmills, Great Britain: MacMillan Press.

Price, Janet and Margrit Shildrick. 1999. "Feminist Theory and the Body: A Reader." New York: Routledge.

Prout, Alan. 2000. "Childhood Bodies: Construction, Agency and Hybridity." Pp. 1–18 in *The Body, Childhood and Society*, edited by A. Prout. Houndmills, Great Britain: MacMillan Press.

Puri, Jyoti. 1999. *Woman, Body, Desire in Post-colonial India: Narratives of Gender and Sexuality*. New York: Routledge.

Qvortrup, Jens. 1994. "Childhood Matters: An Introduction." Pp. 1–24 in *Childhood Matters: Social Theory, Practice and Politics*, vol. 14, *Public Policy and Social Welfare*, edited by J. Qvortrup, M. Bardy, G. Sgritta, and H. Wintersberger. Aldershot, UK: Avebury.

Rako, Susan. 2003. *No More Periods?: The Risks of Menstrual Suppression and Other Cutting-Edge Issues About Hormones and Women's Health*. New York: Crown Publishing Group.

Reuben, David R. 1970. *Everything You Always Wanted to Know About Sex—But Were Afraid to Ask*. New York: David McKay Company.

Richards, Amy. 1998. "Body Image: Third Wave Feminism's Issue?" Pp. 196–200 in *Adios Barbie: Young Women Write About Body Image and Identity*, edited by O. Edut. Seattle, WA: Seal Press.

Rierdan, Jill and Sally A. Hastings. 1990. "Menstruation: Fact and Fiction." Wellesley, MA: Center for Research on Women.

Rierdan, Jill, Elissa Koff, and Jenny Flaherty. 1985. "Conceptions and Misconceptions of Menstruation." *Women and Health* 86:33–45.

Riessman, Catherine Kohler and Constance A. Nathanson. 1986. "The Management of Reproduction: Social Construction of Risk and Responsibility." Pp. 251–81 in *Applications of Social Science to Clinical Medicine and Health Policy*, edited by L. H. Aiken and D. Mechanic. New Brunswick, NJ: Rutgers University Press.

Ruble, Diane N. and Jeanne Brooks-Gunn. 1982. "The Experience of Menarche." *Child Development* 53:1557–66.

Sapir, Edward. 1963. "The Status of Linguistics as a Science." Pp. 160–66 in *Selected Writings of Edward Sapir in Language and Culture and Personality*, edited by D. G. Mandelbaum. Berkeley: University of California Press.

Schwalbe, Michael, Sandra Godwin, Daphne Holden, Douglas Schrock, Shealy Thompson, and Michele Wolkomir. 2000. "Generic Processes in the Reproduction of Inequality: An Interactionist Analysis." *Social Forces* 79:419–52.

Scott, Jacqueline. 2000. "Children As Respondents: The Challenge for Quantitative Methods." Pp. 98–119 in *Research With Children: Perspectives and Practices*, edited by P. Christensen and A. James. London: Falmer Press.

Simmons, Roberta G. and Dale A. Blyth. 1987. *Moving into Adolescence: The Impact of Pubertal Change and School Context*. New York: A. de Gruyte.

Simpson, Brenda. 2000. "Regulation and Resistance: Children's Embodiment During the Primary-Secondary School Transition." Pp. 60–78 in *The Body, Childhood and Society*, edited by A. Prout. Houndmills, Great Britain: MacMillan Press.

Southard, Helen F. 1967. *Sex Before Twenty: New Answers for Youth*. New York: E. P. Dutton & Co.

Snow, Loudell F. and Shirley M. Johnson. 1978. "Myths about Menstruation: Victims of Our Own Folklore." *International Journal of Women's Studies* 1:64–72.

Steinem, Gloria. 1978. "If Men Could Menstruate." *Ms. Magazine*, October, pp. 110.

Stoltzman, Susan Marie. 1986. "Menstrual Attitudes, Beliefs, and Symptom Experiences of Adolescent Females, Their Peers, and Their Mothers." Pp. 97–114 in *Culture, Society, and Menstruation, Health Care for Women International*, edited by V. L. Olesen and N. F. Woods. Washington, DC: Hemisphere Publishing Corporation.

TAMPAX, Incorporated. 1945. "How Times Have Changed: A Manual of Menstruation, Its Purpose, Function, Care." TAMPAX, Incorporated, Palmer, MA.

Tannock, Stuart. 1998. "Noisy Talk: Conversation and Collaboration in a Youth Writing Group." Pp. 241–65 in *Kids Talk: Strategic Language Use in Later Childhood, Oxford Studies in Sociolinguistics*, edited by S. M. Hoyle and C. T. Adger. New York: Oxford University Press.

Tavris, Carol. 1992. *The Mismeasure of Woman*. New York: Simon & Schuster.

Taylor, Jill McLean, Carol Gilligan, and Amy M. Sullivan. 1995. *Between Voice and Silence: Women and Girls, Race and Relationship*. Cambridge: Harvard University Press.

Taylor, Verta and Leila J. Rupp. 1991. "Researching the Women's Movement: We Make Our Own History, But Not Just As We Please." Pp. 119–32 in *Beyond Methodology: Feminist Scholarship as Lived Research*, edited by M. M. Fonow and J. A. Cook. Bloomington: Indiana University Press.

Thompson, Sharon. 1995. *Going All The Way: Teenage Girls' Tales of Sex, Romance, and Pregnancy*. New York: Hill and Wang.

Thorne, Barrie. 1994. *Gender Play: Girls and Boys in School*. New Brunswick, NJ: Rutgers University Press.

———. 1987. "Re-visioning Women and Social Change: Where Are the Children?" *Gender & Society* 1:85–109.

Tolman, Deborah L. 1994. "Doing Desire: Adolescent Girls' Struggles for/with Sexuality." *Gender & Society* 8:324–42.

———. 2002. *Dilemmas of Desire: Teenage Girls Talk about Sexuality*. Cambridge: Harvard University Press.

Tsao, Amy. 2002. "Freedom from the Menstrual Cycle?" *Business Week Online*, May 23, 2002.

Usmiani, Sonia and Judith Daniluk. 1997. "Mothers and Their Adolescent Daughters: Relationship Between Self-Esteem, Gender Role Identity, and Body Image." *Journal of Youth and Adolescence* 26:45–62.

Verbrugge, Martha H. 2000. "Gym Periods and Monthly Periods: Concepts of Menstruation in American Physical Education 1900–1940." Pp. 67–97 in *Body Talk: Rhetoric, Technology, Reproduction*, edited by M. M. Lay, L. J. Gurak, C. Gravon, and C. Myntti. Madison: University of Wisconsin Press.

Voelckers, Ellen. 1975. *Girl's Guide to Menstruation*. New York: Richards Rosen Press.

Wasserfall, Rachel R. 1999. "Women and Water: Menstruation in Jewish Life and Law." Hanover, NH: Brandeis University Press.

Weedon, Chris. 1997 (1987). *Feminist Practice and Poststructuralist Theory*. Oxford: Basic Blackwell.

Weitz, Rose. 1998. "A History of Women's Bodies." Pp. 3–11 in *The Politics of Women's Bodies: Sexuality, Appearance, and Behavior*, edited by R. Weitz. New York: Oxford University Press.

West, Candace and Don H. Zimmerman. 1987. "Doing Gender." *Gender & Society* 1:125–51.

Whisnant, Lynn and Leonard Zegans. 1975. "A Study of Attitudes Toward Menarche in White Middle-Class American Adolescent Girls." *American Journal of Psychiatry* 132:809–14.

Whorf, Benjamin Lee. 2000 (1940). "Science and Linguistics." Pp. 114–21 in *The Routeledge Language and Cultural Theory Reader*, edited by L. Burke, T. Crowley, and A. Girvin. London: Routledge.

Williams, Lenore R. 1983. "Beliefs and Attitudes of Young Girls Regarding Menstruation." Pp. 139–47 in *Menarche: The Transition from Girl to Woman*, edited by S. Golub. Lexington, MA: Lexington Books.

Williams, Simon J. and Gillian Bendelow. 1998. *The Lived Body: Sociological Themes, Embodied Issues*. London: Routledge.

Willis, Paul. 1981. *Learning to Labour*. New York: Columbia University Press.

Wulff, Helen. 1988. *Twenty Girls: Growing Up, Ethnicity and Excitement in a South London Microculture*. Stockholm, Sweden: University of Stockholm.

Zola, Irving Kenneth. 1991. "Bringing Our Bodies and Ourselves Back In: Reflections on a Past, Present, and Future 'Medical Sociology'." *Journal of Health and Social Behavior* 32:1–16.

Index

advertising, 16, 29–30, 40, 53–54, 111, 112

advice literature, 41–43, 46, 57, 122–23

agency: and the body, 23–24, 37, 84–85; feminism and, 134; menstruation as source of, 69, 93, 114, 104, 149–50, 155; and talk, 11–12

AIDS, 45, 106

All in the Family, 55

amenorrhea, 65–66, 70

Angier, Natalie, 71, 74, 88, 95, 151

Archer, Jules, 47, 119

Are You There, God? It's Me, Margaret, 24, 54, 95, 169n2

Aristotle, 42, 46

Ball, Aimee Lee, 119

Beacher, Abraham, 47

Bible, 42, 124

biological reductionism. *See* essentialism

blood. *See* menstrual bleeding

Blume, Judy, 3, 24, 31, 54

body, the, 1–5, 11, 23–24, 79–82, 106–8, 145–53, 161, 164; and children, 6, 16–17, 81, 85, 127–28; female, 2–4, 13–20, 37, 57, 62–63, 72–75, 81–93, 110, 114, 133–34 (*see also* menstruation); and gender, 78–79, 128, 154; male, 16, 50, 57, 73, 95; phenomenology of, 173n22; and power, 37, 39, 40, 48, 73, 83, 84–85; and teens, 7, 10–12, 25, 28, 72, 79, 81–82, 105, 138. *See also* embodiment; medicalization

Boston Women's Health Collective, 102, 107

Brody, Jane, 106

Carrie, 55, 120

Charmaz, Kathy, 68

childbirth, 57–58, 102

children, 39, 50, 64, 71, 84, 89, 155, 164. *See also* body, the, and children

class: and health, 58; and feminism, 133; and menstrual illness, 46–47; of teen participants, 9, 45, 47, 154, 157

contraception, 19, 69–72

Connell, R.W., 23–24, 85

Corsaro, William, 6, 39–40

Coutinho, Elsimar, 70, 71, 72

Cunt: A Declaration of Independence, 134

Curse: A Cultural History of Menstruation, The, 105

Delaney, Janice, 16, 33, 46, 69, 124

DeVault, Marjorie L., 11

DiFranco, Ani, 23

discourse, 2, 89, 102, 132, 154. *See also* language; talk

Douglas, Mary, 86, 120

Elliott, Grace, 123

Elson, Jean, 89–90, 173n22